The Long Journey of Noah Webster

Richard M. Rollins

The Long

Journey of Noah Webster

 University of Pennsylvania Press   1980

Library of Congress Cataloging in Publication Data

Rollins, Richard M.
  The long journey of Noah Webster.

  Bibliography: p. 173
  Includes index.
    1. Webster, Noah, 1758–1843.   2. Lexicographers—
United States—Biography.   I. Title.
PE64.W5R6   423'.092'4 [B]   79–5257
ISBN 0–8122–7778–3

Designed by Tracy Baldwin

For Ann, Rebecca, and Matthew

Contents

Acknowledgments

Many individuals and organizations deserve thanks for the role they played in the creation of this study. Professors Douglas T. Miller, Russel B. Nye, and Peter D. Levine, under whose guidance I began this monograph, often gave their generous advice and helpful suggestions for improvement. The staffs of the Amherst College Library, Bienecke Rare Book and Manuscript Library, Carroll College Library, Connecticut Historical Society, Detroit Public Library, Historical Society of Pennsylvania, the Huntington Library, Library of Congress Manuscript Room, Maryland Historical Society, University of Montana Library, New York Public Library Manuscripts and Archives Collections, New York Historical Society, the Ohio State University Library, Pierpont Morgan Library, Spahr Library of Dickinson College, University of Southern California Library, Sterling Memorial Library of Yale University, Trinity College Library, and the University of Vermont Library all gave freely of their time and cooperation. Especially helpful were Mr. Robert Williams, Mr. Walter J. Burinski, Ms. Jane Sagataw, and Ms. Peg Smith of the Michigan State University Library.

Several scholars read part or all of this study, and thereby donated their time and expertise, as well as their often insightful comments. I would like to thank David Ammerman, Lawrence J. Friedman, Peter D. Hall, Daniel Walker Howe, Bruce Kuklick, Richard Lebeaux, Michael McGiffert, Russell Menard, Richard D. Shiels, Henry Silverman, Thad Tate, Thomas E. Williams, and several anonymous readers for their suggestions. I thank the entire staff of the University of Pennsylvania Press, and especially Tracy Baldwin, Jane Barry, Robert Erwin, Terri Ezekiel, Patrick O'Kane, and Warren Slesinger for their patience, energy, and skill. Part of my research was supported by American Council of Learned Societies Grant No. 18-1851145. Portions of this study were published in *The American Examiner: A Journal of Ideas*, *American Quarterly*, and *Connecticut History*.

Anyone foolish enough to try to fashion a career as a professional historian in the present era cannot survive, much less succeed, without a goodly amount of encouragement and assistance from others interested in, or more established in, academic life. During the past several years contributions by the following people made my life more pleasurable than it otherwise would have been: Mansel Blackford, Karen Blair, Robert Bremner, John Burnham, Les Cohen, Harry Coles, Jeff Demetrescu, Tom Farnham, Larry Friedman, Tom Flynn, John Humins, Richard Jensen, Michael Kammen, K. Austin Kerr, Richard Lambert, Richard Lebeaux, Erick Lunde, Joe Maresca, Doug Noverr, Russel Nye, Richard and Pamela Oestreicher, Gary Reichard, Larry Rudner, Shinsuke Sasaki, Lewis Saum, George Sellement, Dick Shiels, Merritt Roe Smith, Chuck Sorensen, Paul Varg, Tom Williams, and Najib Younis.

Tom Williams, Tim Nugent, Malcolm and Carol Muir, Nelson Lichtenstein, and Karen Blair deserve special thanks. During the 1976–77 academic year I had the good fortune of sharing an office, many important events, and numerous long hours of conversation with them. If there is indeed a community of scholars dedicated to the pursuit of knowledge and improvement of the human condition, they are among its foremost members. As individuals they embody the best of the American spirit. As a group, their intelligence, humor, and kindness delayed the completion of this study for several months, and for that I am grateful. I learned much about history and America from them, and enjoyed doing so.

My personal debts are numerous. My parents, Donald and Barbara Rollins, have always provided love and strength. Richard, Jane, Tom, Ann W., and Chris Featherstone, as well as Walter and Mabel Scott, and Lee and Ethel Featherstone, have added joy to the writing of this study in their own personal ways. Helpful editorial comments were occasionally offered by C. Jane Rollins. Thomas Foghino, Stan and Dawn Hecker, Gordon and Joan Hershey, Stuart Michael Jones, Carol Joy Lappin, Robert and Dina Meissner, Howard and Lorraine Pierce, Maurice and Ruth Seay, and Richard Timmons all added important foundations. My debt to Ann, Rebecca, and Matthew, who constantly remind me what is important and what is not, is indeed great, for it cannot be described here.

Los Angeles
15 January 1979

The good and the brave of all nations are welcome to the
last resort of liberty and religion; to behold and take part
in the closing scene of the vast drama, which has been
exhibited on this terrestrial theater, where vice and
despotism will be shrouded in despair, and virtue and
freedom triumph in the rewards of peace, security and
happiness.
     N. W., 1783

We deserve all our public evils. We are a degenerate and
wicked people.
     N. W., 1836

Introduction

"I have in the course of my life been often obliged to change my opinions."[1]
With these cryptic words seventy-six-year-old Noah Webster acknowledged
that his life had encompassed an extraordinary sweep of events and ideas,
that they had affected him in profound ways. For nearly six decades he had
walked among the men who even in the early years of the republic assumed
mythic dimensions. In 1775 he heard the news of Lexington and Concord
and marched off to fight the British. In the 1780s Webster traveled the length
and breadth of the Confederation strenuously advocating the optimistic doctrines for which he believed the Revolution had been fought: liberty, equality, and a utopian future. George Washington, Benjamin Franklin, James
Madison, and many others paid tribute to these endeavors. As the leading
Federalist editor in New York in the 1790s, Webster became deeply involved
in national affairs, joining Alexander Hamilton, John Jay, Rufus King, Oliver
Wolcott, Jr., and others in their attempts to control, direct, and contain the
flow of events. With these men he voiced strong criticism of many aspects of

American life and the very nature of man. Writing from New England after 1800, he expressed deep hostility toward most of the developments he observed. He believed mankind innately depraved and democracy unworkable. In 1808 Noah Webster experienced a traumatic conversion to evangelical Protestantism. Throughout the final decades of his life, Webster continued his integral role in American life, corresponding with all the social, cultural, and political figures of his day, from Thomas Jefferson and Benjamin Rush to Daniel Webster, Henry Clay, and Andrew Jackson.

Along the way, Noah Webster contributed significantly to the development of American life and became a unique figure in American cultural history. One of the earliest advocates of educational reform, he made the first American attempt to restructure curriculum along nationalistic lines. His *American Magazine* became the first truly national literary and political publication, and his newspapers enjoyed the widest circulation in New York in the 1790s. His *American Dictionary* (1828, 1841), a monumental achievement unduplicated by a single individual in the century and a half since its appearance, and the product of a quarter-century of daily labor, was only one of several he compiled for a variety of uses and audiences. Wherever English is spoken or written, his name is synonymous with correct spelling and authoritative definitions. He also helped build the financial, social, political, and intellectual foundations of schools and colleges, served in the legislatures of two states, held several appointments in local government, edited a special version of the Bible, and actively supported moral reform organizations. In addition to all this he wrote medical treatises still regarded as turning points in their field; numerous essays on politics and Greek mythology; histories of the United States; an important study of etymology; schoolbooks of all kinds; broadsides calling for the abolition of slavery and supporting other social reform movements; texts on moral instruction for the young; and commentaries on religion, economics, foreign affairs, law, and many additional subjects too numerous to list. Few individuals, even in an age of extraordinary personal accomplishment, shared Webster's breadth and scope of interests.

In the past, students of Noah Webster's life and works have largely concerned themselves with celebrating his contributions to the development of an American culture. Indeed, the basic themes dominating all previous studies of Webster stress his buoyant patriotism and his individual achievements. They personify the "great man" approach to history and biography, and in the end reveal little about his inner life or intellectual development.

Nineteenth-century treatments of Webster are filiopietistic, rather than analytical in approach. Two of his sons-in-law, William Chauncey Fowler and Chauncey A. Goodrich, published eulogistic accounts of his life shortly after he died.[2] Horace E. Scudder's *Noah Webster* (1883), part of Charles Dudley Warner's "American Men of Letters" series, was the first serious, scholarly work. Scudder utilized primary sources to narrate the basic story of his birth, writings, and death. While criticizing Webster's personality as aloof and egocentric, Scudder's basic theme was to celebrate his great contributions to the development of American culture.[3]

Three important works published in the first half of this century continued to employ the same approach. The lexicographer's favorite granddaughter, Emily Ellsworth Fowler Ford, lovingly preserved and compiled a valuable two-volume collection of Webster's papers, interspersed between long narrative passages; published at her own expense, these were partly intended as a defense against Scudder's charges.[4] *Notes on the Life of Noah Webster* (1912) attempted to portray him in the most favorable way possible, as a kind, patriotic gentleman of an earlier time. Two major scholarly books appeared in 1936: Harry R. Warfel's *Noah Webster: Schoolmaster to America*, and Ervin C. Shoemaker's *Noah Webster: Pioneer of Learning*. Both concerned themselves primarily with Webster's work in the field of education. Shoemaker examined his pedagogical efforts in detail, within the context of the overall development of American education, and praised him as an early nationalistic reformer.[5] Warfel's scope was much broader, touching on nearly every aspect of his life, and his is still the best traditional narrative of the events in the life of a "great man." Indeed, Warfel's study is a fine example of the search for, celebration of, and often rediscovery of, American culture and heroes in the 1930s. Warfel began writing a history of American nationalism; he ended up writing on a major contributor to American culture.[6]

Recent studies have achieved only limited advances beyond the treatments by Ford, Shoemaker, and Warfel. Two dissertations, Gary R. Coll's "Noah Webster, Journalist: 1783–1803" and Dennis Patrick Rusche's "Empire of Reason," respectively examine Webster's career as newspaper editor and his writings on education, within the celebrationist context.[7]

The Long Journey of Noah Webster is an inquiry into the relationships between the thoughts, feelings, and public contributions of an individual, and the world in which he lived. As such it attempts to carefully examine the details of Webster's private and public lives, in order to establish their connections to the larger trends in American society. Like recent studies of John Adams, Tom Paine, Catharine Beecher, Andrew Jackson, and Henry Thoreau, it assumes that individuals do not live in cultural, social, psychological, or historical vacuums, but that they are firmly embedded in a specific historical context.[8] It diverges from earlier studies of Webster in its approach and conclusions. This is an attempt neither to celebrate nor to condemn him, but rather to understand the ways in which an individual internalized the events, ideas, values, and beliefs of his age, and to show how these affected his work.

Noah Webster endured a long journey through a series of profound psychological, intellectual, religious, social, and political transformations. His life was tightly interwoven with a half-century of tumultuous developments of national importance. The structure and vicissitudes of his changing beliefs and perspectives may be traced through everything he wrote: newspaper articles; letters to friends, family, and opponents; his diary; textbooks; and essays. They appear in his comments on every topic, from economics, to science, to linguistics. His most famous work, the *American Dictionary*, was a summary of his life and experiences as well as a remarkable scholarly achievement. Writing to Thomas Jefferson in 1790, Webster indicated his awareness that his public works carried the burden of his private views of the world. His reading books, he believed, might never be as widely used as his enormously popular spelling book, yet both were vehicles by which he hoped "to diffuse some useful truths; which is my primary object in all my publications."[9]

The truths they reflected varied widely over his eight decades of comment on American life. Like many of the revolutionary generation, Webster began as a supporter of the Revolution, risking his life for a cause that had no assurance of success. He advocated the ideals of universal white male suffrage, complete religious toleration, separation of church and state, abolition of slavery, and equitable division of property.

The social and political events of the late eighteenth and early nineteenth centuries shocked and profoundly disturbed Webster and a number of his contemporaries. Indeed, American society endured an enormous social transformation. American historians are just becoming aware of its scope and intensity, and the traumatic effect it had on individual lives. This metamorphosis in the structure, tone, and pattern of American life produced a new nation, far different from the one Noah Webster had imagined or desired. In his case, American failure to live up to the ideals he internalized in his youth demolished an optimistic belief in the perfectibility of man and led to a drastic change in his view of the world. Webster, like many of the revolutionary generation living in the late 1790s, and especially after 1800, became a severe critic of the emerging pattern of national life. Concerned with what he perceived as a growing chaos and anarchy, he turned to Federalism and then to an authoritarian form of Christianity as a means of imposing social order on a disintegrating world. The only way for America to become stable, he came to believe, was for all her citizens to live passive lives in submission to civil and religious authority. In essence, Webster and many of his contemporaries felt that the world into which they had been born had been a cohesive, deferential one; they sought to restore those qualities through any available means.

The long journey of Noah Webster led him, as similar odysseys led many of his contemporaries, to look back on the America of the pre-Revolution years with admiration, to long for what they believed was a cohesive, deferential world, a golden past. The onetime revolutionary nationalist sought to restore an old order, one that, if it had indeed ever existed, he had been instrumental in overturning.

It was during this latter stage of his intellectual life that Webster executed most of the great works that form his contribution to American culture and society. It is also this period of his life that has so frequently been misunderstood and ill-treated. Webster's intellectual development did not cease in the Revolution, and despite the assertions of historians and biographers, an optimistic American nationalism was not the organizing theme in his understanding of the world or in his written works. This is not to suggest that Webster's entire life can be fairly portrayed in terms of the attitudes he held in the latter stages of his career; such an approach would replace an old, simplistic view with a new, but equally unfair, image.

To properly evaluate Noah Webster's place in the development of American culture and society, one must understand the life of an individual, his written legacy, the world in which he lived and wrote, and the tangled interrelationships of all three in a specifically historical context. That is the objective of *The Long Journey of Noah Webster*.

In this situation of things, his spirits failed, and for some
months, he suffered extreme depression and gloomy
forebodings.
    N. W. on himself in 1781–82

1 Crisis

By any standards, the experiences of Noah Webster's life were extraordinarily diverse and contradictory. Friend and associate of Franklin, Washington, Adams, Madison, Hamilton, Rush, and many other well-known men, Webster achieved monumental success in education, medicine, and lexicography. His name was famous throughout America during the later decades of his life, and by the middle of the nineteenth century "Webster" was itself in daily usage as a synonym for "dictionary." Yet in his youth he was an abysmal failure.

The entire social milieu in which he matured offered ambivalence, uncertainty, and confusion in all the important areas of individual growth. Childhood care produced contradictory desires. Population pressures on land, a problem throughout New England, precluded the possibility of following his father into a farming career. Neither did religion provide him with an adequate foundation of emotional or spiritual strength. His education added to his increasingly antiauthoritarian cast of mind and further set him

7

apart from his family; it also failed to give him a clear alternative career. At the same time, politics and the Revolution made his years in college chaotic and unsatisfying. His relationship with his parents dissolved in 1778. In the years after graduation Webster floated from job to job and from town to town in search of stability and self-definition. In his twenty-third year, all of the traumas, frustrations, and failures of his youth were fused and intensified in his final rejection by a prospective lover. Webster suffered a severe emotional and psychological crisis; he fled home, family, friends, and region in search of a meaningful and fulfilling existence.

Noah Webster was born into an old New England family in 1758. The founder of the American branch of the family, John Webster, had come to Massachusetts Bay Colony in the early 1630s from Warwickshire, England. Like many other Puritans, he fled the wrath of Archbishop William Laud and settled near Boston. There he joined the congregation of Thomas Hooker, following him into Connecticut in 1635. Settling near what is now Hartford, John Webster became a member of the Court of Magistrates and governor of the colony.[1]

Yet John Webster's odyssey was not over. The death of Thomas Hooker precipitated a crisis that lasted ten years, climaxing in 1656 when Webster led a small group of about fifty settlers out of Connecticut and into western Massachusetts.[2]

Obscurity surrounded John Webster in his final years, as it did several generations of his descendants. The Websters were farmers and petty merchants from small Connecticut towns. Noah, Sr., father of the lexicographer, was no different from the previous four or five generations of his ancestors.[3]

Owner of a ninety-acre farm west of Hartford, he lived his entire life in the same area and rose to minor status within the community.[4] His congregational church asked him to serve in several capacities, and the state legislature appointed him justice of the peace between 1781 and 1796. While little of a factual nature is known, it does seem that the elder Webster was a representative Connecticut farmer. He left few written documents of a personal kind, and those that exist indicate a limited education. He married Mercy Steele Webster, of whom even less is known, and together they raised five children.[5]

Childhood is the most difficult period to assess in Webster's life. No primary sources remain that reveal even the slightest information concerning the manner in which he was raised. Little has been written on childhood in late colonial America. We know far more about obscure politicians, the cultivation of tobacco, or the price of land than we do about how Webster's contemporaries were nursed, disciplined, or what games they played.[6] To reconstruct the development of an individual child in Webster's day is virtually impossible.

Yet if his childhood was not dissimilar to those of others of his class, region, and gender, it is possible to make a few generalizations. Above all, childhood in mid-eighteenth-century America produced ambivalence: a yearning for dependence on the family and desire to become independent of external controls.[7]

Earlier New England parents looked on their children as means to greater ends, as perpetuators of their own religious beliefs and social values. Throughout most of the seventeenth and early eighteenth centuries, children were subjected to strict rule and were expected to obey authorities with deference. Child-raising techniques were designed to civilize and tame beings regarded as either highly susceptible to evil corruptions or inherently wicked. Their spirits were to be broken or their natural tendencies would endanger all that their parents worked for. Play was discouraged as connected to sinfulness and degeneration.[8]

Complete submission to parental authority was induced through a variety of practices. Constant lessons in obedience, correct manners, religion, and strict diligence inculcated habitual deference. In extreme cases, bodily chastisement in the form of whipping, burning, and bleeding reinforced these lessons. A more subtle use of shame, guilt, and fear supported the overall system. Parents scared children into submission with terrifying stories. They disciplined by tying children to bedposts and locking them in closets. Common fears of death played into parental hands and were often used to enforce desired behavior.[9]

But by Webster's birth in 1758 a distinct transformation in child-raising attitudes was under way. Many parents continued to emphasize obedience through a regime designed to restrain youthful energies; yet others began to look on children with more tolerance. Mid-eighteenth-century child-raising manuals stressed "prudent government" of children and revealed a growing nonauthoritarian attitude. Two opposing desires emerged: to control and protect children and to give them room for autonomous development. As two New England authors put it, children should be governed strictly within the family fold until they could supervise themselves, at which time, it was hoped, they could follow the lifestyle of their parents in an independent manner.[10]

Prudent government consisted of a less severe discipline yet continued stress on correct, obedient behavior. Now children were treated in a more individualized manner; their age, mental capacity, and temperament were considered. Browbeating and terror decreased. Child-raising manuals now stressed discreet use of the rod; few activities required bodily correction. Rearing must be carried out calmly and gently, and children should be encouraged as much as possible, not reproved. Parents were made aware that severe discipline was often inflicted as a result of their own passions, not their children's behavior. Above all, play should be allowed. Genuine recreation and innocent diversion were permitted, although with supervision.[11]

This ambivalent attitude produced an equally contradictory set of desires in children to become self-reliant yet remain dependent, to remain protected and secure in their parents' household, but also to exert their individualism. The Webster family left no indications that they diverged from this pattern.

The pressures of a growing population on limited New England soil coincided with these changes in child-rearing patterns. Together they helped alter the basic social and intrafamilial relationships, and strengthen the sense of ambivalence in youth. Seventeenth-century fathers had used the distribution of land among children to influence and control the decisions of life: marriage, career, and other plans were formulated around parental values in order to inherit family land. Prolonged periods of dependency, powerlessness, and marginality resulted, coupled with older ages of marriage.

By the early eighteenth century this pattern was dissolving. All across New England succeeding generations found land existing only in limited quantities. Often, as a series of recent studies has shown, they discovered that it was insufficient for their needs.[12]

This "crisis of overcrowding" further loosened the patriarchal hold. With inheritable land dwindling beyond the point of potential subsistence for more than one family, new generations looked outside the traditional models for their livelihoods. Some were forced to learn new trades or move to new settlements, relying on their own labor for subsistence. While fathers became less authoritarian and exercised less direct control, their children experienced a prolonged period of uncertainty over their future, combined with a heightened antiauthoritarianism and desire for self-reliance.

More complex patterns of family life verging on socially atomistic individualism emerged in response to demographic pressures. Children asserted their independence by marrying younger, and moving out of the reach of family control at a much earlier point in their lives. Early births of first-born children indicate increased sexual activity among youth.[13] Youthful assertion in vocational choices, demands for new singing styles in church, delinquency, and other behaviors expressed adolescent desires.[14]

Demographic trends also affected larger social patterns. With land less and less plentiful, occupational structures among nonagrarians became increasingly specialized. Thus at the same time youths were looking for alternative lifestyles, it grew increasingly difficult to find them. Since average land-holdings shrank, a perceptible decrease in the quality of rural New England life appeared.[15]

These factors produced an uncertain and volatile adolescence. Without families to guide, control, and ensure their futures, children were forced into active searches for personal roles in society. They increasingly ignored traditional restraints of all kinds, turning their energies from family and community endeavors to the pursuit of personal gain and individual achievement. Obedience to the physical and psychological demands of the authorities was no longer assumed and was less frequently practiced than before.

New models of behavior emphasized self-assertion, independence, and autonomous individualism rather than self-denial and submission to external authority and communal norms. Youth became rebellious; one author has remarked that parental disgust with adolescent recalcitrance was strikingly common in mid-eighteenth-century America.[16]

Connecticut was strongly affected by all of these developments. An exceptionally high birth rate dramatically increased its population in the years of Webster's adolescence, and made Connecticut the second most densely populated colony in New England on the eve of the Revolution. Large numbers of young people were forced to travel in search of more and better land.[17] The Websters, with five children and only ninety acres of land, were no exception to this general situation.

Similar patterns of change and uncertainty appear in other areas of life. Religion was a central part of life in eighteenth-century Connecticut, and the Websters attended church regularly. The God overseeing Connecticut in Noah Webster's youth was far different from the one who peered down over John Webster's world. He had been a fearful, omnipotent being, full of wrath and anger. But as new generations replaced the original Puritans, God had taken on a less oppressive character. Increasingly, citizens of New England worried over the relationships between men, rather than that between man and God. Over the years the religion of the first generation had mellowed, and now between God and man mediated a book in which man could look for his direction: nature. God seemed less omnipotent and fearsome to Noah Webster's generation, and they marveled at the wonder of his work in fashioning their bountiful continent.

Webster's early religious views were formed as a member of a congregation considered by its own minister as rivaling any in New England in its lack of religious conviction and orthodoxy. In the 1770s, when Webster attended the Fourth Church of Hartford (later called the First Church of Christ Congregational in West Hartford), the Reverend Nathan Perkins could find only one youth with any sense of piety in the entire congregation. Not a single person made a public profession of religious devotion.[18] Webster's early milieu and his religious values are clearly reflected in his only explicit statement of his religious beliefs before 1808. He said that the essence of religion was the universal brotherhood of man, and that "God is Love."[19]

Yet the old system of religion had left a strong residue of certain beliefs and accepted patterns of behavior. The theology of New England gradually softened, but the values and precepts that it was based on and that it had fostered continued. Max Weber and a host of others have long debated the relationship between capitalism and the Protestant ethic.[20] This system of values, primarily abhorrence of extravagance and idleness, and emphasis on work, thrift, and frugality, was widespread in eighteenth-century America. Especially strong was a belief that all individuals should lead honest, moral lives devoted to hard work, not to materialistic enrichment and political manipulation for personal betterment. As Edmund S. Morgan has pointed out, Congregationalists and Presbyterians like Sam Adams of New England and Benjamin Rush of Pennsylvania shared this system of values with Anglicans from the South like Henry Laurens and Richard Henry Lee, as well as with deist Thomas Jefferson.[21] Benjamin Franklin's autobiography is a clear example of these ideas at work in the individual.[22] The Protestant ethic formed an important ingredient in Webster's early years. His belief in these values became so deeply ingrained that it affected everything he wrote and did for the remainder of his life.

There were other, more pessimistic elements of the Puritan residue. The brooding fear of an omnipotent God and the belief that man was helpless and inherently depraved were hard to erase, even after several generations. This underlying uneasiness, though submerged beneath the general optimism of American thought in the late seventeenth and most of the eighteenth centuries, appears in all periods of New England history. The revolutionary generation's perfectionist view of the nature of man as expressed in political essays of the 1770s and 1780s deteriorated under the impact of civil disruption, symbolized by Shays' Rebellion and the French Revolution. In the 1790s Webster succumbed to the cosmic pessimism of his Puritan forefathers as did many others who participated in the second Great Awakening.[23]

But religion was not the center of his youthful concerns. When the farm work slackened during the winter, Webster went to school. Connecticut law provided for eleven months of school, and children under the age of seven attended in the summer while the older ones went in the winter.

In his mature years, Webster made educational reform one of his many preoccupations, and his early school experiences undoubtedly served as a stimulus. The schools of Connecticut in the 1760s were wretched at best. Often housed in dilapidated buildings, the children were in the hands of men and women who frequently could find no other means of making a livelihood. Webster himself referred to schoolteachers as the dregs of society, and his own education was meager. In school, he later remembered, there were no geography or history lessons. The only books available were a speller, a Bible, and a collection of psalms. In his bitter final years Webster recalled (perhaps inaccurately) that he never spent more than an hour actually engaged in reading and writing, "while five hours of the school time was spent in idleness—in cutting the tables and benches to pieces—in carrying on pin lotteries, or perhaps in some more roguish tricks."[24]

Outside the schools the social structure was in the midst of important changes. Seventeenth-century Connecticut had been a conservative, deferential colony. Social rank often dictated church-pew assignments. Men of family, wealth, and education usually rose through local offices to positions in the colonial government, often without making a single political speech. Levellers were abhorred because they jeopardized authority. Each institution melted into and reinforced the others; theology emphasized the wickedness of rebellion against community standards, and preachers savored and planned election-day sermons the year around. The highest civil offices were often occupied by those stationed at the head of the social ladder, and most felt they were there because of the wisdom of God. The total impact was immense. The inhabitants of Connecticut knew exactly where they stood, both in politics and in society.[25]

Much had changed by the third quarter of the eighteenth century. New people migrated to the banks of the Connecticut River, people who had not fled England because of religious or economic oppression. The religious revival of the 1740s pitted friends and neighbors against one another in debates over social and political questions as well as theological points. The Old Lights, relying on traditional concepts of social order as well as a less enthusiastic religion, gradually lost ground in Connecticut to the new emphasis on internal authority and law. Over the years, the new group coalesced and became accustomed to thinking in antiauthoritarian terms. Civil leaders had opposed their movement as well as the religious establishment. Respect for all forms of authority was weakened by the very actions of civil and religious leaders, and this occurred amidst the demographic problems already described.[26]

By the time of Webster's adolescence a new social order, fragmented and potentially explosive, was emerging in Connecticut. Divine authority had been undercut by the controversies over the Awakening, and men could now oppose civil officers without fear of eternal damnation. A significant shift in the perception of the relationship between ruler and ruled had taken place. God was still the final source of authority. Yet now the emphasis was placed not on the duty of the ruled to obey the rulers, but on the obligation of the rulers to serve the people. Dissent and internal conflict of an antiauthoritarian nature were legitimized.[27] As all citizens were no longer dependent on rulers, so sons were no longer completely dependent on fathers for their livelihood. Instead, a more balanced perception of intrafamilial relations enhanced self-determination.

Religious, demographic, and economic factors all indicate that Connecticut was a traditionally based yet changing society. Imperial politics, increasingly important after 1760, also emphasized the less cohesive, volatile nature of Webster's milieu. In 1765 Parliament passed the Stamp Act, requiring that all paper goods sold in the colonies be taxed. The governor, Thomas Fitch, took an oath to enforce it over the objections of most of his council. In September, a mob captured the man who shouldered the direct responsibility for collecting the revenues, forcing him to resign his commission on the threat of death. The same mob, calling itself the Sons of Liberty, then met with the governor and informed him that unless he refused to honor the act his house would be "levelled with the dust in five minutes."[28] Connecticut was thoroughly aroused, and for the next year town after town met and condemned the Stamp Act until it was repealed. From then until the outbreak of the war, Connecticut stood beside Massachusetts in opposition to England. When the Port Bill was enacted, Boston was fed with supplies from Connecticut. In 1776, Thomas Fitch was voted out of office, an act virtually unthinkable in previous years. He was replaced by an antitax man.[29]

Amidst the growing strain of prerevolutionary events, Noah Webster began to express interest in matters less routine than daily farm chores. In 1772 he informed his father that college attracted him. This decision was difficult for the family and undoubtedly caused tensions, since they lacked adequate financial resources to support advanced education. Yet the Websters were in the same situation experienced throughout the region; demographic reality dictated that only one family would be able to continue to live on the farm. His brother Abraham elected to move west in search of better opportunities, and eventually became a farmer in upstate New York.[30]

The elder Webster hesitated but finally agreed to do what he could for his youngest son. In the autumn they went to the Reverend Nathan Perkins, who tutored Webster in the subjects necessary to prepare him for college.[31] A year later he entered the grammar school run by Mr. Wales of Hartford. The following year he applied for admission to Yale and was accepted. It was an expensive proposition, but the elder Webster mortgaged his land to send his son to college.[32]

Noah Webster entered college as one of the first of a movement that reached major proportions after the Revolution. Thousands of youths flocked to New England colleges. They were not the sons of the rich or of city dwellers, but products of the trend that had been developing over many decades: children of small farmers too poor to provide land for the next generation. New schools, such as Williams, Middlebury, and Amherst, sprang up to accommodate them.[33]

The tiny campus in New Haven housed a small but dynamic institution. Just eight years before Webster arrived the system of seating students in class according to their social standing had been abolished. A system of alphabetical seating was substituted, giving the school a more democratic air. Former students had spent two days each week studying theology, a subject on which Webster spent less than one day a week. During his years at Yale an anticlerical faction called for specific reforms toward a more practical curriculum, and some of their plans were successfully implemented. In Webster's years a few literary societies appeared, open even to freshmen. Yale substituted English for Latin in classroom exercises, and formal debates over the morality of slavery and the legality of opposition to England kept students astir. A new concern for mathematics, astronomy, physics, and anatomy slowly forced more changes. It was an exciting period, one in which a young man from the country was exposed to many different ideas, and especially to the belief that progressive social change was possible and even necessary.[34]

Yale introduced Noah Webster to the Enlightenment. Not a coherent system of philosophy put forth in one treatise, it was instead a way of thinking, a diverse group of assumptions and beliefs clustered around reliance on human reason. The modes of Enlightenment thought could seldom all be found in the writings of one person; yet they all saturated the culture as a whole. The possibility of social change, and change in a progressive manner, was assumed. The emphasis on reason, or man's ability to use his own mind to understand the universe without recourse to supernatural explanations, characterized nearly all mid-eighteenth-century thought.[35]

The Scientific Revolution of the previous century provided the foundation for enlightened thought. The critical spirit of scientific methods discovered by a host of Europeans influenced all areas of inquiry. God was the architect of the universe, and through the study of his creations one could learn all the important secrets. All phenomena, from the stars to the smallest insect, were believed to function according to logical and rational principles. They could be understood and reduced to the certainty of natural laws as specific and ironclad as mathematical formulas.

Inspired by Bacon, Locke, and especially by Sir Isaac Newton's synthetic work, the American Enlightenment observed, experimented, and tested new theories about the physical world. Jefferson wrote a zoological and botanical treatise on his native state; Franklin invented practical tools for the betterment of mankind; Noah Webster studied potatoes, the nature of dew, and winter weather, as well as human diseases.[36] Nearly all the figures associated with eighteenth-century America—Benjamin Rush, Tom Paine, John Adams, and even George Washington—exhibited a deep interest in the natural world and its regularity of operation.

Webster indicated his interest in science in a paper delivered in 1778 as the culmination of his formal education. "A Short View of the Origin and Progress of the Science of Natural Philosophy" traced the intellectual history of the Scientific Revolution and celebrated the accomplishments of Copernicus, Galileo, Descartes, and others. His hero, however, was clearly that "great genius," the "immortal Newton." No other subject, said Webster, could furnish more pleasure for a speculative mind like his own "than that of Natural Philosophy."[37]

The enlightened students of Yale conceived of human nature in optimistic terms. Man's fate was no longer predetermined by an arbitrary being. It was the natural result of the environment and could thus be encouraged and advanced by man himself simply by bringing it into line with natural law. Evil and depravity were religious fictions invented by priests and their cohorts to control the populace; whatever evil there might be was the result of natural causes. More importantly, men had the power to improve their environment through science, education, and reason, and many Americans during the Revolution believed that there was no better place for this to occur than in America.[38] In the next decade Webster would write essays on

America as an "empire of reason." A great many Europeans shared this sanguine view of the young republic's future. The noted English radical Richard Price, one of the most widely reprinted authors in America, believed that the Revolution was the dawn of a "new era in the history of mankind," while Goethe, Schiller, Lessing, and Kant sang German praises of the New World.[39]

Old ways took on new meaning when seen through the lens of the Enlightenment. The covenant system of the Puritan forefathers now looked very much like the compact system of government that many Englishmen seemed to believe had been discovered by John Locke. But now obligations of the state and the individual were not handed down by God. Instead they seemed more like natural devices by which man could put his world in order. The most important concept of all was natural rights. They were not granted by God but were part of man because of his very humanness.

The Enlightenment, as two recent studies have reminded us, was not incompatible with Calvinist values.[40] Many Americans, and Webster was one, combined their belief in reason and progress with attitudes and ethics derived from Calvinism. England seemed in its death-throes, diseased beyond hope and engulfed by luxury, money, and vice. America must be kept virtuous. Its leaders, therefore, must be unselfishly devoted to the good of the whole, and moral beyond a shadow of a doubt. The public good could only be served by men who were free of private temptations, full of industry, and simple in ambition as well as in lifestyle. Thus the yeomen farmers, whom Jefferson called the chosen people of God, were the heroes of the second half of the century.[41] They were the people on whom the republic would be founded; the ultimate hero in an age of heroes, of course, was that stoic, plain farmer from Virginia, George Washington.[42]

The need for heroes also led down another path, one that pointed back to the past. Numerous examples were dredged up out of the ancient world and used as models for the new one. The newspapers, political pamphlets, theater, poetry, and in fact virtually all areas of American culture in the late eighteenth century were saturated with references to the ancient republics. People wrote letters to newspapers and articles, signing themselves "Camillus," "Phocian," "Cicero," or "Publius." Plutarch, Polybius, Solon, and Lycurgus were quoted on most important occasions as if the spirits of the past republics could ensure success for the new one. When Webster finally began to write, long after he left Yale, all of the characteristics of Enlightenment thought appeared in his work. His essays stressing America's utopian nature, man's capacity for reason, morality, and heroic endeavor were often signed with classical pennames, including "Honorius," "Orpheus," "Curtius," and his favorite, "Cato."[43]

Thus at Yale the young farmboy became a nascent intellectual. He had been prepared by his milieu in the sense that the social, religious, and political trends of the era all stressed individual decision-making and self-determination in a manner quite different from those of the previous century. All produced, to a limited extent, an antiauthoritarian cast of mind that allowed Yankees like Webster to question external authority, to assume and believe that one should actively engage one's mind (and spirit) with the world. The dominant teaching of the Enlightenment was the same. By the time he graduated, Webster was an intellectual not merely because he had read books and received a college degree, but because his experiences before 1778 taught him to think analytically and critically.

Young Noah Webster's first year away from his father's farm was a momentous one. His classmates formed, in the opinion of the most recent historian of the college, "one of the greatest classes to graduate from Yale."[44] Webster struck up friendships with Josiah Meigs and Oliver Wolcott, Jr., future secretary of the treasury. His closest friendship was with Joel Barlow, who, like Webster, came from a small, poor Connecticut farm and who became one of revolutionary America's foremost poets.

In February 1775, while political tensions with England increased, the students of Yale began preparing for combat. They formed a militia company and drilled enthusiastically under the eyes of two regular soldiers. Breastworks were under construction when on 21 April a courier arrived with the long-awaited news that colonists had exchanged fire with British troops. Captain Benedict Arnold quickly assembled the company on the college green and marched up to the powder-house, seizing the stores of arms and ammunition. The whole company then marched off toward Boston, dressed in scarlet coats, white breeches, black leggings, and fur head-pieces.[45]

The sixteen-year-old farmboy was quickly swept up in the war. Classes were dismissed and did not meet again for about six weeks. Yale became a center of rebellion, and one alumnus regarded it as "a nursery of sedition, of faction, and republicanism." Those suspected of loyalism were drummed off the campus.[46] In June, two distinguished-looking men on their way to join the troops around Boston stopped for the night at the home of Isaac Beers, a local tavern owner. The students discovered that one of the men, George Washington, would take over command of all the militia then encamped near Boston. The Yale company turned out to drill in front of the Beers residence, an event Webster remembered for the rest of his life. Sixty years later he recalled that he was among the musicians who led Washington and Charles Lee out of town.[47] The next month the usual commencement ceremonies were canceled and not resumed until after the war.[48]

The rest of Webster's college days were even more chaotic. Classes were suspended twice in 1776, once because of disease and once because of a lack of food. His entire third year was spent not in New Haven but in Glastonbury, after the corporation decided that the town was too susceptible to invasion. Each class and its tutor was sent to a different town, and in April 1777, the library was broken up and dispersed to prevent its being ransacked or burned by the British. In January 1778 the school told the students that those who could keep up their studies at home or elsewhere need not return. Webster came back only to pick up his degree.[49]

Webster joined the army twice during his student days. In 1776 he marched to Canada where one of his brothers was fighting. In the fall of 1777 he joined his father's militia company to fight against Burgoyne.[50] As they were making their way up the Hudson valley amidst what Webster described as "terror and devastation," a courier informed them that Burgoyne had surrendered. Frustrated yet relieved, they turned around and went home.[51]

The antiauthoritarian spirit affected life at Yale. In April 1776, the students petitioned the corporation to renounce Naphtali Daggett, the president of the school, a quite unusual act in early American education.[52] Later that year, after returning from the battle of Long Island, Webster's friend Barlow wrote a parody of the Book of Chronicles satirizing life at Yale and Daggett.[53] In 1777 two of Webster's classmates were about to be punished for some now unknown crime when Noah and twenty-five others, in a "premeditated and preconceived combination," walked out of chapel. This was a serious offense that shocked the school officials, and the entire group was given the option of signing a confession of their "audacious contempt" or taking the consequences. They chose to admit, in writing, that their conduct had been "utterly inexcusable, entirely Criminal, and highly affrontive, an Example tending to the Subversion of all good Order." They publicly condemned themselves and promised to "Avoid all such like disorderly Behavior" in the future.[54] And that was not all. In August of the same year Noah and the rest of his class were drafted to serve in the continental army. They were not opposed to the war or to fighting, and most of them served at least once during the war. Yet they all refused to be drafted on the grounds that it was an infringement by the government on their rights. Claiming what may have been the first student-deferment in American history, the class of 1778 hired a lawyer and took their case to court.[55]

Webster's college education, even though it probably entailed no more than two years of actual on-campus study, significantly altered his values and his life. By 1778 he was no longer a farm boy, but was deeply interested in science, literature, philosophy, and politics, not in business or agriculture. His major concern in college had become intellectual growth, not preparation for a vocation. His senior thesis, "Whether the Destruction of the Alexandrine Library, and the Ignorance of the Middle Ages caused by the Inun⊥ of the Goths and Vandals were events unfortunate to Literature," shows his orientation. Moreover, the abbreviated and chaotic nature of his Yale experience left him dissatisfied. "The advantages enjoyed by the students," he once said, "during the four years of College life were much inferior" to those enjoyed before and since the Revolution.[56]

Thus when Webster graduated in 1778 he was in somewhat of a dilemma. Interested in a subject matter which failed to prepare him to earn a living, he could only return to his father's farm. But this too was unsatisfactory. The other children resented his education and the favoritism implied in his father's support.[57] Greek, poetry, and revolution made farm chores seem an excruciating bore; it was quite evident that he did not belong there. Indeed, demographic reality prevented him from remaining there.

His arrival in the house was unpleasant for all concerned. His father, after all, had mortgaged the land to send young Noah to college, and now he seemed not only unfit for the farm, but unprepared for anything else. Frustration and anger caused an incident that Webster remembered vividly for the rest of his life. Indeed, it was the only conversation with his father he ever recorded or referred to in all his voluminous writings.

"Take this," said the father, handing his son eight dollars in nearly worthless continental currency: "You must now seek your living; I can do no more for you." These words reflect and summarize his sense of failure and rejection by the standards of New England society. Their tone clearly implied disgust and dismay. In effect, his father and family had bluntly rejected him. The stern command threw him into what he described as a "state of anxiety." He promptly closeted himself in his room for three days, contemplated his uncertain future, read Samuel Johnson, and felt "cast upon the world."[58]

For all practical purposes, this was the end of Noah Webster's relations with his family. No evidence remains indicating that he ever returned for more than a brief visit. The debt to his father remained unpaid, and in 1790 the elder Webster was forced to sell his farm.[59] The son's correspondence rarely mentions the family, and he evidently communicated with his parents mainly through his brother Abraham.[60]

Like so many others from his background, Webster turned to schoolteaching to earn a living. Virtually penniless and without a family to fall back on, he took a position in Glastonbury. Schoolteaching in revolutionary America was generally an unpleasant means of employment; yet he remained until the summer of 1779. He then decided to become a lawyer and secured a position as an aide to Oliver Ellsworth, later chief justice of the Supreme Court. However, he could not repay the debt he owed to his father on his small salary. In the fall of 1779 he took a second teaching position in Hartford.[61]

During the winter of 1779–80, Webster began to think about the role of education in society. It was the beginning of a lifelong interest in the topic, and from the first he believed that education was a means to a greater end. He said that schools had been neglected by Americans in terms of both their physical situations and their possible use as a tool of socialization. Ignorance could only bring tyranny, he felt, and thus the school was an important institution. The schools must be improved so that the new republic could fulfill her mission of establishing "civil and religious liberty."[62]

As Webster became increasingly critical of and alienated from the schools in which he found himself, he took time to put his thoughts down on paper. The buildings were generally run down and poorly heated, an obvious source of difficulty. In addition, the tables were too low for the children to write on and there were no locks on the drawers in which the books were stored. Classrooms were often crowded, and it was impossible for one teacher to instruct seventy or eighty children in one room as many were forced to do. Twenty or twenty-five would be a better number. Individualized instruction, said Webster, could then take place.[63]

Most appalling to the young schoolteacher were the authoritarian methods used by American teachers in general. He observed that most teachers either tried to frighten children into paying attention, or tried to force them to learn. Webster warned that children would never enjoy learning as long as they were dragged "along under the lash of a master's rod, without any delight in books."[64] Instead the teacher should be less of an authority figure and offer incentives, some "alluring object" for students to reach for. Schools must change, in physical as well as mental ways, and Noah Webster urged all Americans to support their local schools no matter how much it cost. A good education, he believed, was the best legacy they could give their children.[65]

In the spring of 1780 he moved to Litchfield as an assistant to the registrar of deeds and once again began to study law. After a year he took the law examinations with twenty other prospective lawyers, and much to the surprise of all, no one was admitted. Local lawyers had been alarmed at the thought of that many new people competing in an already overstocked, depressed business, believed Webster. Instead of trying again in Litchfield, he rode back to Hartford and soon passed the same examination there.[66]

But passing the examination did not guarantee security, and Webster's search for his niche continued. The war had decimated the practice of law in Connecticut, and as Webster himself said, "no good prospect of professional business presented itself."[67] He tried to set up an office in Hartford, but could not make enough to live on and pay his debts to his father. The few cases he did manage to attract brought only meager fees, and the profession turned out to be as overcrowded in Hartford as it was in Litchfield.[68]

By summer it was apparent that he was not going to succeed in the legal field. Once again, in desperation, he turned to teaching. This time he decided to open his own school. Sharon, Connecticut, near the New York line, seemed like a promising town, and there he offered a school of the highest quality. Education, his advertisement said, was "essential to the interest of a free people." Webster attracted the children of Whig refugees from New York City and taught Grammar, Latin, Greek, French, Geography, Composition, Mathematics and Vocal Music.[69]

Webster enjoyed life in Sharon, and for a while it looked as if he had found his niche. The school was in a house owned by John Cotton Smith, later elected governor of the state. Smith's nineteen-year-old sister, Juliana, had organized a small literary circle, not unlike the one to which Noah had belonged in college. The society reawakened his literary interests and further stimulated his political thinking. It even published a small magazine, *The Clio: A Literary Miscellany*, to which he submitted a few small poems.

In Sharon he found a means of survival amidst intellectual stimulation, and he thrived. One Sharon resident fascinated the young schoolmaster: the Reverend John Peter Tetard, a learned European and a Huguenot. With Tetard he studied French, German, Spanish, and Latin, as well as history. Reading Tom Paine's *The Crisis* sharpened his democratic and nationalistic tendencies. In September he dashed back to New Haven to pick up a Master of Arts degree, awarded almost automatically by Yale in the eighteenth century, and returned to discuss Rousseau's *Social Contract* with Tetard. Their conversations revolved around the rights and responsibilities of governments and the basic structure of society, as well as the problem of human slavery. During his college years Webster had become convinced that universal white male suffrage was necessary in America in addition to complete religious toleration. Tetard reinforced his convictions.[70] His antiauthoritarian stance, planted in his youth and nurtured at Yale during the Revolution, was strengthened by his experiences after graduation.

His stay in Sharon was exciting for another reason. He had always been fond of female company, and in Sharon he met several intelligent and beautiful women.[71] Webster and Barlow had been known as socialites in New Haven, but this was the first time he had ever been involved in a serious relationship. Juliana Smith was the first to draw his attention, but when she rejected the poetry (which she called "doggerel") that he had submitted to *The Clio*, he fell in love with another.

Rebecca Pardee represented the final failure of Noah Webster's adolescence. He fell deeply in love with her, and for a time she returned the feeling. The summer and early fall of 1781 was the happiest time since college for Webster, but it did not last long. Unfortunately for him, she had previously had another relationship with a man who was then an officer in the continental army. When he returned, a triangular affair developed and Webster was soon excluded from her company. Her rejection precipitated a drastic move: in October he abruptly and without warning closed his school and left Sharon.[72]

One of the most significant stages of any human life, including Noah Webster's, is late adolescence. This was no less true in the eighteenth century that it is today.[73]

The essential characteristic of this period between childhood and adulthood is role experimentation and a quest for a positive sense of inner identity, a search for acceptance and a niche in society that is both firmly defined and seemingly unique. It is a time when it is important to the individual that the society in which he exists somehow communicate to him a sense of meaningfulness, that he develop a sense of achievement and function within the greater society. Webster clearly failed to achieve any of these goals. The inability to settle on an occupational identity was especially disturbing. He floated from job to job, all of which were low in pay and status. Always financially insecure and in debt to his father, he clearly did not enjoy teaching, the work he fell back upon by default. He moved seven times in three years, unable to feel at home for long in any single place. When he tried to break away from teaching and practice law, he failed again. His sense of failure was compounded because neither his family and traditions nor his religion was strong enough to provide him with a sense of being an integral part of any larger whole. His education had made him hostile to both. During the three years after Yale, Noah Webster felt progressively rejected by all the significant figures in his life: his father and family, the community as a whole, and his first love.

His feelings of rejection and failure intensified a sense of instability and uncertainty about the future. Indeed, every phase of his youth—childhood, religious experiences, early education, the social structure of his home state and its demographic pressure on his family, his years at Yale, the Revolution, even his familial and interpersonal relationships, revealed uncertainty, change, and even incoherence.

All of these elements added up to an overwhelming sense of anxiety and confusion about his identity, significance as an individual, and relationship to the rest of the world. In the fall of 1781 he experienced a profound psychological and emotional crisis, one that propelled him toward a new life.

He left Sharon in October. Five full decades later, after a long lifetime of traumatic experiences, incredible events, and enormous achievements, he remembered the anguish and bewilderment of this period as vividly as anything he ever lived through. The memories of his mental state were so strong and clear that he described them with an intense power. For some time he wandered aimlessly through Connecticut, drifting from village to town in search of "mercantile employment." Of course he was unprepared for such work and failed again. New England as a whole seemed hostile, so he decided to travel south or west, with no real objective in mind. He ended up in Goshen, New York, about twenty-five miles west of the Hudson River.

Looking back on this moment, an aged Noah Webster recalled having but seventy-five cents in his pocket. He was alone, "without money and without friends." He had no ambition, no easily marketable skills, no sense of personal direction, and, seemingly, no future. He utterly lacked self-confidence. In Goshen, his youthful spirits failed. For several months, as he remembered half a century later, he "suffered extreme depression and gloomy forebodings."[74]

All power is vested in the people. That this is their
natural and inalienable right, is a position that will not
be disputed.
    N. W., 1785

2 *Revolution*

Webster's crisis was not an end but a beginning. For amidst the loneliness of his self-imposed exile in Goshen he found a way to achieve a sense of meaning and self-definition in his own life by fusing it with a cause: the nation as a whole and its struggle to establish its own identity.

From this period on, throughout the next six decades, Webster's life centered on the use and manipulation of words. He built his entire world on and around words. They served him in two distinct ways. He used them to further a variety of causes, to influence the behavior of other people, and even to change American national life. The specific details of the causes he wrote in favor of, and the precise nature of his relationship to those causes, varied widely. Yet the fact remains that between 1781 and 1843 Noah Webster was primarily engaged in the manipulation of words. He began using them to influence others, and ended up trying to change the very meaning and structure of the words themselves. Words also came to serve Webster as his primary means of communication with the world outside his immediate family. They became virtually an extension of his personality, a screen through which he contacted, or filtered out, the rest of the world. Writing words, as he told George Washington in 1785, became a central part of his existence: "I wish to enjoy life, but books & business will ever be my principal pleasure. I must write—it is a happiness I cannot sacrifice."[1]

Out of Noah Webster's crisis emerged an individual who perceived himself as a propagandist for the Revolution, and who espoused an ascetic, utopian, and antiauthoritarian ideology. For Webster, the Revolution was neither a simple rebellion against colonial rule, nor a revolution from the bottom up.[2] It was both of these and much more, containing elements personal and national in scope.

To the cause of revolution Webster brought enormous talent and energy; in fact one historian has called him the most effective propagandist of the 1780s.[3] His books, pamphlets, essays, and even personal letters written in Goshen and Hartford (to which he moved in 1783) were polemical in tone and devoted to spreading the principles for which he believed the Revolution had been waged. An analysis of his thinking reveals that it was divided into three categories. First, there were general themes, usually abstract in form and often not strongly articulated but nevertheless assumed, revealing connections to his adolescence and the colonial American past. He probably held most of these ideas as early as 1775, and perhaps earlier. Second, Webster addressed specific issues and advocated certain changes within American society that were directed towards improving it. Finally, Webster's central belief in education led him to some unusual conclusions about the methodology for implementing large-scale reforms.

Webster's revolutionary ideology, often confused and superficial, was far from original. The narrative presented here is vastly more logical and ordered than anything he personally wrote. Like the event itself, revolutionary ideology stemmed not from a single cause or overriding issue, but from a complex interaction of social, economic, political, religious, and psychological factors. It reflected all of them and was thus sometimes ambiguous, even contradictory. Overall, it outlined an idealized, abstract model, one that most Americans believed they could and should live up to.

His own crisis triggered his essays. A mind in such a state as Noah Webster's was during the winter of 1781–82 is potentially an ideological mind. A person in the midst of a crisis like his eagerly seeks confirmation of the self in the form of rituals, creeds, and programs. He needs to realize a clear comprehension of his own life within the context of an intelligible pattern of existence. Much like a religion, the ideology that Webster grasped centered on a utopian simplification of history and his own newly developing sense of identity. In the most general terms, it constituted a synthesis of an idealized model of the past and utopian dreams for the future. Indeed, at times it is not clear if he is writing about a condition that existed in the past, or one that exists in the present, or something that he believes should be done in the future.

If Webster's ideology was often hazy, it was also thoroughly modern in nature. The cumulative effect of the social, religious, and political trends of mid-eighteenth-century America created a modern personality, and the young propagandist was a good representative figure. He shared with his generation a set of characteristic attitudes and behaviors that marked his work as a secular form of millennialism. Above all, his generation believed in the enlightened concept of man's capacity, even duty, to improve his natural and social environment. A new world of simple goodness lay in America's future. They welcomed new experiences and change in all areas of life. Webster exhibited a personal ambition for himself and his children far beyond anything his father had ever dreamed of. He also symbolized the revolutionary era's increasing desire for independence from authority figures in all walks of life. The ideology he and others espoused reflected all these traits, and in its widest scope was deeply humanistic and majoritarian. All Americans could and should look forward to a rosy future with confident hopes of progress and prosperity. Webster surely did.[4]

It was in this optimistic atmosphere that the argument over the structure of the English empire occurred, first in England and then in the colonies. The resurgence of imperial authority after 1763 was not just a series of political and economic events. As two historians have pointed out, revolutionary literature indicated that many Americans were prepared by social trends to see the struggle for national liberation in personal and family terms, to oppose the symbolic parental power as they themselves sought to exert control over their own lives.[5] The family analogy appeared everywhere; Americans perceived Britain as a tyrannical parent imposing its will on a newly matured and unwilling son. John Adams summed up this attitude when he said that the real revolution occurred before the war commenced, in "the minds and hearts of the people." Americans had been raised as children with a "habitual affection" for their "mother country," a "kind and tender parent." Yet by the Revolution that had dissolved, and "their filial affections ceased and were changed into indignation and horror. This radical change in the principles, opinions, sentiments and affections of the people, was the real American Revolution."[6]

The writings of Noah Webster exhibited this analogy. The strained relationships between parents and children throughout New England, and in his own life, prepared him to perceive events in generational terms. His personal break with his father gave his arguments added power and emotional force. He believed England had "grown old in folly, corruption and tyranny." For America "in her infancy" to continue its relationship would "stamp the wrinkles of decrepit age upon the bloom of youth." Americans were like mature sons, able to defend themselves.[7]

A passage in one of his earliest essays, written less than four years after his traumatic conversation with his father, is especially striking. The intricate relationship Webster weaves between the family model and the imperial question clearly demonstrates his sensitivity to both issues. The English "call us *children*," he noted, and were sure that severance of "such near relations" would be "*unnatural.*" This was false; Americans considered "abuses on the part of a parent as a symptom of coldness and ill-will" that alienate "the affections of a child." Americans, having experienced "jealousy, distrust, envy" and other quarrels, deem independence from their parents "*natural.*" America had "gloried in a connexion with the parent state" and "during her minority" had "endured the rod of proper authority with patience and submission," borne "the temporary abuses of a haughty, peevish parent, with total silence, or remonstrated with marks of duty and respect." Webster explained the events of the years before 1776 in terms that could have come from a modern textbook on adolescence and family relations. The children suffered through the meanness of harsh parental direction and even put up with serious injuries. When the final break came, Americans experienced "that mixture of joy and regret, which one virgin feels when she quits the parent to embrace the lover."

He did not stop there, but described the years after 1776 in a manner that with a few small changes could have been a description of his own independence in Goshen:

> Children, after a few months separation, forget the parents—contract other friendships—grow fond of their new situation—and are unwilling to return to a state of obedience. America, driven by necessity to abandon the parent state, has felt her affections alienated—she has formed more agreeable and advantageous connexions—she is fond of her new situation—and is unlikely to revert back to a state of dependence, as the bride to quit the partner of her heart, for the company of sullen age. . . .[8]

An important indicator of the decline of patriarchal influence throughout the English-speaking world was the growing emphasis on contractual relationships. For as patriarchalism in the family lost its appeal and power throughout society, so did the ideas of royal absolutism and passive obedience. As two scholars put it, "by mid-century, when the Revolutionary generation was coming to maturity, the traditional pattern of prolonged filial subordination and dependence would appear to have been broken."[9] A parallel development in imperial relations was the insistence by the colonists on firm contractual agreements.

The question of the British Constitution became one of the central

points in Whig ideology.[10] Before the Revolution the Whig concept of constitution did not center on a specific written document like the one produced
later in Philadelphia. Instead the word itself was a symbol for an entire system of values and governmental operations. It meant the fundamental laws,
institutions, and traditions, and most importantly, the moral principles
which they thought the commonwealth had been founded upon. Englishmen in the eighteenth century generally believed that this marvelous system
preserved the rights under which they prospered. Those rights were the
foundation of British liberty. In America, Sam Adams believed that these
principles were based in nature and protected by God, to be applied universally to all mankind. His cousin, John Adams, said that they were "the most
perfect combination of human powers in society which infinite wisdom has
yet contrived and reduced to practice for the preservation of liberty and the
production of happiness." On the Continent, Montesquieu himself, perhaps
the most influential of all the French *philosophes*, declared that it was indeed
a beautiful system.[11]

Over and over again throughout the years of turmoil, American
Whigs reiterated that one of the central ideas for which they fought was the
preservation of the British Constitution. They believed that it was being undermined by the king, his court, and Parliament. Beginning in the 1760s with
James Otis, virtually all cried out over the loss of liberties and the subversion
of the Constitution, indicating that what they sought was a return to the old
ways. Some believed that there was a conspiracy of those surrounding the
king, while others insisted that it was Parliament which was trying to destroy
the society. By 1775 most agreed that the English system of government was
rotten to the core.[12]

The idea of contract was central to Webster's conception of the essence of the Constitution. Under the old system, the king had been obliged
to provide protection for the colonists, who in turn owed him their loyalty.
King George, he believed, had, before the Declaration of Independence, attempted to impose some "unconstitutional and oppressive laws" on the colonists. He had withdrawn his protection, confiscated property, and thus had
forfeited all right to their allegiance. The king's claim that the colonists owed
him unconditional submission was in itself an "infraction of the compact
between the King and his subjects, which dissolves every tie of allegiance,
and [was] an insult to the rights of humanity, which the free sons of America
cannot fail to resent with unabating indignation." But the corruption, he
believed, went deeper than the attitudes of the king. Parliament also sought
to limit traditional liberties, and they acknowledged their own guilt, he felt,
when they repealed their own acts in the 1760s.[13]

Webster undoubtedly knew that his ideas fitted easily into a long tradition of English and American Whig thought. Like Sam Adams, Thomas
Jefferson, John Adams, Tom Paine, James Otis, and innumerable others,

Noah Webster drew on a rich heritage of opposition to authority and agitation for social change going back at least to the Glorious Revolution of 1688. Men like John Trenchard, Algernon Sidney, Thomas Gordon, John Locke, and James Harrington wrote political propaganda which became and remained central to American thinking right up to Lexington and after. The English radicals, including the revolutionary generation's own contemporaries, John Wilkes, Richard Price, and Joseph Priestley, stood for a solid belief that government, by its very nature, was a necessary evil, hostile to human happiness, which must be scrupulously watched and battled at every turn. They fought for adult manhood suffrage, freedom of the press, elimination of rotten boroughs, complete religious toleration, and binding instructions as well as residential requirements for representatives.[14]

Webster's *Sketches of American Policy* (1785) clearly indicates his specific debts to French radicals as well as English Whigs. He had reexamined Rousseau's *Social Contract* and read a new essay by Richard Price during January of that year. Rousseau's influence on Webster had always been strong, and he admitted that he had "imbibed many visionary ideas" from the French *philosophe*.[15] The concept of the General Will, as well as Rousseau's millennialist spirit, appeared often in his work. Price's influence was new, but no less potent. "Many of my observations, particularly on religious tests and establishments, and on the liberty of discussion," Webster explained, "have been anticipated by that respectable writer, so distinguished by the justice and liberality of his sentiments and by his attachments to America."[16] Indeed, when Webster sent Price a copy of his *Sketches*, Price replied that it would help spread revolutionary principles.[17]

The influence of enlightened values also appears in the young propagandist's work. Belief in reason and the common man pervaded everything he wrote. A quotation from *Hamlet*, act 2, scene 2, illustrated his emphasis on rationalism. "What a piece of work is man," said his 1785 reader, "how noble in reason! How infinite in faculty and in form and moving, how express and admirable! In action how like an angel! In apprehension how like a God!" Man could indeed perfect himself, and America would be the place where he would do it, especially if all her citizens would learn to read with one of Noah Webster's essays or books. Reason, he felt, was the key to progressive change. "Let reason go before every enterprise," and if children followed this classic rule, America would indeed become a utopia.[18]

The enlightened young men of the Revolution who used their powers of reason and looked around them to see the birth of a new nation also looked into the past and found that the past justified their cause. History was, they discovered, cyclical in nature; as one nation declined in power and eminence, another inevitably took its place, as Rome had replaced Greece. "The birthday of a new world is at hand," said Tom Paine, and most Americans believed that the Revolution was the beginning of a new cycle.[19] Noah Webster echoed this idea:

Nations, like animals, have their birth, grow to maturity, and decay. Constitutions which began with freedom, end in tyranny, and those which are founded on the wisest maxims of justice and virtue, always crumble to pieces by the imperceptible influence of their own Corruptions.

Not to go ahead would be unthinkable. America must take up the torch of civilization. To subject the colonists "to the corrupted tyrannical system of British politics," he added, "would be to stamp the wrinkles of age on the bloom of youth, and to plant death in the vitals of the infant Empire."[20]

The green fields and hills of Connecticut made America, when compared to the rest of the world, look obviously superior. Descriptions of not only England but Denmark, South America, Asia, Africa, Arabia, and Rome flowed from Webster's pen. They were beastly places, unfit for good republicans to inhabit. On the other hand, America and her future glittered and shone under present and future suns. It was the only country on earth where all governments were calculated to promote the "happiness of mankind."[21] America had been chosen by nature as though it specifically intended to baffle the last efforts of tyranny. It was almost as if some mysterious hand had "reserved one part of the world from the yawning gulf of bondage," out of the reach of all evil.[22]

One of the most significant assumptions that Webster made in all his essays was that Americans were and should be ascetic revolutionaries. Again and again he stressed the quality of virtue: truth, hard work, and frugality. For Noah Webster, like Sam and John Adams and numerous other Americans of their generation, was essentially a Puritan revolutionary seeking not profit and self-glorification, but a pure and austere way of life.[23] As Webster had submerged himself in the cause of the greater community, so too should all others.

This ideal was embodied in the main character of Joseph Addison's famous play, *Cato* (1713), a pseudonym widely used among revolutionary propagandists. Cato was the ultimate ascetic hero: a public man of high moral character and personal honor. He criticized the materialism, corruption, and pretentiousness of English social circles.[24] Webster used Cato as a penname on several occasions.[25]

America seemed a veritable paradise to Cato. It welcomed all ascetic revolutionaries fleeing from the degenerate way of life that was Europe:

The good and the brave of all nations are welcome to the last resort of liberty and religion; to behold and take part in the closing scene of the vast drama, which has been exhibited on this terrestrial theater, where vice and despotism will be shrouded in despair, and virtue and freedom triumph in the rewards of peace, security and happiness.[26]

One of the keys to the strengthening of this past and future utopia was the equal distribution of property. Webster expressed gratitude that America was being settled by peasants who came to live on their own private land, and that there were no barons, dukes, princes, or other forms of nobility invested with European-style grants of property and power. Future happiness could be secured by allowing every person to purchase and possess as much as he could in fee simple. This was, he believed, "the only method to preserve the liberties of America, for that virtue and public spirit which are the essential springs of a republic depend solely on an equal distribution of property."[27] His own historical enquiries led him to believe that unequal property caused almost all the civil wars that had torn nations to pieces, from ancient Rome to seventeenth-century England. "The great fundamental principle upon which alone a free government can be rendered permanent," he repeated, "is an *equal distribution of property*."[28]

From his Hartford room, Webster gazed westward toward the future of the republic. Millions of acres stretched farther than he could possibly see; his hopes soared. The West assured, as Thomas Jefferson would point out in his first inaugural address, enough land to supply the good yeomen farmers on whose shoulders the republic would stand for thousands of generations. The West produced a new kind of ascetic individual, believed Webster, a man stronger and more opposed to aristocracy than any European peasant.[29]

Intoxicated by dreams of a future utopia, Webster contemplated the confiscation of landed estates. Without clarifying his thoughts, he noted that even as he wrote, there were some large estates being divided more equally in every part of the new nation. That move helped equalize the distribution of property, and destroyed any ill-founded respect for aristocracy that might be still in existence.[30]

In fact, he now believed that a thorough annihilation of all distinctions of rank was necessary to build a truly republican world. Distinction was inconsistent with the nature of popular government because it always led to quarrels over power and privilege. The only distinctions of rank that should be allowed in America were those arising from natural differences in merit. "Whenever a man or body of men establish to themselves a share in government independent of the people, and when they are no longer responsible for their conduct," he warned, "a state may bid adieu to its freedom."[31]

The evils of unequal property were obvious to him, as were those of established religion. "Next to the feudal system," he said, the establishment of religions had done "the most mischief of any event or institution on earth." Perhaps the worst period in the history of man, as far as he was concerned, had been the Middle Ages in Europe, when both systems were united and "the terrors of superstition were added to the sword of the civil magistrate, to depress the mind and bind the human race in extreme servitude."[32]

Separation of church and state was necessary in the new utopia. Webster saw the two as different forms of government; one dealt with the temporal happiness of man, the other with his spiritual redemption. The messengers of salvation should not be allowed to sit in judgment of commercial and political affairs, nor should those involved in politics have any voice in church matters, let alone actively support one specific sect. The two different types of government could not be reconciled, and to attempt to do so, he believed, was to attempt "to mix oil with water, or to make the most discordant sounds in nature . . . harmonize." He feared their cooperation, for each made its subjects in its own field "sufficiently slavish." But of the two, the clergy were by far the more dangerous. They hid their lust for domination behind the guise of saintliness and had consistently deceived people in the past. The "ambassadors of Christ" had too often "joined the terrors of eternal damnation to the iron rod of civil magistrates in order to extend an unlimited authority over the persons, the purses, and the consciences of their devoted vassals."[33]

Along with strict separation of church and state, Webster advocated complete religious toleration. He looked back at Europe and saw happiness, commerce, and population restricted by unnecessary disputes between obscure sects. The progress of mankind was cramped and the human mind chained by religious superstition. In contrast, America had been founded on the idea of universal toleration. All religions were welcome here, and all sects lived together peacefully. Toleration was the capstone of freedom and would raise America "to a pitch of greatness and lustre, before which the glory of ancient Greece and Rome shall dwindle . . . and the splendor of modern Europe shall fade into obscurity."[34]

The establishment of religious qualifications on suffrage, office holding, or in any other area clearly appeared repugnant to him, so he saved his strongest attacks for them. They were "glaring absurdities" and had "introduced more disorders into society, than all the political motives that have activated tyrants" throughout history. They were another form of slavery, "an insult to humanity, a solemn mockery of all justice and common sense." Some areas were better off than others, and Webster examined each state, discovering that toleration was most prevalent in Pennsylvania and the Middle Atlantic states. New Englanders were the worst offenders and caught the brunt of his attack. Every citizen of that area, and of course he was one, should be indignant at the persecution of Quakers and others that had taken place there.[35]

While a deep antiauthoritarianism pervaded all that he wrote, so did a feeling of confidence in the ascetic revolutionary Americans. Webster clearly believed that man was naturally moral and thus freedom must be extended as far as possible in all areas of life. Political rights were no exception. "The people will never make laws oppressive to themselves," he wrote, and if the values that he held were widespread all would be well:

> When . . . the sovereign power resides in the whole body of the people, it cannot be tyrannical not because it is barred by physical necessity, but because the same power which frames a law, suffers all the consequences, and no individual or collection of individuals will knowingly frame a law injurious to itself.[36]

"All power," he stated, should be "vested in the people." That was their "natural and unalienable right." Equalization of justice was quite important; no individual or class should be subject to a law which it had no voice in framing or which all were not required to obey. All laws must be general in application. Specifically, all male citizens, regardless of wealth, should be made to pay taxes and serve in the militia. Under the Websterian system, all laws could be nothing else but fair; they would be made by the people themselves, since "the essence of sovereignty consists in the general voice of the people."[37]

Frequency of elections was also important. Webster was a firm believer in the widely held Whig maxim: "where annual elections end, tyranny begins."[38] Americans, he believed, elected men of merit, not men of wealth or hereditary titles. His own observations of elections gave him confidence that those with abounding desire to gain office for their own self-benefit would be the choice of none. Free elections, held regularly, would act to safeguard the rights of the people. The more often they were held, the better.[39]

Yet despite the superabundance of land, despite the basic goodness and reasonableness of her citizens, America suffered one major flaw: human slavery. On this point Webster stood in advance of many of his contemporaries.[40] Few would agree with his statement that "the abolition of slavery is a matter intimately connected with the policy of these states." To Noah Webster slavery was repugnant to human nature on every conceivable level. It was an evil, pernicious system, the bane of industry as well as morals, and in addition to its human horrors it supported luxury and indolence. Those who owned other human beings were marked by a "haughty, unsocial, aristocratic temper, inconsistent with that equality which is the basis of our government and the happiness of human society."[41]

Slaveowners were portrayed in the same terms that he used to describe the unruly, tyrannical English political fathers. The connection in Webster's mind between slavery and politics was obvious: if Americans as a nation should not be enslaved by England, neither should one individual be owned by another. Abolition of slavery was the logical extension of all points of his beliefs. America could not become a utopia with the stain of slavery, nor could Americans perfect themselves in his ascetic image until they stopped exploiting human beings. The logic that compelled the freedom of one demanded that all be independent. "A nation which is subject to the will of an individual is a nation of slaves," said Webster, whether they be white or black.[42]

Slavery must be abolished, and soon. The northern states would hardly feel the effects of immediate emancipation, but the South was another story. He knew that it would suffer; its social and economic structure would be devastated. But that was a small price, he felt, when compared to the utopia which America could and should become. The future of all must be counted as more important than the present of a few, and so the move must be made now.[43]

All of the principles which he advocated, believed Webster, could be brought together in a specific form of government. Like John Adams, principal author of the Massachusetts Constitution of 1780, and Thomas Jefferson, who wrote one draft of the Virginia Constitution of 1776, he believed that a basically republican system, divided into balancing centers of power, was necessary. No other form "would be reconcilable with the genius, of the people of America; with the fundamental principles of the revolution; or with that honourable determination which animated every votary of freedom to rest all our political experiments on the capacity of mankind for self-government." The chief magistrate should be solely executive in power, with no legislative voice, as in Pennsylvania. He had a clear idea of what he thought would be the most practical system of government. It would be a "government, where the right of *making* laws, is vested in the greatest number." He seemed to be heralding the feelings of many who would later ratify a new federal constitution when he said that "a representative democracy seems . . . to be the most perfect system of government that is practicable on earth."[44]

The methodology of reform necessary to guarantee internal social change and construction of an ideal form of government, thought Webster, was education. In this belief he was virtually alone; no other figure, even Thomas Jefferson, consciously advocated the use of education as a tool of change as strongly or as publicly as Webster during the 1780s.[45] Robert Coram, a strong egalitarian who called for the establishment of free public schools as a means of abolishing class distinctions in 1791, consistently praised Webster as a model spokesman on education.[46]

In 1784 he tried to establish a school with a tuition scale based on the relative economic status of the individual pupil. Those with enough money would help pay for the education of orphans and poor. He was quite bitter when it failed. The rich citizens of Hartford had enough money to support education for all, he believed, but they preferred to waste it on luxuries instead. One remedy would be to tax the rich to pay not only for education, but for the costs of government and other social services as well. The poor, who then paid the heaviest tax burden, should not be taxed at all, since they could least afford it. "Let the honest, the poor, and the laborious be exonerated from the burden," he said.[47]

Thus when Noah Webster began to construct the first system of American education while living in Goshen in 1782, he clearly had much more than reading, writing, and arithmetic on his mind. Teaching in revolutionary America had led him to believe that the only way of ensuring the type of broad social change he wanted was through a general diffusion of knowledge. The main books used in schools throughout the colonies, and especially the grammar and spelling books, were woefully inadequate. He would write new textbooks that would emphasize not only changes in education, but internal social change as well. Furthermore, cultural independence from England, necessary for the establishment of a truly utopian form of society in America, would be strongly emphasized. His new American form of education would then be an end in itself and a means to greater ends as well.

The first part of his plan for an American system of education called for a new spelling book to be used on the elementary level. He had developed and practiced his ideas while teaching in Connecticut and New York, so the book was not difficult to put together. The work was finished by the summer of 1783, but finding someone willing to publish it was another matter. The spelling book market had been dominated by an Englishman, Thomas Dilworth, and no one seemed willing to challenge his hegemony. To make matters worse, Webster was unable to bear the expense incurred while traveling from printer to printer in search of a publisher.[48] Indeed, most of the people he talked to discouraged him. Only his two friends, John Trumbull and Joel Barlow, consistently said they believed he had any real prospect of success.[49] Finally, after a year of planning and preparation and six months of carrying the manuscript across New England in search of a publisher, he made an agreement with the printers of the *Connecticut Courant*. Hudson and Goodwin would put out the little book, if Webster would pay for the paper, ink, and labor and grant them exclusive rights to publish any new editions. It was not a good deal, but no one offered a better one. On 7 October 1783, the first of 5,000 copies rolled off the press.[50]

Webster's speller, soon commonly known as the "blue-backed speller," became one of the most popular books in early national America. The small book, simply bound in blue cloth, achieved phenomenal success. Webster had originally intended to call it "The American Instructor," but Ezra Stiles, who examined an early manuscript version, suggested a more classical title: *The Grammatical Institute of the English Language*.[51] Eventually this little speller found its way across the Mississippi River and into virtually every hollow in the southern mountains, as well as nearly every community in the northern states. The first edition was sold out in nine months. Two more appeared in 1784, and then came an avalanche. At least 404 editions had appeared by Webster's death in 1843. Indeed, the blue-backed speller may very well have been the most widely read secular book in eighteenth- and nineteenth-century America. One and one-half million copies were sold by 1801, twenty million by 1829, and at least seventy-five million by 1875. Probably no less than a hundred million have been sold altogether. Webster would have been incredulous had he been told that as far into the future as 1936, 153 years after the original publication, editions of his speller would still be used in American schools, and that in 1975 two editions would still be in print.[52]

As he told a friend, the book was a means of gaining the widest possible audience for certain ideas and beliefs. Webster had pondered the problem of reaching a mass audience and even considered writing an "abstruse philosophical" work, but had rejected the idea because it would only be read by "a few, and its utility seldom [would] reach further than the philosopher's head." What he had to say deserved widespread attention. Perhaps, he thought, a little fourteen-penny volume would "convey much useful knowledge to the remote, obscure recesses of honest poverty." He had no idea how wildly successful he would be when he said that he hoped his speller would be "like a star" casting "its beam equally upon the peasant and the monarch."[53]

The blue-backed speller was not just a dry series of school lessons: it was also a revolutionary broadside. Its rhetoric reflected Webster's personal life and revolutionary ideology. All of the themes of Webster's work—youth versus age, asceticism, cultural nationalism, enlightened reason and the perfectibility of man, and antiauthoritarianism—can be found amidst spelling instructions.

This 119-page book advocated drastic reforms. In the previous eight years, Webster believed, greater changes had "been wrought, in the minds of men . . . than are commonly effected in a century." The citizens of the New World had submitted to the authority of Great Britain, to laws which were "a ridiculous compound of freedom and tyranny" for far too long, he stated in the opening pages. They had been overpowered by wicked men, by a nation full of vice and error. Americans should now be "astonished at the former delusion" and should break free from the evil ways of England in politics, religion, and literature. It was the duty of America "to attend to the *arts of peace*"; to correct errors and defects wherever they were found, but also to introduce improvements into "civil policy." They must act boldly and seize the time. "Europe," he charged, had "grown old in folly, corruption and tyranny—in that country laws are perverted, manners are licentious, literature is declining and human nature debased." The torch of liberty must now be picked up by the New World; the whole future rested on her shoulders.[54]

He repeated his belief over and over again that to continue in the old ways of Europe would be to defile and poison America. A reformation in all areas of life must be made. Above all, Americans must be ascetic:

> It is the business of Americans to select the wisdom of all nations, as the basis of her constitutions, —to avoid their errours, to prevent the introduction of foreign vices and corruptions and to check the career of her own —to promote virtue and patriotism, —to embellish and improve the sciences, —to diffuse the uniformity and purity of language, —to add superior dignity to this infant Empire and to human nature.[55]

In short, America must become a utopia.

One way to achieve that superior dignity would be to develop a language sufficiently different from that spoken and written in England. Through the use of Webster's speller, cultural as well as political independence from the old world would be increased. "Amercia must be as independent in *literature* as she is in *politics*," he declared to a friend, "as famous for *arts* as for *arms*, and it is not impossible but a person of my youth may have some influence in exciting a spirit of literary industry."[56]

Webster was unafraid of tinkering with the basic structure of the language. The English grammarians had taken rules from Greek and Latin and applied them to their language. He would remake the language by drawing grammatical rules from common American usage and then make appropriate changes. Peculiarities which existed in each state or section would be wiped out, and a single accurate system of pronunciation and spelling would be instituted.[57]

The exercises in his speller would "inspire youth with a contempt of the unmanly vices of mankind and a love of virtue, patriotism and religion."[58] He left no scheme unplotted, and even outlined specifically when the speller should be used in the schools for its greatest advantage. In order to further a sense of American nationalism, he introduced a "Chronological Account of Remarkable Events in America" in the last pages of his book.[59]

The second and third parts of his system were somewhat more difficult to politicize. His grammar book[60] concentrated on vowels, verbs, and other technical subjects, while the capstone was a new kind of book with new and interesting types of material to help students learn to read. It included literature, drama, and oratory, and was a new concept in American education. For the first time, when they picked up Noah Webster's reader, the children of New England and America would be exposed to Shakespeare; excerpts from *Hamlet* and *The Merchant of Venice* could be easily studied in one-room schoolhouses from Massachusetts to Georgia.[61]

Included were several essays written during the Revolution containing what he believed were the noble, just, and independent sentiments of liberty. The emphases were on youthful rebellion and America as a utopia, as well as the ability of man to perfect himself through his powers of reason. There were words which all American schoolchildren should learn by heart; he was excited at the prospect of gaining a wider readership for them. The "rising generation" could now soak themselves in the spirit of the Revolution and its rhetoric, and Webster was convinced that they would go on to live their lives by certain ideals. They would also be stimulated by the words of one "Thomas Payne," whose *The Crisis*, number five, written in praise of American virtue in 1776, was included.[62]

By 1785 Webster had emerged from his crisis as a propagandist for the Revolution. Toward the end of the war and shortly after it, he strongly and sincerely advocated broad social change. His own life became bound up with the cause of what he believed were the principles of the Revolution. The ideology he espoused was a utopian synthesis of past and future cast in antiauthoritarian terms. It included, among other points, equal distribution of property (including confiscation of some estates if necessary), complete religious toleration, and especially cultural independence. America should become a utopia where all men could live in happiness. The culmination of his efforts was a new system of education which would indoctrinate those who had not passed through the experience of the Revolution itself, and thus ensure that these principles would be embraced by an intelligent public.

Too much health is a disease . . .
Too much liberty is the worst tyranny.
    N. W., 1786

3 Balance

In the spring of 1783 Noah Webster left Goshen and moved to Hartford, where he remained until early 1785. He took lodging in a boardinghouse and again attempted to practice law with little success. He did not return to the restrictions of his parents' house, though he did occasionally visit them. Instead, he enjoyed the social life of the town. His diary records the life of an educated young man, full of parties and dancing, courting young ladies and association with the "Hartford Wits." He read and discussed poetry with Timothy Dwight and Joel Barlow, attended local government meetings and participated in every aspect of town life.[1]

In Hartford he began to rethink some of his beliefs and develop new ideas. He had come to identify his life with that of the Revolution: in it he believed totally, firmly, and unquestioningly. Yet beginning in 1783 a series of events challenged some of his beliefs and changed the direction of his thinking. Most notable among these were the convention in Middletown,

Connecticut; Shays' Rebellion in Massachusetts and his own observations of the political and cultural atmosphere of Virginia and the South.

While Webster remained basically optimistic about America's future, he came to hold an ambivalent attitude toward authority and freedom quite in keeping with his experiences. Concern emerged over the failures of the Confederation. Criticism of Americans for their inability to live up to his abstract idealized model of ascetic revolutionary behavior grew in his mind. At the same time, he began to move in the social and intellectual circles of nationally prominent men. His acceptance by men of the stature and power of Washington, Franklin, Madison, and their friends made him feel part of the national leadership. With these men as his new models of achievement and moderate behavior, Webster began to identify his life and work with preservation and stability, not disruption and change.

Webster expected that the victory of the Revolution would bring happiness and joy to all men. Instead it seemed only to bring problems and worries as serious as those faced before 1775. The Articles of Confederation appeared too weak to deal with the postwar situation. Far from a moral republic, the new nation was full of bitterness and dispute. Thirteen separate and sovereign units were held together by a unicameral legislature in which each state had one vote. That body was virtually helpless, without the coercive power to raise taxes and enforce what legislation it managed to pass. Each state proceeded to write laws and form commercial treaties with little or no regard for its neighbor. Thirteen different judicial and commercial systems operated without any centralized direction, and Webster found that he personally suffered because of the situation. There was no national copyright law, and the Continental Congress consistently failed to pass one. Thus each state had separate regulations regarding the distribution of royalties from his books; it was nearly impossible to stop people from selling them or pirating them without paying him.[2]

The Confederation faced its first real crisis in 1783. The financial basis of the new government, always shaky at best, began to crumble, sending shock waves up and down the country. The Revolution had been supported by issuing nearly uncountable sums of paper currency; the Congress itself, between 1776 and 1780, had spewed forth at least $200,000,000 in scrip. The effect was disastrous. By 1779, the official rate of exchange between the new continental dollars and specie was 40 to 1, while the real market value was more like 100 to 1.[3] Since Congress had no means of raising money through taxation, it could only rely on loans and requisitions from the states, and they simply had their own problems to worry about.

The army was measurably affected by these problems. The same troops that had fought, often without sufficient food, clothing, or arms, were now on the edge of revolt. Soldiers in the field, it seemed, had always been the last on the list of concerns, and experienced financial difficulty throughout the war. Indeed, in 1780 Congress had been forced to pass a special measure to head off wholesale desertion by its officers. A bonus of one-half of a regular officer's current pay, to be paid for the rest of his life, had been offered to each officer who would agree to remain in the service for the rest of the war. The offer had been accepted and had been sufficient to retain their services. But in December 1782, more rumblings were heard. The army itself threatened to lay down its arms when peace was achieved. A few officers had mumbled about replacing Washington with someone "less scrupulous," but he had managed to quash the movement without any real friction.[4]

"Commutation," as the agreement to pay the officers a lump sum equal to five years' full pay came to be known, was not entirely popular. Noncommissioned officers presented petitions asking for similar bonuses while the "war men," those who had enlisted for the duration of the conflict, demanded immediate discharge. By the end of April 1783, Washington reported to Congress that his men were rioting, insulting their officers, and demanding discharge. In late May, Congress tried to raise enough money to pay the men for three months and instructed Washington to furlough as many as possible. More open threats were heard, and the officers demanded that the army be kept in camp until accounts were settled. Washington refused and dismissed them all, saying that the government had done everything it could to provide for the men.

The problems of Congress and the army did not end with the latter's dissolution. Six days later several hundred men from Pennsylvania surrounded the state house in Philadelphia where both Congress and the Pennsylvania Executive Council were in session. They kept the politicians cooped up inside all day long, pelting them with stones and insults. Terrified, Congress emerged late in the afternoon amidst a jeering throng. Once out the door they kept on going and did not stop until they reached New Jersey, from which they never returned.[5]

The reaction to commutation touched off a series of protests up and down the coast. Crowds gathered to shout their disapproval and conventions of citizens met to draw up resolutions in Virginia, New Jersey, and New York. James Madison believed that disaffection with Congress had grown by the late spring of 1783 to the point "as to produce almost a general anarchy."[6] In May some officers founded the Society of Cincinnati, a hereditary social order, to foster relationships and care for the more unfortunate among themselves, as well as the families of deceased officers.

Discontent was especially strong in New England. In the summer of 1783, all the Massachusetts state congressmen who favored commutation were voted out of office and a new delegation, all of whom opposed it, was elected. The Rhode Island legislature refused even to consider honoring the measure, and many people in that state thought that the principles which it embodied were quite similar to those Great Britain had tried to impose on the colony in the previous decade.[7]

The clamor seemed to reach its peak in Webster's home state. The Connecticut Assembly formally opposed the bonus, and specifically provided that no part of the revenues raised by impost could be used to pay the officers. By late summer, numerous town meetings had passed resolves condemning the payments as well as other grievances. Lebanon, for example, claimed that the pension was "contrary to the Genius of this State," and that it was "unconstitutional, injurious, impolite, oppressive, and unjust."[8]

In September, a special, extralegislative convention was called, and twenty-eight Connecticut towns sent representatives. "Commutation is the Jig," wrote one citizen, and the whole country seemed to be joining it.[9] Held at Middletown, the convention met three times between September and April, calling each time for investigation into the legality of the officers' bonus and asking the Assembly to oppose it. They also drew up a list of nominees for the upper chamber of the state legislature and denounced the Society of Cincinnati as an order of nobility.[10]

The Middletown Convention had a strong impact on Connecticut. Under pressure from this body and from rumors connecting his name with war profiteering, Jonathan Trumbull resigned the office of governor. He had been in office for fourteen years, the only governor to serve through the entire Revolution. At about the same time the tenures of three national representatives (two of whom, Oliver Ellsworth and Oliver Wolcott, were personal friends of Webster) ended, and three new candidates, all convention sympathizers, were elected. They took their seats in January 1784.

Noah Webster's immediate reaction to the convention was bewilderment and fear. He could not really comprehend why it happened, but he struggled to make sense out of it for himself and for his neighbors as well. Anger filled his mind as the differences between his hopes and American realities widened, and especially when he thought of the possible consequences of what he saw going on around him. He was fearful that America's utopian opportunity would be lost and that the morass of corruption that was Europe would be copied on this side of the Atlantic. Frustrated, confused, and bitter, he responded as he did to all the important events of his life: he wrote. Indeed, Webster wrote obsessively: it was his primary means of relating to others and of sorting out the world as a whole. He once told George Washington: "I wish to enjoy life, but books & business will ever be my principal pleasure. I must write—it is happiness I cannot sacrifice."[11] During the last half of 1783 he filled Hartford's *Connecticut Courant* with attempts to analyze the Middletown Convention and all it stood for.

Webster was clearly afraid that the aim of that "nest of vipers" was basically to undermine the principles of the Revolution.[12] His anxiety and the harshness of his essays were increased by his identification with those ideals. The representatives were scoundrels, he said, "men of intrigue." They sought to replace those who had fought for the same cause he had fought for. If they succeeded, every "man of ability, of liberal and independent sentiments," would be extricated from places of power, replaced by men who were "tyrants at heart." Any person who supported them had to be an "unprincipled demagogue."[13]

The delegates looked suspiciously like Tories. While traveling through Connecticut in the fall of 1783, Webster talked to many citizens, often inquiring about the representative they had sent to Middletown. He was told that in general the delegates had not attended the various meetings of freemen in most towns until after the war had ended, but that they now seemed to be trying to control the meetings. Many of them, he stated, were "avowed tories." They had now switched tactics, and openly attacked the very men who had been the leading patriots, accusing them of being tyrants.[14] In March of 1784 he wrote to Sam Adams, asking for his views on the problems which then plagued Massachusetts as well as Connecticut. The troubles, said Webster, were "headed by a few designing characters, principally tories," who had for a long time been trying to "throw the state into confusion." Adams agreed.[15]

Webster was entirely opposed to the convention. Some delegates charged that the officers had extorted the promised bonus. But Webster pointed out that they had not known about it until after it had been passed. In support of his point, he quoted Washington, who said that the officers had known nothing of the bonus until Congress passed it. Another voice from Middletown wailed that the entire army should have been discharged, a second one raised, and no bonus paid to keep them at the front. Webster dismissed this as perfectly ridiculous. The convention proclaimed that the fledgling Society of Cincinnati was a threat to Liberty, and Webster laughed at this suggestion. "From such a society of men as little is to be feared as from the order of Masons, a convention of physicians, or a company of merchants."[16]

The logical conclusion to the events of 1783, including the convention, he believed, was quite obviously anarchy. If the current flow continued a few more months, he "would not give a farthing for the best interest of the state." The word "anarchy" was to him the most dreadful of all; "despotism is far preferable to it." The consequences of anarchy were fatal, for it was "inevitably followed by tyranny."[17]

When the Middletown Convention adjourned in the spring of 1784, Noah Webster felt greatly relieved. In the April elections, convention nominees were soundly defeated. Trumbull's former deputy-governor was elected to replace him, while an entire slate of anticonvention men gained seats in the Assembly. Six days later, a federal impost was approved to fund the bonus. Writing in the *Connecticut Courant*, Webster noted the death of the factious spirit:

> Yesterday se'night about five o'clock p.m. departed this life in the eighth month of his age, MR HOBBY CONVENTION, a person of

43

great notoriety in this State. His death was attended with violent spasms and convulsions, produced no doubt by the rigour of a strong fiery constitution, struggling with that *new* and fatal *disorder* called *Reason*. His remains will be *decently* interred in May next, and his funeral eulogium will be pronounced by Mr. Government.[18]

The events of the early 1780s had shaken Webster's faith in the people. They had indicated to him that Americans were easily deceived by anyone who could speak well and make a show of being virtuous. "I pretend not to lay down rules for other people," he said, while recommending that no one vote for candidates who actively solicited support. He had listened to people during elections, hearing them say they would vote for a man because he was *"next in course"* or because they simply thought that he would "do enough." He had begun to suspect that people had forgotten that their right of self-government had been a principal issue in the Revolution. Americans no longer seemed to care enough about government to pay close attention to their leaders.[19]

In his more reflective moments, Webster thought about the ways in which governments are constructed and stabilized, and one element in his revolutionary idealism disappeared. He had believed that Montesquieu was essentially correct when he said that governments, in order to rest on popular approval, must be based on public virtue. Now the events of the day had forced him to doubt the existence of public virtue. Webster concluded that he and Montesquieu had been wrong; that virtue could not form a stable basis for government.[20]

"Self-interest," he now declared, was "the ruling principle of all mankind." Adam Smith's economic theories were universally applicable, and if implemented would lead to widespread human happiness. When the self-interest of a majority of individuals merged to pursue the same object, it was mystically transformed into something quite different, patriotism or public spirit. Any particular interest that clashed with it could be labeled *"selfishness."* Thus, one impulse, self-interest, produced both negative and positive effects. In a time of danger, as the Revolution had been, the private interest of all individuals merged into a unified whole to resist a common enemy. When that common opponent disappeared, schisms in the pursuit of interests again appeared, and Webster theorized that this was what was happening in 1783. "This accounts for the capricious, fluctuating conduct of the people at the present time," he declared. So long as the British posed a threat, many were willing to sacrifice their personal fortunes for the common good, but now cooperation was not seen as an important value. The financial burden of taxes, inflation, and military bonuses drove people further apart. "Their estates and their liberties are secured," or so they believed, and "not one penny extraordinary will they pay, unless it is extorted from them by law."[21]

As a direct reaction to this new sense of doubt, Webster began to contemplate a means of controlling political events. Like the rest of the revolutionary generation, he had opposed the centralized government of England, and so this move did not come easily. The thought of rearranging and reinstituting a system which awarded power to a single man or a small body of men was an alarming one. Yet others had come to the same conclusion. In 1783 Washington sent a circular to all governors. Fearing "anarchy and confusion," he called for a "Supreme Power to regulate and govern the general concerns of the Confederated Republic, without which the Union cannot be of long duration." Tom Paine, a man as different from Washington as revolutionary America could produce, had called in 1782 for unification of the thirteen states under one central government. In *The Crisis*, Paine said that it was on the "movement upon one center, that our existence as a nation, our happiness as a people, and our safety as individuals, depend." Writing in February 1784, Webster saw centralization as one cure for the ills of the body politic. The current government "by committee" must end, for "the dignity, safety and happiness of America" were "inseparably connected with the union of all states." Cooperation must be achieved, and if a supreme authority had to be reconstructed, this time on this side of the Atlantic, so be it. "A Continental Union must feel, at all times," believed Webster, "the necessity of unanimity and vigor in all our federal operations."[22]

Webster's conceptualization of the nature of the new government emerged in early 1785. His *Sketches* symbolized his dualism. It contained four essays, the first three of which indicated his identification with America as a land of freedom and promise. The fourth was a call for a stronger centralized form of government within which they could be successfully administered. To Webster and others of his generation, any government must institutionalize the principles of the Revolution within a framework of a more stable national organization. *"Too much health is a disease,"* he remarked, and *"too much liberty* is the worst tyranny."[23] The essence of the new government was an emphasis on checks and balances, and his support of it was a reaction to the events of the 1780s. All states must be organically related, all must be equal in influence in national circles. If a single state could nullify or reject a measure passed by Congress, they would not be united for long.[24] Webster urged all those who would read his *Sketches* to consider themselves as inhabitants not of a single state or town, "but as *Americans.*" Provincial views must be subordinate to continental ones. Self-interest, the ruling principle of mankind, must not be allowed to become a provincial interest, but must be merged into a *"national interest."*[25]

Webster was dismayed when he examined the Confederation. Every positive measure toward reform and stability was defeated, enormous debts were unpaid, commerce was restricted. Those were the fruits of the Articles, and each state grabbed for what it could get. "The whole body, linked together by cobwebs and shadows," was "the jest and the ridicule of the world." Something must be done, and a stronger government was his answer to the chaos of the confederation. "On an energetic continental government principally depend our tranquility at home and our respectability among foreign nations."[26]

Yet there was a distinctly provincial tone to Webster's nationalism. The most perfect government that he knew of, and the one that he felt would be the best pattern for the central government to reflect in its construction, was the government of Connecticut. Indeed, the new government that he envisioned for America was nothing more than Connecticut writ large. The whole body of freemen would be the supreme authority on which all power would rest, although it would be exercised through a system of representatives. These delegated authorities would make all laws applicable to the whole nation. The governor would be elected by the freemen, with subordinates commissioned by him as judges, sheriffs, and other civil officers. "If the representation of the freemen is equal, and the elections frequent, if the magistrates are constitutionally chosen and responsible for the administration," he declared, "such a government is of all others most free and safe."[27]

Thus Noah Webster's *Sketches of American Policy* encompassed two very different impulses. This ambivalence perfectly reflected his youth and adolescence. On the one hand, Webster still advocated and believed in a basic revolutionary ideology. The extension of human freedom and self-control still drew his support. Yet he also felt a definite need for order and stability. The stronger, centralized government that he envisioned would embody these two concerns in a balanced system. It would then resemble the harmony of nature's planetary systems, a machine that worked like a clock. He planned to travel through the middle and southern states, and these were the basic ideas he wanted to discuss with others interested in the fate of the new nation. He spent the early spring of 1785 preparing for his journey.

Packing extra copies of his *Sketches* along with copies of the three volumes of his *Institutes*, Webster left Hartford in May. In addition to distributing and discussing his ideas, he intended to secure copyrights for his books in as many states as possible as well as to agitate for state and federal copyright laws. Since he was still an unemployed schoolteacher and unsuccessful lawyer, he probably also planned on meeting as many influential people as possible; reputable contacts might make it easier to secure wide distribution and acceptance of his books. In addition, knowing almost no one and having little money to secure the necessary lodging and meals raised apprehensions. Work would have to be found from place to place, and he thought he might be able to give a series of lectures in the towns he visited. If he could draw a large enough audience they might even pay for his transportation costs. Writing to a friend, Webster expressed fears that he would not be as welcome in the South as someone from Europe, for he had no reputation to precede him, and there was a natural dislike for northerners.[28]

The trip was a strenuous one. Over the next year and a half, he traveled up and down the Atlantic seaboard. During that time his *Sketches* appeared in print in New York, Philadelphia, Baltimore, and Charleston, and he gave his lectures in virtually every center of population in between.

On 18 May 1785, he reached Alexandria, Virginia, and the next day he introduced himself to George Washington. Mount Vernon had by then become a stopping place on the tours of many American travelers,[29] and so Washington was probably not surprised to see an unemployed schoolteacher of whom he had never heard mention. The general's reception was pleasant; he even indicated that he was impressed. Webster presented him with a copy of his *Sketches*, and the remainder of the day was spent in talking about the need for a strong central government, as well as agriculture, education, and the necessity of abolishing slavery. They spent the evening in a laughter-filled game of whist, and before he left, Webster asked Washington to endorse his *Institutes*. Replying that he had not read them, the general declined.[30]

For the next four months Webster traveled in the South. A ride on a sloop between Baltimore and Charleston took twenty-seven days. He stayed in South Carolina for only two weeks, and returned to Baltimore almost bankrupt. He had incorrectly estimated how long he could live on what he had taken with him, and so in Baltimore he decided to offer his services as a singing master in order to survive. Enough students were gathered, and in September his school successfully opened. At the same time he began to write the lectures which he planned to use as another source of income.[31]

In October Webster was off again, with greater success. He roamed from New Hampshire to Richmond, stopping to lecture in any town with enough people to warm a room. His subject was the English language, and his talks were marked by an increasingly nationalistic tone. In Philadelphia, Dover, Boston, and Newburyport he called for a more drastic and complete separation from England. He proposed his new American language as a tool of cultural independence, and was full of ideas about how it could be developed and implemented.[32] Along the way he dined with many dignitaries. James Madison, to whom Washington had sent a copy of the *Sketches*, lauded his work and said that Webster was a major factor in the passage of a copyright law in Virginia. Webster met the presidents of virtually every major American college, including Harvard, the College of New Jersey, Dartmouth, and Yale. All had favorable words for his work. With Benjamin Franklin he discussed the need for a total reform of the alphabet, one of the sage's fondest projects. With Washington, whom he visited a second time, he spoke of education and nationalism. He discussed many topics with Tom Paine. David Rittenhouse, Benjamin Rush, David Ramsay, Aaron Burr,

Samuel Lathem Mitchill, Roger Sherman, Simeon Baldwin, Timothy Pickering, and John Dickinson all offered him encouragement. By 1787 his books were being read, printed, and sold in every major American city, and the precocious Yankee peddler had indeed become, almost overnight, without family influence or financial backing, the "schoolmaster of America."[33] At times his audiences swelled to three hundred, and when he spoke in Philadelphia, newspapers as far away as Boston reported the event.[34]

It was a rewarding nineteen months, but not all of his experiences were pleasant. For one thing, he did not like the South. His sense of asceticism and ethical morality was offended by the lifestyle of the Virginia gentlemen whom he visited, especially by the gambling, horse racing, and other forms of what he considered "dissipation." A ball he attended, given by one of Washington's nephews, had cost £18, and that shocked him. When one Maryland senator confided to him that only about 10 percent of the plantation class could read and write, Webster was astonished: "O New England! How superior are thy inhabitants in morals, literature, civility and industry."[35] He emphasized his asceticism when he sent to Washington a copy of Timothy Dwight's "The Conquest of Canaan," an epic poem celebrating the Revolution. Webster pointedly commented that he could recommend it to "every friend of America and of virtue."[36] He was most shocked by the elections he witnessed in the South. While Connecticut had a long history of peaceful elections, the South stood sharply in contrast. There men sought every advantage in an election and even begged the citizens to vote for them. He noted that election days south of Pennsylvania often degenerated into "mere riots," and almost always they were a source of disputes which ended with bloody noses "and sometimes with greater violence."[37]

Yet even New England had not been peaceful during his journey. Indeed, western Massachusetts had been in virtual rebellion during most of the decade. By the fall of 1786, many parts of New England were plagued with economic difficulties. The burden of local and national debts, combined with monetary chaos, produced armed bands who attempted to stop various civil proceedings. In August a convention not unlike the one in Middletown three years before met in Hatfield, Massachusetts. The delegates demanded that the state government issue paper money in large amounts as a cure for the economy, and listed nine other grievances. In the course of their meeting they managed to denounce virtually every branch of the government as well as every person in it. Later that month a mob prevented the Court of Common Pleas in Hampshire County from meeting, while in September another crowd forced a court in Worcester County to adjourn. Similar events occurred across the state and in November an organized army of over two thousand discontented citizens began regular drilling and other military preparations. Henry Knox, former commander of artillery under Washington, wrote a widely publicized letter claiming that the men under arms numbered between twelve thousand and fifteen thousand and that they proposed to march on Boston to secure a common division of property. In January 1787, the rebels, led by Daniel Shays, were easily suppressed by state troops, but the damage had been done. Many Americans were genuinely aroused, afraid that his rebellion was only a dark portent of worse events to come. Those who sought a stronger government found wider acceptance of their ideas, and a convention meeting in Annapolis recommended that another convention be held to consider major changes in the Articles of Confederation.[38]

Webster personally felt the shock of social unrest. In June of 1786 he stopped momentarily in Hartford in the middle of his tour. He had been received warmly and decided to deliver a lecture in his home town. As in other cities, he advertised that it would cost two shillings to attend, though he had presented a few free tickets to members of the state legislature. An angry mob gathered outside the church he was scheduled to speak in, interrupting his performance by loudly protesting the cost of admission and the free distribution of tickets to politicians.[39]

After this incident he continued on to eastern Massachusetts where he found himself in the middle of Shays' Rebellion. Deeply troubled, Webster reacted strongly. In September he wrote a normal business letter to his publishers, calmly discussing minor publishing agreements. At the end his tone dramatically changed when he began berating the protestors with highly emotional language. "I would fight the insurgents," he said, should they attempt to stop the court in Salem, in Ipswich, or in Newburyport where he was lecturing. After relating a few details of some of the actions, he wrote to a friend that "the mob is headed by some desperate fellows, without property or principle."[40]

Without law, feared Webster, people would cease being "free and safe." The ultimate implications of such lawlessness frightened him:

> The same principle which leads a man to put a bayonet to the breast of a judge, will lead him to take property where he can find it, and when the judges dare not act, where is the loser's remedy? Alas, my friends, too much liberty is no liberty at all. Giv [sic] me anything but mobs: . . . I would shoot the leader of a mob, sooner than a midnight ruffian.[41]

Yet good men, and he still believed all men were basically good, obeyed and respected the law. Not all dissidents, he stated, were of low character. Many well-meaning people were led into opposition merely by false information. The truth, diffused among the people at large, would soon restore tranquility.[42]

Shays' Rebellion, believed Webster, pointed out the need for strong government to curtail lawlessness. "The Devil is in you," he had heard clergymen say to the mobs over and over again, but he knew that the devil was not the problem. If anything, it was the jealousy of Congress among the states that was devilish, as well as the general weakness of the confederation. One state could stop the others from adopting measures to control financial ills. The obsession of some people with fancy clothes, baubles, and trinkets added to the instability of the situation because it wasted precious funds on unnecessary items. Disrespect and loss of faith in the law only made things worse.[43]

Webster still encouraged all men to "shake off every badge of tyranny," and he still firmly believed that "the best way to make men honest, is to let them enjoy equal rights and privileges." Citizens must not suspect the Shaysites of being rogues. Oppressive laws must be avoided. "Leave force to govern the wretched vassals of European nabobs," he wrote, for it had no place in America. Men must deal with problems through laws which would improve man's already "excellent nature." In short, he believed that "no man will commence enemy to a government which givs [sic] him as many privileges as his neighbors enjoy."[44] Yet mankind must not be given too much liberty. People who enjoy a great amount of freedom often carry it to the point of being licentious, he observed. It was this excessiveness that was dangerous.[45]

In November 1786, Webster ended his trip in Hartford. It had been a huge success; his name was known in every state. Yet he was not happy: doubts about the ability of man to live by his own laws in a republican government plagued him. It was quite possible, he thought, that "people in general are too ignorant to manage affairs which require great reading," and so his system of education took on greater importance. Consequently he now gave his publishers the right to sell all his works at even lower prices in order to increase their circulation. Webster was not making much in royalties as it was, and claimed that it did not matter to him. He wished only to "live an honest man. I wish to do justice to all men and I am frequently obliged to do it at a great loss."[46]

Even more troublesome were the mild doubts beginning to surface about the liberty for which he believed the Revolution had been fought. He was once as strong a republican as any man in America, he noted, but "*Now a republican is among the last kinds of governments I should choose.*" Instead he would prefer a limited monarchy, for the capriciousness of one man could be opposed by the many and be corrected. The "ignorance and passions of a multitude," as recent events had shown, were more difficult to control.[47]

Thus Webster found himself in the middle of an intellectual dilemma, the solution to which was not far away. His revolutionary optimism and fervor were shaken, but not entirely destroyed. The journey had been in some ways disturbing, but it had also had two significant results. He had found acceptance among a class of men symbolized by Washington and Franklin, and he had become completely convinced of the need for strong government. The new Constitution, created by Madison, Washington, Franklin, and others, would provide the solution to the problem.

In the winter of 1786–87, Noah Webster attempted to analyze the problems of the new nation. Americans were unhappy, he claimed. All were surprised at the disappointment. Property was unsafe, taxes were unbearably heavy, and no changes appeared on the horizon. Things actually seemed to be getting worse, and even the Revolution now appeared incomplete since there were still signs of English influence in the speech, manners, and opinion of many Americans. What had gone wrong?[48]

Webster concluded that these troubles stemmed from the nature of the Revolution itself. It had occurred too fast; it had broken something quite fragile which held society together. There were habits and customs, and not necessarily British ones, which had been challenged along with foreign authority, and that was not good. Drastic change, said the former revolutionary, must come slowly. Innovation of course was necessary, but the events had shown that it should be organic, the "natural progress of society," and should come only when people were prepared. "Nothing can be so fatal to morals and the peace of society," he said, "as violent shock given to public opinion or fixed habits." The drive for freedom from tyranny in the 1770s had changed to a total opposition to authority in the 1780s. "The restraints imposed by respect and habits of obedience were broken . . . and the licentious passions men set afloat." Only a long series of prudent and vigorous measures could correct the flow of passions which the Revolution had unleashed. Someone had to take a stand, and Noah Webster volunteered: "I reprobate everything that wears the least appearance of opposition to lawful authority."[49]

In April he moved to Philadelphia. He had been offered a position teaching English, but there was an even more important reason for going to Philadelphia in the spring of 1787: The Constitutional Convention was about to meet. Although not a delegate, he was nevertheless quite interested in the proceedings. Since he had traveled up and down the continent stumping for a central government, perhaps he might now exercise some influence. In any event, many of the people he had met would be in the city, and he knew that Benjamin Franklin for one would welcome him warmly. Webster had made a special trip to Philadelphia to meet the aged genius during the previous winter, and the pair had talked over their shared ideas on language reform. Despite the difference in their ages, they had another interest in common; as Webster put it, both were fond of "visiting the ladies."[50]

The influence of Franklin and his friends had been profound. In their company and recognition he had found something for which he had been looking. They all treated him cordially and respectfully and exhibited a keen interest in his work. Here were people who were gracious, intelligent, and thoughtful, and for the first time in his adult life he felt as if he was really doing something valuable and constructive. These were the kind of men with whom he felt comfortable, who appreciated his work, who should lead the new nation. He sought their companionship, advice, praise, and hospitality. As he talked with this national class of men he found confidence, direction, and meaning.

The convention itself excited him. They were all here, the best that America could summon. They had been elected by the people, he believed, and thus this convention rejuvenated his belief in the masses. Here was living proof that it could work, Middletown and Daniel Shays notwithstanding. The fears and doubts of the previous years were assuaged, at least temporarily, by this remarkable gathering. All summer long he listened to the delegates discuss important issues—important not just for Philadelphia and Noah Webster, but for the rest of the world, whose hopes and dreams rode on their shoulders.

It seems, too, that those who came to the convention had a certain respect for Webster. His name appeared frequently in the Philadelphia papers along with the news of deliberations. There were a few disparaging remarks. The president of the University of Pennsylvania called him a "retailer of nouns and pronouns" and "a fomenter of rebellion," while another man wrote ten lengthy articles criticizing his *Institutes*. But the overwhelming comment on Webster was favorable.[51] In addition, he had met and fallen in love with Rebecca Greenleaf, the sister of a wealthy merchant, James Greenleaf. Two days after the opening of the convention, George Washington, by now virtually a god in America who would soon be declared president by plebiscite, paid his respects to Webster by visiting him at home. During the course of the summer Webster dined and held conversations with David Rittenhouse, Abraham Baldwin, Pelatiah Webster, Timothy Pickering, Benjamin Rush, James Madison, John Fitch (on whose steamboat he rode during its maiden voyage), Edmund Randolph, Rufus King, Oliver Ellsworth, William Livingstone, and many other "convention gentlemen." He had done all he could to pave the way for the gathering, and the members evidently recognized his contribution.[52]

On 15 September, two days before the close of the secret proceedings, Noah Webster's nationalistic endeavors were officially recognized. Thomas Fitzsimmons was the most inconspicuous member of the Pennsylvania delegation, which included Franklin, George Clymer, Jared Ingersoll, Thomas Mifflin, Gouverneur and Robert Morris, and James Wilson. He had spoken only twice during the entire summer, but now wrote to Webster asking for his help in the ratification process. "I consider the moment, as the crisis that will determine whether we are to benefit by the revolution we have obtained," said Fitzsimmons, "or whether we shall become a prey to foreign influence and domestic violence."[53] Like Franklin, who said he was astonished at the quality of the new system,[54] Fitzsimmons believed that it was "the best which human wisdom could devise." He thought Webster's powers were "eminently useful," and urged him to exert himself on behalf of the new government.[55]

Webster responded enthusiastically. Here was a chance to put in writing the fruits of his conversations with the delegates as well as his own observations and experiences. It was also a chance for him to feel as though he was a member of the national class. In fact, he spent three weeks thinking about all that had happened in the previous twenty years and organizing his thoughts. His reaction to the new Constitution was not haphazard scribbling; it displayed the effects of his entire life. Hints of his old revolutionary idealism, the fears aroused by the Middletown Convention and Shays' Rebellion, all shone through his essay in a complex maze of hopes and doubts, of ideals and realities. In early October he wrote a final version, and on 17 October Pritchard and Hall published his *An Examination into the Leading Principles of the Federal Constitution*. It was dedicated to Benjamin Franklin, who Webster was sure would agree with all he said.[56]

The new government institutionalized the kind of balance between freedom and stability he had advocated since 1785. It was an *"empire of reason,"* the best man could devise. Its origins lay in the wisdom of all the ages, in freedom and enlightenment. The people were the source of power, he proclaimed, not military might or superstition foisted by clergy. Majority rule was the most basic law of the land, while the idea that no man should be bound by a law to which he had not given his consent was also fundamental. But since each man could not possibly be present to give his specific consent to every piece of legislation, the concept of representation was employed in the new Constitution, and representation was "the perfection of human government." The House of Representatives was the guardian of the privileges of the people. Under this system there was no possibility of corruption or tyranny; he was still convinced of the basic goodness of all mankind. If a representative misbehaved, he could simply be voted out of office. The people, on the other hand, must act in conformity to the will of the majority. Each man must bind himself to "obey the *public* voice" and thus the liberty of each individual would be equally protected.[57]

At the core of the new system were two factors which he felt had been at the heart of the Revolution as well: equal distribution of property and frequent elections. "In which does *real* power consist?" he asked. His answer was short and plain: property.[58] Laws barring entail should be made in every state, for *"a general and tolerable equal distribution of landed property is the basis of natural freedom."* This was the very soul of the republic. Freedom of press, trial by jury, the right of habeas corpus, and all other secondary considerations, according to Noah Webster, were constructed and dependent upon a general distribution of real property among all classes of people. When property was equally held, no great combinations or families could control the government, and America was the only place on earth where this was possible. "No lords strut here with supercilious haughtiness or swell with emptiness," he said, "but virtue, good sense, and reputation, alone, ennoble the blood, and introduce the lowest citizen to the highest office of the state."[59] The *"right of election"* was also a principal bulwark of freedom, and the new Constitution guaranteed that right. "Americans!" he pleaded, "never resign that right."[60]

All of these concerns would be balanced by and within a strong, centralized government. To combat economic chaos, this authority could organize and regulate; the defense of all states would be made easier. Mutual concessions of the kind built into this system were necessary if America was to avoid anarchy ending in a Cromwell or a Caesar. It was a balanced government in all ways; large and small states had influence, and neither property nor number was overly powerful. The Senate made sure that passions, which could sweep through the lower house of Congress, would be checked by wisdom and experience, which he assumed would be lodged there. Indeed, the various checks and balances in the new system were wonderfully constructed to provide restraint on the passions of men from doing harm to themselves. "In turbulent times, such restraint is our greatest safety," while "in calm times, and in measures obviously calculated for the general good, both branches must always be unanimous."[61]

Noah Webster was clearly a firm and dedicated supporter of the new Constitution of the United States. His support was neither accidental nor superficial. He had come to this position as the result of a long series of events and some very strong emotions. The Constitution, he believed, embodied the best ideals for which the Revolution had been fought, and was worthy of "the ashes of our slaughtered brethren" who had died during the war. It also created an authority strong enough to prevent anarchy and was thus a cure for "our own suffering." When he thought of the new system, he could not help but think of the symbol which had been emblazoned on many flags during the conflict, and which had been designed by Benjamin Franklin: a divided snake over the words "UNITE, OR DIE." He wanted his fellow citizens to support the new system. "Let us, then, be of one heart, and one mind. Let us seize the golden opportunity to secure a stable government . . . " This government would bring man closer to the utopia of his dreams. He was convinced that it was the answer:

A HOUSE DIVIDED AGAINST ITSELF CANNOT STAND . . . CONSOLIDATION MOST ASSUREDLY INVOLVES OUR PROSPERITY, FELICITY, AND SAFETY.[62]

*A PROMPTER is the man who, in plays, sits behind the
rehearser, and with a moderate voice corrects him when
wrong, or assists his recollection when he forgets the next
sentence. A Prompter then says LITTLE, but that little is
very necessary and often does MUCH GOOD. He helps
the actors on the stage at a dead lift, and enables them to
go forward with spirit and propriety.*
     N.W., 1791

4 *The Prompter*

With the end of the Constitutional Convention, Webster decided that his
usefulness in Philadelphia had ended. New York looked more promising,
and there he began the first truly national and reform-oriented publication in
America. Unfortunately the magazine ran less than a year before it failed,
and in the winter of 1788–89 he retreated to Hartford, where he remained
until 1793.

Throughout these years, Webster perceived himself as a prompter,
pointing out America's faults in a moderate tone while advocating the basic
positions he had articulated in 1785 and solidified in his 1787 essays on the
Constitution. No significant intellectual transformation occurred. Assuming
the Enlightenment doctrines, the positive nature of man and a utopian future
for America, he spoke of the extension of human rights and progressive (if
moderate) social change through humanitarian reform. All these could be
achieved through a stronger centralized government.

The new nation needed a national voice, he decided in the autumn of

1787, one that would tie the various threads of the country together. He admired Josiah Meig's *New Haven Gazette* and Mathew Carey's *Columbian Magazine* in Philadelphia, but they did not fit the image of what a truly national magazine should be. He believed he could found a broadly appealing national paper, without financial support. Original essays on every conceivable topic would be included along with the latest political, commercial, and cultural news from all corners of the country. History, geography, satire, poetry, science, and peculiar customs would grace its pages. Indeed, there would be something for everyone, and all would be written in nationalistic tones.

The end of the year was consumed in seeking subscribers. He wrote to people up and down the Atlantic coast, asking for encouragement. Much time was spent looking for a printer, since Webster had neither the energy nor the inclination to do the physical work of placing the ink on the page. In January 1788, the first issue appeared. For the next ten months, the *American Magazine* was Webster's main occupation.[1]

In the course of editing the *Magazine*, Webster commented on many diverse subjects. He personally wrote and edited histories of the discovery of America, essays on the possible origin of ancient buildings, poetry, gothic and sentimental stories of European romance, theological tracts, and essays on agriculture, botany, and law. Writing under the pseudonym "Giles Hickory," he personally fought for the new Constitution, and also expounded on economics and education.

Giles Hickory reaffirmed much of what Noah Webster had already said in favor of the new system of government. By its very nature, all mankind had the right to "enjoy life, liberty, and property." Laws should be made by the consent of the governed, and the key to good representation was the freedom of election. Government was a sacred contract which neither party should break, and the basis of the laws made by the people's representatives should be *"a regard to the greatest good which can be produced to the greatest number of individuals in the state."* The "collective sense" of the whole must be followed.[2]

But new questions had arisen about the Constitution, and he did his best to answer them within this framework.[3] A few convention delegates had refused to sign the document, most notably Elbridge Gerry, Edmund Randolph, and George Mason. In general, the opponents feared centralized power. They believed that the new federal government would be too strong, that too much power had been given to the president and the Senate.[4] They were convinced that state sovereignty would be obliterated.

The Constitution, in the mind of Noah Webster, was now synonymous with stability, progress, and order, and the Anti-Federalists were a real threat. Their objections were echoes of the cries first raised at Middletown in 1783 and in Massachusetts in 1785–86. They stood for anarchy, and must be beaten back, or the work of utopia building could not go on. He noted that extralegal mobs had not disappeared, that they were still active. One riot in which a jail had been taken over by men armed with rifles particularly disturbed him.[5] In his eyes the decade of the 1780s had seen a continuing breakdown of respect for authority, and with that came a certain amount of disillusionment.[6]

The Anti-Federalists advanced specific arguments that Webster tried to refute. They called for an unalterable constitution and a bill of rights as safeguards against future evils. Both of these were useless, as far as he was concerned. Government took its form and structure from the values and habits of the people.

The people would have no difficulty making changes. The delegates to the convention were not infallible, and must not be allowed to make laws which would be oppressive to future Americans.[7] Following this train of thought, a bill of rights would simply be "*absurd.*" The present generation had no right to tell the next what privileges they may or may not have. Those decisions must be left up to them. America was not Europe, and there was no one here to fear. Barriers "against our *own* encroachments against ourselves," he thought, were ridiculous. Those who attempted to construct them were "Don Quixotes fighting windmills."[8]

By 1788 Webster's nationalistic vision led away from self-control. The Anti-Federalists raised a call for the right of local instruction of representatives, to which he was adamantly opposed. Again the fears raised by Middletown and Daniel Shays were at work. Webster felt that this issue boiled down to whether, in a free state, there ought to be any distinction between the powers of the people or electors, and the powers of the representatives in the legislature. The correct division, he felt, lay in the abilities of the legislators themselves. The people in the towns and villages, some hundreds of miles from the Capitol, could not possibly have all the information necessary to make a sound judgment on every vote in Congress. As he had said before, although the opinions of the people should be collected, they should not be allowed to bind the representatives to a specific action. "When the people are well informed their general opinion is perhaps always right," but the simple and obvious fact was that they were not always well informed. The people often had only partial knowledge, at best, of the facts in any situation.[9]

The problem of instruction rested on a general misunderstanding of the common conception that power resided in the people. This incorrect interpretation, he said, had been one of the principal sources of discontent and disorder. For power to directly reside in the people, all would have to attend conventions on every issue, and with four million people in the country, that was of course impossible. Instructions also were inadequate; the representatives must be free to negotiate. "In short, the collected body of Representatives is the collected sense and authority of the people."[10]

The *American Magazine*'s views on education were heavily oriented toward reform. By 1788 Webster had become a leading voice in American education.[11] While his political and economic writings may have been over-shadowed by the *Federalist Papers* of Hamilton, Madison, and Jay, his agitation for educational reform was surpassed by no one. Every issue of the *Magazine* carried at least one article on the subject, ranging from general calls for change to specific programs. Foremost in Webster's mind was the necessity of using education in the struggle for freedom. "Americans unshackle your minds, and act like independent beings," he wrote. "You have been children long enough, subject to the control, and subservient to the interest of a haughty parent." A broad program must be formed and acted upon, for the national character, like the national government, was not yet formed, and education could be used to inculcate the ascetic values of virtue, liberty, and patriotism in all Americans.[12]

No mere shouter of slogans, Webster always prompted his readers with specific suggestions on how to build a useful system. One of the central problems, as he knew from his own experience, was the poor quality of instruction. Parents wished their children well educated, which was difficult when their teachers were "clowns." He felt that in many states the school laws were still "monarchical"; no provision was made for teaching the children of people too poor to send them to school, and thus only the rich obtained even the meagerest education. This situation must be changed. Most important for the new nation, however, was that its system of education be made practical. Dead languages were useless for farmers or merchants, and should be replaced with basic courses in English. Since all students were not exactly alike, each should be allowed to formulate an individualized plan of study. Students should obtain a minimum level of competence in mathematics and grammar, and then be allowed to pursue a course connected with their destiny in life. In the classroom, he added, rote memorization must be eliminated. It did not teach ideas nor help develop patterns of thinking. This program was indeed visionary, since it depended on a system of public education that did not exist.[13]

All this applied to male education; Webster also advocated increased education for females. His attitudes closely paralleled those of his friend Benjamin Rush and many others.[14] In essence women were held naturally inferior to men; males should engage in politics, labor, war, and other masculine activities, while women were naturally suited for submissive domestic routines. As man's companion, they restrained vice, refined society's manners, and in general reformed male habits. These role limitations were rigidly and nearly universally held in early national America. To deny them would undermine female happiness.

Above all, Webster and his contemporaries sought to harness the moral power of women and their influence on children. Indeed, the primary concern in Webster's early writing on women's education was not really women; it was their role in shaping the character of future Americans, both male and female. All sorts of positive reforms could be accomplished if women would raise children as hard-working and moral patriots.[15]

Women's education should differ from that afforded men. Females should not be taught to deal with abstract metaphysical questions, read or write novels, dabble in foreign languages, or even prepare for the world of business. Like men, women should be taught to write and speak good English. Moral character could be inculcated through the study of housekeeping, domestic economy, and child-raising.[16] Thus the education of both sexes could be tools of national development.

Participation in the "Grand Procession" held in July to celebrate the adoption of the Constitution symbolized Webster's nationalistic prompting. New Yorkers paraded up and down the town in orderly groups, divided according to their occupation. It was a happy event. Tailors marched beneath a giant flag on which sat Adam and Eve, surrounded by a chain of state-named links around the word "majority." Tanners, curriers, skinners, cordwainers, and furriers marched among giant statues of Washington and even more colorful flags emblazoned with federal eagles with wings spread; large horse-drawn stages depicted work, or scenes of heroism symbolic of past episodes in the life of the new republic. The procession, containing at least five thousand people, was over a mile and a half long. Among the throng marched Noah Webster, proudly numbered as a member of the Philological Society which he had helped to found the previous March. His group was dressed uniformly in black, and he marched at its head, bearing a large scroll "containing the principles of a Federal language."[17]

Despite his involvement in national questions, life in New York was not altogether pleasant for the young editor. The *American Magazine* was unsuccessful and began to fail almost immediately. He was becoming increasingly well known in high circles and now corresponded regularly with men of prominence like Franklin,[18] but he was not becoming more popular. As early as 1786 he had been stung by charges of excessive vanity and egotism.[19] The recognition won by his lectures, pamphlets, and magazine swelled his ego; he dropped the names of his famous acquaintances with regularity in his everyday conversations. Now thirty years old, he was becoming arrogant, vain, contentious, and generally unpleasant. One potential subscriber referred to him as "the monarch," and "a literary puppy," who was downright "intolerable."[20] The few friends he had made in New York grew tired of his egotism, and by the fall of 1788 even they disliked his company. Writing to one of them shortly after he had left for New England, Webster remarked bitterly that "it is a satisfaction to find a few friends whose attachment is not shaken by slight faults or popular opinions."[21] On top of this, he strongly wanted to marry Rebecca Greenleaf, but his lack of financial stability brought nothing but discouragement from her family.[22]

In addition, Webster himself felt a growing sense of alienation. He believed his magazine was beneficial to all Americans, and its lack of financial support upset him. His prompting appeared to bring only negative results. Few seemed to pay attention to what he was saying, and he recognized that he was losing friends because of his growing bitterness. As his situation deteriorated, he described his emotional reaction to his future wife:

> I sometimes think of retiring from society and devoting myself to reading and contemplation, for I labor incessantly and reap very little fruit from my toils. I suspect I am not formed for society; and I wait only to be convinced that people wish to get rid of my company, and I would instantly leave them for better companions: the reflections of my own mind.[23]

In October he left New York. The magazine's circulation had dropped to a mere 200,[24] and he was growing anxious to see Miss Greenleaf. He officially closed the magazine and fled to New England. Stopping only briefly to see his parents in Hartford, Webster reached Boston in December.[25]

He was in a state of bewilderment. One observer during this period described him as "unstable as water."[26] Once again, he found himself with no place to go, no one to turn to, and no real plans for the future. He knew only one thing for sure: that he was in love and that he wanted "the happiness of a friend whose interests should be mine."[27]

His task, then, was to gain financial solvency. The effort to find a viable means of supporting a wife became the most important thing in his life. As he told James Greenleaf, "Becca is all that is good and to *me* that is dear. If happiness depends on a Union of souls, I am sure we have the most flattering hopes."[28] Since his lectures were the most successful project he could fall back on, and since there seemed to be an interest in subjects national and educational, lecturing was the only thing he could think of to do. He spent the next four months revising his notes and arranging for the publication of his lectures.

By spring he had managed to find a publisher but still had no income. He returned to Hartford in May, where he believed he could make enough money to support a family. He again attempted to practice law, and his books began to provide a little in royalties, so that by fall he was almost solvent.[29] A small loan from his future brother-in-law helped, and in October of 1789 he married Rebecca Greenleaf.[30]

With marriage came the first stable period of his adult life. For the next four years he felt at home in Hartford and concentrated mostly on making money and participating in the local social life. Hartford in the late 1780s and early 1790s was one of the cultural centers of the young republic, and Mr. and Mrs. Noah Webster enjoyed themselves, dining with the leading citizens. They socialized with John Trumbull, Chief Justice of Connecticut Jesse Root, and Peter Colt, the state's treasurer. Their social circle included many of the young lawyers about town and the Friendly Club, which included Dr. Samuel Hopkins, Dr. Mason F. Cogswell, Theodore and Timothy Dwight, and David Humphreys.[31]

Most important of all was Webster's family. During the entire course of his long and publicly turbulent life, his relationship with his wife and family remained singularly positive and supportive. Indeed, it stood in stark contrast to his relationship with the rest of the world. The births of his eight children were joyous occasions;[32] their education and general upbringing were among his deepest and most absorbing interests. When he moved to New Haven in 1798 and found no schools suitable for them, he began one of his own.[33] He spent hours and hours with his children, singing, reading, laughing, and playing;[34] with them he had a relationship that was warm and full of positive, loving feelings. Webster was not given to expressing these kinds of emotions, and quite possibly never mentioned his family in public. Yet when one daughter died giving birth in 1819, both he and Rebecca were despondent for many months.[35] They then raised the grandchild as if she were their own. Another daughter was evidently retarded; yet Webster never spoke of the burden. William, his only son to live past childhood, suffered from "a native imbecility of mind." Of him Webster often said, "He is my only son, and you know I love him."[36] His letters to his wife were filled with questions about his children. "I love my children," he often wrote. Rebecca Webster once wrote to her children that "Papa longs to see you all. I heard someone conversing in the drawing room the other day and found him standing before your portraits . . . we often talk together (your father and myself) of our singular happiness in our sons-in-law and daughters and such a promising batch of grandchildren."[37] Indeed, from the scant written information that survives, it almost appears that there were two Noah Websters. The cold, cantankerous, authoritative, and self-righteous public man shielded a private, sensitive, warm, and loving family man. It was this private side to which he retreated at crucial times, as in 1788–89 and 1798. His family was a refuge, and when his relationship with them was threatened in 1808, he endured his most profound crisis.[38]

The security of his family relationships often gave him the strength to write, and while in Hartford he continued to advocate the development of a national language. Webster felt that in publishing his *Dissertations* he was going out on a limb. "I shall assert some strange things," he wrote, "some of them will be proved; and others, the world will say, are left unsupported." He was about to attack a few gods, and was prepared for the reaction. "Some great men, with whose works I have taken liberties," were standing with their mouths open, "ready to devour the child as soon as it is born." But he would go forward anyway, for "an author's brats are doomed to be the sport of a mad world."[39]

Noah Webster's *Dissertations on the English Language*[40] was not the product of hasty thoughts. As early as October 1785, he had written to Timothy Pickering that he had begun a major reformation of the language.[41] For two years before that he had been thinking about grammatical reforms which his teaching experiences had made him believe were necessary. His *Dissertations*, as he himself acknowledged, were the fruit of ten years' labor.[42]

Webster had some strong ideas about changing the language. He felt that the grammars of Johnson, Horne Tooke, and others, as laudable and honored as they were, had done more damage than good. The heart of their mistake was that they had tried to base the English language on rules derived from Latin grammar. To adopt Latin or Greek rules was absurd; they must be based on the language itself. Yet that was a difficult task; he knew quite well that languages were not fixed, concrete things, and the rules must be flexible enough to flow with the changes in the language. A perfect analogy, he thought, was an attempt to build a lighthouse on a floating island. New words appeared, old ones disappeared, the changes in usage, emphasis, and even pronunciation occurred continuously. Yet when examined closely, all languages contained analogies to others, and it was on this principle that he based his work.[43] He hoped this line of investigation would lead to the necessary rules for the use of the language.

His proposed reforms had a practical purpose. It was not an accident that this work was dedicated to Benjamin Franklin, who shared his interest in language reform. His praise of the sage exhibited the qualities which he himself valued most and tried to live by. Franklin was the hero of the book because he had not labored at useless systems or theories which would serve no purpose but to confuse his readers; he thought up no "unintelligible speculations in theology and metaphysics." Instead, Franklin seemed to Webster the enlightened Puritan *par excellence*. He had lived by a plain doctrine, never far from some useful business or some practical truth. Collecting facts and applying them to useful purposes had been his hallmark, and that was what Webster intended to do in his *Dissertations*.[44]

The central concern of this work was his theory of etymology, the development of language. The study of the true derivation of words, as he defined it, had been an accepted scholarly activity in Europe. John Horne Tooke and Dr. Samuel Johnson, the great English lexicographer, were the best known etymologists, but no American had emerged as a leading theorist and student of the subject. Webster's interest had been sparked by his attempts to organize and analyze the language and to make it easier to understand, especially for young students. His trip south in 1785 had originally given him the opportunity to put his observations down on paper. He had since revised them.

He believed that language had evolved slowly, over long periods of time. At the beginning, he thought, there had been only one language, spoken by different tribes of people living in what was now Europe. That first language had been basically "Phenician or Hebrew," and from it had developed the different languages: Celtic and Gothic. People had migrated from Asia Minor into Russia and northern Europe, and by comparing similar "radical" or common words, he found that the two languages had developed into no fewer than twenty-four others. Over the years, certain words had taken on different meanings, and new events, objects, and inventions peculiar to each culture had originated new terms. Different peoples advanced at different rates of speed, and their languages gradually separated. Yet a few words remained constant in sound, structure, and significance.[45]

Elaborate diagrams graced the pages of his work, setting forth the precise path taken by various dialects.[46] Webster's main interest was the development of English, which he believed could be easily traced. The original inhabitants of northern Europe had spoken Celtic, and four hundred years of Roman rule had not substantially altered it. But then the German tribes had invaded Britain in the fifth century, and among them was a tribe of Saxons. "The universality of the conquest is demonstrated by the total change in the language," he wrote, "there being no more affinity between the Saxon or English, and the ancient British, than between any two languages in Europe." The ancient British had fled to Wales, where they still remained as proof of his theory, speaking what he believed was the purest descendant of the original Celtic. The language, he believed, had been static until the twelfth century, when gradual changes began that were recognizable in contemporary speech.[47]

This account of the evolution of language led Webster directly to the principal message of his book: the need for a truly American language. He was acutely aware of the fact that the new nation had been and would continue to be settled by emigrants from many lands. Through a national language the differences in sectional dialects would be lessened and all citizens would eventually speak the same tongue. These Americans, he prophesied, would eventually number a hundred million. This fact alone was sufficient reason to systematize the language.[48]

But there was an even more important reason for establishing a common and distinct tongue. "*A national language* is a brand of *national union*," he wrote, and sincere efforts must be made to render all citizens national in outlook and character. Americans had not yet become sufficiently independent; they still exhibited an "astonishing respect" for the customs, manners, arts, and literature of Europe.[49] But Webster had lived through the previous decade, and he believed that Americans were susceptible to change. Their minds had been awakened to the possibilities of reform in every area, and language was no exception. New inventions had aroused attention, and expanded and invigorated the "intellectual faculties." "Here men are prepared to receive improvements," he believed, which would be rejected by nations whose habits had not been shaken by similar events. As he had said in 1783, now was the moment to embark on new adventures:

NOW is the time, and this the country, in which we may expect success, in attempting changes favorable to language, science and government. Delay, in the plan here proposed, may be fatal; under a tranquil general government, the minds of men may again sink into indolence; a national acquiesence in error will follow, and posterity be doomed to struggle with difficulties, which time and accident will perpetually multiply . . . . Let us then seize the present moment and establish a *national language,* as well as a national government.[50]

The idea of basic changes in spelling and the alphabet was not entirely new. In his first spelling book Webster had opposed the drastic change in this area others called for, such as the omission of the "u" in *honour, colour,* and so forth. That was an unnecessary step brought on by a "rage of singularity," he believed. If any letter should be dropped in those cases, it should be the "o," which was silent.[51] By 1785, however, he had begun to think about the possibilities for greater coherence in spelling as a means of speeding up the development of a national language.[52] By 1789, with encouragement from Franklin, orthographic reform had become a central part of his agitation for a national language. All superfluous letters would be dropped. In situations in which a letter had a vague or inconsistent pronunciation, a fixed, specific sound would be represented by a new character. Points would be placed over vowels to distinguish their fluctuating sounds.[53] Thus *publick* would become *public, neighbor* would become *nabor, hed* would be substituted for *head,* and so on.

In a collection of essays published in 1790, Webster put his ideas into operation:

> In these essays, ritten within the last year, a considerable change in spelling iz introduced by way of experiment . . . . The man who admits that the change of housbande . . . into husband, iz an improovement, must acknowledge also the riting of *helth, breth, rong, tung, munth,* to be an improovement. There iz no alternativ. Every possible reezon that could ever be offered for altering the spelling of words, still exists in full force: and if a gradual reform should not be made in our language, it will proov that we are less under the influence of reezon than our ancestors.[54]

Webster's nationalistic prompting extended from language into the area of economics. Again and again throughout the years between 1787 and 1793, in newspaper articles and private letters, he encouraged a whole series of new directions which he thought should be taken in that sphere of life. In December 1791, Secretary of the Treasury Alexander Hamilton delivered his "Report on Manufactures" to Congress. Hamilton had visionary plans for building a new and aggressive American economy. The new nation, believed the secretary and his chief assistant, Tench Coxe, must construct a modern, national economic system along the lines of Great Britain's. Most Americans were farmers, and so incentives for manufacturing must be instituted in the form of tax breaks, liberal government bounties, protective tariffs, and high guaranteed profits. Northern ships should carry southern agricultural products to new factories. Women and children should be allowed to work in manufacturing plants and mills, since otherwise there would be insufficient labor to run the plants. This new national economy would benefit everyone, they claimed, from farmers and merchants to carpenters and soapmakers. And, of course, Hamilton had a few other devices that he would like to see implemented, including a bank, a mint, and an extensive system of credit.

Noah Webster fully supported the Hamiltonian system. Many of the same ideas had crossed his own mind. Manufacturing would be good for the poor as well as the rich, for they would be able to find employment, and this would make them better citizens in the long run.[55] Bounties on wool as well as material for sails should be offered. "Let the monied man assist the artisan," he argued, "let the wealthy give the manufacturer a reasonable credit for his wool, that the manufacturer, in turn, may give a reasonable credit to the merchant in his cloths." A society should be established to promote the arts and sciences, which could then disseminate manufacturing advice and ideas. A national bank would make more capital available and perhaps attract foreign investments. Roads must be improved to carry the new goods, and so Webster drew up plans for a canal between Boston and Hartford.[56]

He also advocated several significant movements toward progressive social change and the expansion of human freedom. He applauded the outbreak of the French Revolution in 1789,[57] and on the first day of the next year he sang its praise in verse:

Fair Liberty, whose gentle sway
First blest these shores, had cross'd the sea,
To visit Gallia, and inflame
Her sons their ancient rights to claim.[58]

His opposition to slavery was strengthened and extended during this period. The *American Magazine* carried his abolitionist poem, "The Negroes' Complaint," a romantic, anguish-filled narrative of the life of a slave (Maratan), who had been captured in Africa, separated from his lover (Adila), and shipped across the Atlantic. Halfway across the ocean, Adila appears "as the mist that hangs light on the wave"; she beckons Maratan to join her and escape the fate for which he is headed:

She beckons, and I must pursue.
To-morrow the White-man in vain,

65

Shall proudly account me his slave:
My shackles I'll plunge in the main,
And rush to the realms of the brave.[59]

During or shortly after his trip through the South, where he undoubtedly watched slaves at work, he met Anthony Benezet in Philadelphia.
Benezet was a Quaker pioneering in antislavery agitation, and he awakened
Webster to the cause, as well as to the contradictions implicit in his vision of
American utopianism and the existence of people in chains. By 1789, Webster actively supported the abolitionist society in Philadelphia. He was in
frequent contact with Benjamin Rush, writing about the "progress of justice
and humanity towards the poor Africans,"[60] as well as ordering part of the
proceeds of his *Dissertations* to be given to the antislavery movement in Pennsylvania.[61] His revulsion against slavery had both moral and economic foundations. It was an evil of the worst kind, and he quoted Washington as
saying that it was unprofitable and counterproductive. Agriculture, they
both believed, was successful in a directly inverse proportion to the number
of slaves involved.[62]

The question of emancipation was a difficult one, for Webster as for
many other Americans. Several possible plans were put forward, but none
seemed to solve the problem.[63] Liberating all the slaves at once, it was widely
believed, would bring chaos. Webster rejected the possibility of freeing them
gradually and allowing them to live with whites, for that would risk discord
of the greatest kind. There was only one solution he felt was acceptable:
colonization. Yet even that route aroused deep fears within him, for in the
amount of time that it would take to find a suitable place and begin the
process, he believed, the "blacks would all be blended with the whites;
the mixed race will acquire freedom and be the predominant part of the
inhabitants of the south."[64]

Despite his dilemma over the question of the proper means of implementing emancipation and his fears of the mixing of the races, he continued
his attack on slavery. Later in the year, he published a book which was, on
the surface, just another reader for schoolchildren. In fact, *The Little Reader's
Assistant*[65] was an early abolitionist tract. Indeed, in a letter accompanying
the copy he sent to Thomas Jefferson, Webster acknowledged that although
he did not expect it to become widely used, "yet it may diffuse some useful
truths; which is my primary object in all my publications."[66] Among the stories of Columbus, the founding of New England, and others drawn from
American history were two concerning slavery. "Lamentation of an old female Slave" was a long narrative about a woman captured and enslaved by
whites while on her way to church. It included a graphic description of a
slave ship and fifty wretched years of bondage under cruel masters. The
other, "Story of the treatment of African Slaves," was even more alarming.
In it slaves were marked for identification with hot irons applied to their

cheeks, and driven through the desert. The slave ships, in all their filth and horror, were luridly described. The blacks in Webster's stories were not pathetic, debased creatures, but strong figures, capable of rebellion. "Sometimes they rise against their cruel masters, and attempt to regain their liberty," he wrote, "but for this, they are stabbed on the spot or beat and mangled in the most barbarous manner; or tied to the ropes and scourged with whips and chains." He described atrocity after atrocity. There could be no doubt about where his sympathy lay, despite his own fears of emancipation:

> Shall the barbarous and unlawful practice always prevail? Are the negroes brutes? Or are they *men*, like ourselves? Have not the negroes the same right to steal from us our wives and children, transport them to Africa, and reduce us to bondage, as we have to enslave them? If there is justice in heaven, vengeance must fall upon the heds [sic] of men who commit this outrage upon their own kind.[67]

In 1791 he helped found an abolitionist society in Hartford, and in November 1792, he delivered his strongest attack. In a speech which was later published, he tried to go beyond mere rhetoric and attempted to present an actual program for the destruction of the evil. All those who heard him or read his pamphlet, he believed, knew in their hearts that slavery violated the basic rights of humanity. It was such an obvious injustice that many elaborate essays had been written stating the case against it, and so he could not waste time rehashing that aspect.[68] Instead of attacking slavery on moral grounds, as he had previously done, Webster employed another tactic. The defenders of the system called on more down-to-earth economic justifications, and so slavery must be dealt with on the basis of its role in the everyday operations of society.

Its effect on the slaves themselves was perhaps the most pernicious part of bondage. When men of any race were prohibited from exerting themselves in their own behalf, they became mere machines, acting only when compelled. They also became insolent, villainous, cruel, deceitful, and lazy. Thus all the peculiarities that Webster and almost all other white Americans saw in the slave were not inherent, but due to their condition. This was a logical extension of the environmental determinism that stemmed from the underpinning of Enlightenment thought, John Locke's *Essay on Human Understanding*. As proof, Webster presented another stereotype believed by writers on Africa, who agreed that blacks were innocent, contented, joyous, hard-working, and inoffensive people.[69]

Oppression of blacks had ultimately to end in revolt. For a man who was profoundly shocked at the Middletown Convention, the specter of angry blacks fighting for their freedom was quite alarming. Hardened by severe labor, exasperated at insults, and disciplined in cruelty, normally humane people become "doubly ferocious," he believed, "and their insurrections are marked with more than savage barbarity." This happened not only in America, but everywhere that slavery as an institution had ever existed. Greece, Rome, France, and Germany had witnessed cruelty and murder from both slaves and masters, regardless of race.[70]

The effect on masters, he thought, was equally odious. Those who held the rod of tyranny became equally hardened and cruel. The civilized man who owned other men quickly became a savage, and all the other attributes of slaves gradually infiltrated the master class; especially obvious, he felt, was the spirit of revenge and oppressive instincts exhibited by the children of slaveowners.[71]

Webster found the effects of slavery on agriculture (which he generally referred to as "industry") to be equally profound. When one man labored for the benefit of others, he would not be nearly as industrious as when he worked for himself. Freeholders produced much more than slaves. He provided a wealth of statistics comparing the annual production of slave and nonslave states to prove it. His figures, he believed, proved that there was a direct positive correlation between the rates of production and three factors: lengths of leases, rent levels, and taxation. Furthermore, this correlation held true in Europe as well as in the United States. "The actual produce of a country is nearly in exact proportion to the degree of freedom enjoyed by its inhabitants," he concluded.[72]

The prompter realized that there was no alternative to emancipation. By 1793 he believed he had solved the problem. Immediate emancipation would have disastrous effects, and no one advocated that drastic course. All cultivation south of New York would halt, and thousands would be impoverished. Famine would occur, followed by bloodbaths between the races that would depopulate the entire region. Colonization, he now decided, was too costly and impractical; the slaves would not go without resistance anyway.

Webster urged Americans to raise the slaves gradually to the status of free tenants. The wealthier slaveowners should begin by giving small groups of slaves sections of land to work for themselves. He argued that this plan had worked in Poland, and with the contribution of agricultural knowledge from whites, it could work in America. It would "answer the double pupose of giving freedom to a miserable race of men, without injuring their owners and [without] obstructing the cultivation of the country." He felt that this was a sound, practical, safe way to deal with the problem of slavery without upsetting the social structure; it seemed quite fair to all concerned. If Americans followed his plan, slavery would be "utterly extirpated in the course of two centuries, perhaps in a much shorter period," he believed, "without any extraordinary efforts to abolish it."[73]

While his antislavery efforts consumed much time and energy, other humanitarian reforms also received his support. His long term of unemployment made him realize that not all men could find such sedentary ways to earn a living as the practice of law. Those whose jobs required them daily to face conditions they could not control encountered dangers from which they could not escape. Merchants could insure their ships and their cargo, he noted, but the men who also sailed in the ships could not replace their lives. Thus in 1792 Webster recommended that the good citizens of Hartford establish a "Charitable Society." Its purpose would be to relieve the distresses of the laboring poor who were "of good deportment and industrious." Widows and orphans would be assisted and a good education provided for the children. Those laboring poor who had families too large to support on what they earned should be given financial assistance.

Reform of penal laws also attracted his attention. Cruelty in criminal punishments was widespread in the new nation, and he felt it contradicted the nature of republicanism. Capital punishment was mere revenge. Webster denied that it could be justified under any circumstances. Instead he suggested more and better means of detention and rehabilitation.[74] Finally, his society would provide financial assistance for the laboring poor who were too old to work any longer.[75]

Between 1789 and 1793, Noah Webster played the role of a prompter, always urging the country on toward humanistic reform and national development. In all fields, from politics and education to economics, language, and antislavery, he advocated broad concepts as well as specific measures in his attempts to improve life.

Yet he was not always satisfied with his role as a behind-the-scenes prompter. Life in Hartford was pleasant enough, but he yearned to be near the center of activity. He was not yet financially stable, and still required some assistance from his brother-in-law. By 1793 he felt, as he had put it when he first moved to Hartford four years before, "out of the sphere of information," cut off from the "bustle of public life."[76] In the spring he began to look around for some way to move either to New York or to Boston, a way to return to a more publicly active life and make money as well.[77]

Let us never forget that the cornerstone of all republican governments is, that the will of every citizen is controlled by the laws or supreme will of the state.
      N. W., 1798

5 *Rejection*

The breakup of the authoritarian world-order of feudalism, monarchy, absolutist religious institutions, and the habit of deference has produced in western cultures a form of freedom dialectic in nature. It is freedom *from* the authoritarian bonds of Church and state which gave man limitations and a sense of security and unity with the rest of the world in which he lived. It is also freedom *to* emerge as strong, integrated, self-reliant individuals.

The dissolution of these primary ties creates anxieties and a feeling of aloneness and powerlessness which is intolerable and must be assuaged. When man breaks free from one set of coherent, ordered relationships with the rest of the world and perceives that his former security has been severed, he must reorient himself and seek to create secondary bonds between himself and the rest of society. In one way or another, man realizes that he must face the world outside himself without recourse to an omnipotent force. The response to this situation may take two basic forms. An individual may seek to unite himself with others through constructive exercise of his emotional and intellectual capacities, as Webster had in the 1770s and early 1780s. He may also fall back, give up his freedom, and try to overcome the resultant anxieties and aloneness by submitting to an authoritarian political, social, or religious system.[1] By the late 1790s Noah Webster had chosen the latter, for himself and for postrevolutionary American society as a whole. It was, in effect, a reaction to the political and social turmoil of the late eighteenth century following the Revolution, the loss of patriarchal authority throughout society, and his own conclusions concerning the nature of man and American inability to live his ascetic ideals. By 1798 he had begun a search for a means of limiting and restricting the behavior of his countrymen.

Anxiety over social and political events was widespread in early national America. Many Americans believed that the forces of human passion unleashed by the Revolution at home had spread to France with disastrous results. The widespread use of the guillotine after 1793 caused some who saw the events in France as a dark portent of the American future to conclude that stability could never be restored to western civilization. Surely the political rhetoric of the 1790s, hysterical at times and characterized by one historian as "phrenzy," can be understood as a product of anxiety over the process of social change.[2] Strong authority figures are often a product of the release from domination, and George Washington has long been viewed as America's father-figure, guiding the republic through the disorders of youth.[3] Indeed, the seemingly chaotic events of these years, including the response to civil unrest symbolized by Shays' Rebellion, the Whiskey Rebellion, Fries' Rebellion, and so on, the establishment of extrapolitical organizations such as the democratic societies which sprang up in the 1790s, as well as the beginnings of the first political parties, all appear as logical attempts to form secondary social bonds.

In recent years, numerous historians have turned their attention to various aspects of early national America. They portray "that peculiarly seminal period" (as Rush Welter calls it) as a time of enormous upheaval in all areas of life.[4] The powerful, dynamic forces unleashed by the Revolution brought the beginnings of modernization to every phase of society.

The transformation is impressive. All recent studies cite at least one and often several developments as the bases of anxiety in a particular area of American endeavor.[5] Political independence and the general dispersion of human freedom; expansion of white male suffrage; real urbanization complete with slums, poverty, crime, and social violence; the first factories and beginnings of industrialization; a growing belief in progress defined in technological and material terms; class tensions and divisions; the emergence of a free-market capitalism and its related values of competition, avarice, status, and success; immigration and cultural pluralism; a perceived decline in religion and the influence of the clergy; and massive demographic shifts: all seemed to occur simultaneously, producing tremors that threatened and actually undermined traditional values, social relationships, and old ways of life. Their cumulative effect brought enormous fears, often a frantic search for cohesion and stability, and a deep longing for social control.

While no single historian has yet examined these related phenomena in a systematic manner, David Hackett Fischer may soon do so. In a legendary unpublished manuscript, Fischer has outlined his plans for a massive fifteen-volume treatise encompassing all phases of American social history, from the beginning to the present. In his introductory book, he concludes that between 1790 and 1820, "an age of social revolution," American society was transformed in every conceivable category of activity. This sudden revolution "of enormous power and sweep—a revolution as powerful and complete as any in recorded history"—was the most dramatic ever, far more so than the French Revolution. It had a "manic quality"; for a privileged few it was a lark, but its effect on most Americans was profound, even terrifying. For most "ordinary normal human beings, it was a private hell—an agony of inner disturbance. . . . All our signs of psychic trouble rose to extraordinary heights."[6]

Fischer's impressionistic overview of social patterns is divided into ten categories. In all ten, the years between 1790 and 1820, or thereabouts, constitute what he calls a "critical period": the moment when "things hang in the balance" and decisions which form the future are made. In every area Fischer traces significant transformations. American demographics, including fertility and marriage patterns, death rates, attitudes toward death, and immigration, began to exhibit modern characteristics. The beginnings of intensive urbanization, the rank-size of cities, and migration rates all produced a modern distribution. An intensive growth of the national per capita production level, a vast banking system, and new patterns of ownership of the means of production added up to a transformed economy. Social stratification, measured by a growing inequality of wealth and new determinants of status, increased. The modern political system, indicated by an expansion of the electorate, a decline of elitism, and changes in office holding, emerged in nascent form. The development of voluntary associations and individuation produced a new national comity. Modern social pathology, marked by alcoholism on a grand scale, prenuptial pregnancies, more homicides, and widespread prostitution, appeared. Transformations of educational systems, American religion, and the development of the ideology of domesticity produced a new process of socialization. In law, the number of lawyers, law schools, treatises, law libraries, journals, and penal practices all increased dramatically, indicating a new role in society. Old forms of social thought dissolved under the pressure of these trends, and new ones appeared. Even the American language itself, says Fischer, was transformed and modernized, so that old forms of verbal comprehension were outmoded.[7]

This massive transformation profoundly affected Noah Webster. By the end of this phase of his life, he had rejected virtually every positive attitude toward social change. He reversed his view of human nature and began looking for an authority to which he and the rest of the American people could turn as a means of reestablishing a deferential world and ensuring social stability.

Reentry into public life was neither disturbing nor difficult. By the summer of 1793 Webster was ready to return to a more active life. His law practice was still a struggling venture; he did not enjoy it enough to invest the energy necessary to make it more successful. National politics still interested him; in fact he could not suppress his desire to participate in debates over important issues. Despite his isolation in Connecticut, Webster managed to keep up with the events in Philadelphia and New York, where the government was now lodged. He also retained his contacts in many influential circles. Thus when an opportunity to return to the center of power and activity appeared in 1793, he accepted it.

Webster's willingness to return is not surprising. He was, after all, still a believer in the future of America, a firm nationalist who felt strongly that he must do everything possible towards the construction of a new world characterized by freedom and virtue. His ego would be served by the attention which would be given him. Moreover, moving to New York seemed to offer a real chance for financial success. For quite some time, the city had been without a journalistic outlet for the loosely knit group of men, led by Alexander Hamilton, John Jay, and Rufus King, whom we now know as Federalists. A newspaper, they believed, was needed to combat the work of Benjamin Franklin Bache in Philadelphia, Thomas Adams in Boston, and Thomas Greenleaf in New York, all of whom ardently opposed the Washington administration. Friend of federal principles and advocate of federal culture, the former editor of the *American Magazine* was a logical choice. He had experience, was learned in the business of words, and most importantly, had a proven ability to use political invective. Webster was approached, and he replied that he needed a minimum amount of financial support; a deal was made. Each of the three leading friends of the central government, plus nearly ten others, would "loan" him $150. In the early summer he prepared to move.[8]

Perhaps in anticipation of what was to come, Webster retired to his study in Hartford early in the summer of 1793 and wrote out a summary of his political views. He was, he believed, a "true republican," and it seemed to him that other "true republicans" would believe in the same logical, obvious principles that he did. The ideas he espoused were essentially the same early Federalist lines that he had followed since the mid-1780s, and serve as a convenient point from which his development may be measured.

"True republicanism" was, to Webster, a coherent and simple program. Those who qualified as true republicans opposed war because it was the most terrible calamity that could befall mankind. War wasted energy, caused the shedding of human blood, and disrupted all commerce and order. True republicans were friends of the French Revolution, and ardently wished her freedom, civil liberties, and a sound constitution. They also knew that neutrality was necessary for the survival of America, and thus favored Washington's neutrality proclamation. At home, true republicans supported a republican form of government because of its liberty and stability. Most importantly, true republicans believed that equality consisted of an equality of rights, not of an equal division of property, as he himself had written so often in the past. The Revolution had destroyed hereditary ranks and titles, and all offices must now be filled by men according to their "*talents* and *virtues*." Finally, all true republicans realized that there was no need for extra-legal political groups like the democratic societies. There existed simply no evil, no opposition, and no corruption of a magnitude sufficient to warrant their existence. Thus the societies which had recently sprung up in Philadelphia and New York were useless and could even be dangerous if they proceeded to nourish discontent, jealousy, and mistrust of the country's leaders. He believed that these groups could cause a serious weakening of the government in the face of danger, especially if war with either France or England threatened.[9]

Despite these dangers, Webster still celebrated America in 1793 as a veritable utopia. Here the mind of man was as free as the air he breathed; here laws applied equally to all. Property was distributed fairly. All religions were tolerated, and no state-supported church demanded payment of lordly exactions or tithes. In comparison to Europe, it was a land of freedom and prosperity for all. Everyone could find employment, even the poorest could accumulate wealth:

> Here no beggarly monks and fryars [*sic*], no princely ecclesiastes with their annual income of millions, no idle court-pensioners and titled mendicants, no spies watch and betray the unsuspecting citizen, no tyrant with his train of hounds, bastards and mistresses, those vultures of government, prey upon poor peasants and exhaust the public treasury of the nation.[10]

Before leaving Hartford, Webster also took time to expand his comments favoring the course of the revolution in France. Much had happened in that country since 1789, including the rise and fall of governments, riots, and beheadings of royalty. Americans had written a great many words about these events and had exhibited much concern. Webster detected the beginning of a change in attitude toward the revolution from positive to negative.[11] He attempted to reverse this trend. Americans, separated by thousands of miles of ocean from the *ancien régime* and living amidst bounty unknown in Europe, could not realize the horror of peasant life before the revolution. He detailed the crimes committed by the monarchy in lurid fashion, defending the rebellion as a desperate response to tyranny and as an extension of the Revolution in America.[12]

Webster left Connecticut for New York City in August. He had chosen to live and work in public in a very volatile atmosphere. New York's political majority, staunchly Federalist in the early part of the 1790s, gradually became Republican. As the town divided, the political process itself became increasingly characterized by bitterness and caustic rhetoric. Just a few days after Webster arrived, one major newspaper carried the charge that Vice-President John Adams had attempted to subvert the republican form of government embodied by the Constitution. "Was he to embrace a stinking prostitute, and endeavor to palm her on the people of America for an unspotted Virgin," it read, "he would not . . . act a more infamous part than he has done."[13] This sort of atmosphere intensified throughout the decade. New Yorkers hung John Jay in effigy for his treaty and stoned Alexander Hamilton. Webster would write about it all in his newspaper.

An incident involving the French minister, Edmund Genet, immediately revealed the tensions and passions in the city. When Genet arrived in America in 1793, he was perceived by many as the very embodiment of the French Revolution praised highly by Webster and by most Americans.[14] Young, headstrong, handsome, and bellicose, Genet loudly voiced slogans calling for rule by the people, and went even farther by attacking George Washington. His arrival elicited large demonstrations by the democratic societies, newly organized groups of people friendly to France and in general opposed to the Federalist administration.[15]

By the time Genet reached New York City on 7 August, Washington and Jefferson had already decided to have him recalled. Manhattan, however, welcomed Genet with wild parades; thousands of people marched through the streets singing the *Marseillaise*, wearing cockades and shouting democratic and revolutionary slogans. The ship that had brought Genet to America, *L'Ambuscade*, had sailed into New York harbor ahead of the minister, emblazoned with similar slogans.[16]

On 12 August Noah Webster stepped into a political whirlwind. It was, says his biographer, "one of the most excited days" in the history of the metropolis. During the previous four days "a whirling mob of fanatics" had controlled the streets, marching, shouting, and singing in Genet's honor.[17] Financial support for his paper was still being negotiated, and since he had no permanent quarters, he fought his way through a large pro-Genet demonstration to Bradley's Tavern and secured temporary lodging. Unfortunately for Webster, it was also the home of Edmund Genet.[18]

The two met a few hours later. Webster had heard reports of Genet's activity and progress while he was packing in Hartford, but had paid little attention. There were other, more serious concerns on his mind, and thus when Webster and Genet were introduced at dinner, all seemed pleasant, with only minor apprehension on Webster's part. Yet in a few minutes, Webster was enraged. A United States frigate, the *Concord*, had recently taken a few ships as prizes. Genet stated loudly that the incident proved that the entire United States government, including President Washington, was under the influence of England. He said that he believed, and could prove, that the officers of the government were involved in a plan to subject the United States to English rule, and that the Americans would soon be slaves again. One minister's aide remarked, in French (obviously thinking that no one in primitive New York could speak his language), that "General Washington is making war on the French nation." Webster, unable to control his temper, stood up and shouted at the French party that they were quite mistaken; it would be impossible to subject the independent farmers of America to England, or for that matter, any other foreign power. Furthermore, he said, the executives knew quite well that it was impossible, and would never dare try such a frivolous scheme for fear of losing their jobs. Webster questioned Genet: Did the French minister really believe that Washington, Hamilton, Jefferson, and Knox were fools? Genet, undoubtedly with a faint smile on his lips, replied that "Mr. Jefferson is no fool." Webster was livid with rage.[19]

The Genet incident marked the beginning of the most important change in Webster's life. As the French Revolution moved into a more radical phase, it gained an increased importance in his mind. Its excesses frightened him and began to symbolize all that was wrong with man and the world as a whole. His analysis of its essential character led him to rethink his conception of the nature of man, which in turn commanded fundamental changes in his view of all else.

"Almost every man who espoused the cause of America in her struggle for independence," he said in the spring of 1794, "is now friendly to the revolution in France." Yet the guillotine was in use in Paris, and mob action in Philadelphia and New York brought visions of headless men and women to his mind. He saw a growing spirit of selfishness all around him, opposition to lawful authority and even to law itself. His own shop was threatened several times by mobs, and to Webster it seemed that society was disintegrating. Was this what republicanism was like? He certainly hoped not. "A King of France and a Mob in America have committed equally an outrage on the *liberties* of *others*," he thought; "it is an attempt to subdue *opinions* the right of which is sacred and inviolable."[20] Not law, but passion and despotic will seemed to reign. The tables had turned. In Europe the aristocracy believed their rights in danger from freedom of discussion. In the United States the democratic societies slandered all those who opposed anarchy. They had become "the tyrants of America."[21]

What really frightened him, however, was the guillotine. Its use was now regular in France, and to one who had grown up in the quiet hills of Connecticut, its bloody work was terrifying. It had "filled France with human blood," and been used unmercifully against anyone who differed with even the slightest whim of those in power.[22] Webster had had occasional doubts about the nature of man, but now those doubts turned to fear:

Is man a tyger [*sic*], a savage, restrained only by law and a little education, but let loose from these, delighting in war, in death and all the horrid deeds of savage ferocity? . . . inflamed by passion, what is he but a beast of prey? A more ingenious animal indeed; for the beast has the teeth, the horns, and the poisonous sting that nature gave him to destroy his adversary; but man has improved upon the works of Nature and *invented* numberless weapons of destruction. One part of men are forging bloody instruments to slay another part, and a third, more fortunate perhaps, amuse themselves with staring at the horrid spectacles.[23]

The Terror in France increased Webster's anxieties. "*Quem Deus vult perdere, prius dementat*! [Whom God would destroy, he first makes mad!]," he wrote to a friend upon hearing of the beheading of Marie Antoinette.[24] By mid-1794 he believed that the revolution was unfortunate no matter which way it turned. If the Jacobins failed, Webster predicted to a friend, there would be a reaction even more oppressive than the *ancien régime*. Tyrants would appear who would make Louis XIV look quite tame. Liberty would be extinct. Either way, human nature would be degraded, the human mind subdued, and France in general would be destroyed. "There is no other alternative," he moaned.[25]

These fears aroused by the events in France produced specific ideas concerning American foreign policy. The new nation, he now believed, must resist the poison of French ideas and avoid involvement in European affairs at all costs.[26] He felt that Marat and Robespierre were the heads of a large conspiracy, organized in local groups spread all across France. They had the country in their control, and he was sure they had their eye on America. Vigilance must be kept, for those who opposed the Washington administration and who built "Magical systems, castles in the air" could easily become their dupes.[27]

The revolution absorbed much of Webster's time. He contemplated its nature, and its long-term effects on France and the world, determined to understand its cause and to discover a method of control. In March of 1794 he produced one of his most extraordinary essays. *The Revolution in France*[28] was an uneven document; brilliant insights were followed by verbosity and near hysteria.

The Revolution in France marked a turning point in Webster's life in at least two ways. His studies of literature and economics during the previous twenty years had displayed a sensitivity to time and development, but this was the first conscious attempt to view a subject as a product of its past. In this essay, Webster strove to accomplish what he thought a good historian should achieve. From this point on, Webster utilized a historical approach in all his work. Time and development, and more importantly, theory and explanation, were the bases of his studies of language, science, and literature; even his essays on politics and religion were historical in nature after 1794.

Webster's methodology did not consist of simply gathering facts and splicing them together. He was sure that his assignment was not merely to narrate the chronological sequence of events, although he did not neglect that aspect of any problem. Instead, he believed that his job was to explain the real action of history, to examine the "why" of any situation as well as the "who, what, where, or when." He was not the narrator of a dead past, but a central part of the whole process:

> It is conceived to be the duty of the historian . . . not merely to collect accounts of battles, the slaughter of the human race, the sacking of cities, the seizure and confiscation of shipping, and other bloody and barbarous deeds, the work of savage man towards his fellow men; but to discover, if possible, the *causes* of great changes in the affairs of men; the *springs* of those important improvements, which vary in the aspects of government, the features of nations, and the very character of man.[29]

Even more important was the change in his social views. With this essay, Webster's support of progressive social change virtually vanished. Nearly everything he had written before had emphasized the need for an extension of human freedom and human rights. Even his essays on government and on the Constitution after 1787 had been cast within the framework of an improvement in the human condition, although he favored change in a structured manner. After 1794, he would never again agitate for an extension of man's freedom or for his right to make decisions for himself.

The French Revolution was, he believed, a radical advance in human freedom; it had broken forever the primary ties which held society together. The authority of the Church and the state (in the form of the monarch) had been overthrown. The essence of the entire matter was that the revolution was not merely a change in the political or economic institutions. It went much farther and much deeper than that.

The revolution represented a basic change in the mind of man. Habits of deference and obedience had been shattered. Political, social, and economic changes were secondary manifestations of a deeper, more profound intellectual change. It was "attended with a change in *manners, opinions,* and *institutions,* infinitely more singular and important, than a change of masters or of government," he said.[30] Revolutionary thought, or "French principles," was a new world-view, based on atheism and materialism, which threatened the "Supreme Intelligence" which man had traditionally perceived to be at the center of all creation. The French would instead substitute "*matter* and *motion*" in their explanation of all things, and thereby destroy the entire structure of man's knowledge of his world, including, of course, the laws based on that world-view which controlled the passions of man.[31]

Webster's invention of a new word emphasized the clash between the events in France and his own intense Protestant ethic. Here, in fact, was the heart of the matter. It was becoming clear that human freedom brought deep changes that he was unwilling and unable to accept. The events of the 1780s and 1790s had destroyed Webster's optimistic view of man and replaced it with a belief that man was innately evil and depraved. The French Revolution cut man loose from all restrictions and unleashed his wild nature. The second clause in the sentence introducing his new word, "demoralizing," both defined what he meant and indicated the depth of his analysis of the profound nature of the revolution. It had removed all means of social cohesion, all sources of authority. The emerging French rebelliousness and anti-authoritarianism was clearly the true nature of man and foretold an awful future. The revolution in France was "demoralizing": it brought a "total change in the minds of the people."[32]

The concept of reason formed the center of revolutionary ideology. In the 1780s Webster had placed many of his hopes for America on man's ability to use his own mental powers to achieve social change. Now, the use of "reason" by the Jacobins had given it an ominous meaning. To Webster, "reason" became a codeword which summarized all their rhetoric about freedom, rights, matter, and motion, as well as their attacks on religion and civil authority. The man who a decade earlier had seen America as an "Empire of Reason" now felt that reason itself threatened all order, stability, and all of civilization. Robespierre's crowning of a prostitute during the Festival of Reason gave it an even more satanic edge. Those who celebrated reason would worship anything, it seemed, and were the *"least rational"* of all beings.[33] Reason itself was merely a *"blind superstitious enthusiasm."*[34] Paine, Godwin, and those who relied on it in their political theories were ignorant visionaries.[35] Because they deluded men into false hopes and thereby created more turmoil, they were "a pack of scoundrels." They undermined stability and order, and were therefore "refuse, the sweepings of the most depraved part of mankind."[36]

Faction was another disruptive manifestation of reason.[37] Without guidelines other than their own minds, men often entered into personal quarrels over trifling subjects, and these grew into senseless, irrational, dangerous, and explosive battles. Both sides assumed they were correct, and it was usually not long before victory became submerged beneath the growing hostilities of two often equal parties. Exasperation resulted, and the stage was set for the entrance of a demagogue. This was the point that Webster believed France had reached by 1794, and there seemed to be no way to stop the flow of events. He predicted that the end result would be unprecedented tyranny. The victorious party would inflict a cruel revenge on their opponents, and do so with the words "liberty" and "reason" on their lips.[38]

In changing man's beliefs and ideas, the revolution attacked government at its foundation. Without government, there could be only bloody chaos. America had her Constitution as a "sheet anchor" (a term he had used in the 1780s to describe the rights of man), and without that document it would be "afloat among the surges of passion and the rocks of error."[39] Jacobinical ideas could "spring up any moment, and unexpectedly spread devastation and ruin at any time, in any place, and among any class of citizen."[40] America as well as Europe was threatened.

Piety now took on more importance in his thoughts. "Religion has an excellent effect in repressing vices, in softening the manners of men," and consoling them under the pressure of calamities.[41] But the revolution had a devastating effect on the social role of religion. Looking back, Webster believed that the *philosophes* led by Voltaire and Rousseau had seen the Church as a tool of the monarchy and an instrument of tyranny and ignorance. They had attempted to destroy the Church along with the *ancien régime*.[42] The Jacobins had gone even farther, turning their attack on the Church and monarchy into an attack on Christianity in general. They had abolished the sabbath, substituting one day in every ten as a day of rest, and had thus disrupted man's mode of reckoning time. Fear of death had been a tool of the clergy, and so the Jacobins had denied the immortality of the soul by depicting death as mere sleep. Notre Dame had been converted to a temple of reason, and Jehovah himself had been replaced by the omnipotence of the nation-state.[43] The social role of religion had been severely shaken, and perhaps even destroyed.

As the revolution continued, Webster's fear verged on paranoia. An acquaintance had witnessed a gathering of high officials, including Aaron Burr, at which an attempt to overthrow the government had been planned. Webster dutifully reported the story to his good friend Oliver Wolcott, Jr., then secretary of the treasury.[44] The continuously increasing number of immigrants flooding into America represented a threat of subversion, since Webster believed that they were all democrats, if not outright Jacobins.[45] When a church burned in Philadelphia, Webster immediately became convinced it had been set ablaze by subversive elements and said so in his newspaper. A few days later he formally retracted his statement and apologized for jumping to conclusions.[46]

Again and again he lashed out at the bogeymen of French principles. They were spread by the intrigues of democrats and spies, and the result, he repeated, could only be anarchy and bloody chaos.[47] In the end, a form of tyranny even worse than monarchy would prevail under a popular military figure.[48] Already at work in the west, French agents in America sought to "*sever the United States*" and control the commerce of the entire world.[49] He pointed out specific areas in which conspiracies were actively being carried out.[50] In fact no area seemed free of subversion. "I am convinced that they formed as early as 1792, the vast project of a general Revolution," he wrote in 1796, "and have since added to their views the design of conquests as extensive as the Roman Empire, in the plenitude of the Greatness of her power."[51]

The French ministers in Philadelphia were suspected of secretly organizing armies.[52] Webster firmly believed they were interested only in "confiscation, blood, and conquest."[53]

Fear of spreading revolution dictated certain political conclusions. Legislative action, he believed, must be taken to combat the growth of Jacobin-inspired democratic societies. Since the South, through Jefferson and Madison, had close connections with France, it must be carefully watched. He expected opposition to the central government to appear there, and even predicted a movement toward separation of the region from the northern states. The Jay Treaty represented to Webster a move toward internal as well as external peace, and thus he encouraged its acceptance despite the heavy criticism leveled at it. Above all, America must do everything it could to oppose foreign influence and avoid being tricked into European alliances.[54]

Indeed, the editor of the *American Minerva* (which became the *Minerva* and then the *Commercial Advertiser*)[55] strongly criticized any opposition to authority. The bitter clash over Federalist foreign policy deeply disturbed him. There was, he felt, little need or justification for opposition to the central government. After all, the officials at the highest levels were all veterans of the Revolution and the Confederation and staunch supporters of the Constitution. Their integrity was unquestionable. Moreover, he felt that most of the measures passed under the new government benefited all citizens. There had been opposition to funding and assumption, but those policies had eventually proven sound. The events of the years since 1789 seemed to indicate that opposition to the Constitution had also been unjustified. Indeed, to his mind, the success of the Federalist programs was decisive proof that any form of opposition to leadership must be wrong in principle.[56] To his way of thinking it was "mad work."[57]

As might be expected, he supported John Adams in the election of 1796. Adams's simplicity of manners, deferential character, and concern for constitutional principles made him a mirror image of Webster, and Adams's emphasis on neutrality ensured the editor's support. When someone accused Webster of conspiring with Hamilton to deprive Adams of certain votes and thereby elect Pinckney, Webster was outraged.[58]

Webster realized that his ideas were undergoing fundamental changes. In 1797 he sent a copy of his *Sketches* to Jedediah Morse, and could not resist commenting on the changes in his political principles and attitude toward dissent. "I was once a visionary and should now leave out a few ideas contained in it," he noted.[59] Furthermore, his analysis of local elections reinforced his view that ownership of property was directly related to stability and virtue. He found that the Federalist candidates received a majority of votes from men who held assets of £100 in property. It was true, he said, that "faction has found materials to work among the poor and the ignorant."[60] Fear of social revolution also changed his evaluation of the past. History, which a decade before had led him to envision a utopia in the future, now seemed to be merely "a history of crimes, follies and contradictions."[61]

With these judgments, Webster's belief in America began to crumble. As the torrents of political slander that characterized the late 1790s[62] poured down around him, as Federalists accused Republicans of Jacobinical subversion and Republicans accused Federalists of monarchism, the editor began to believe that corruption and moral turpitude had made severe inroads in every area of American life. He saw the highest officers of the government lie, cheat, and swindle to advance their own interests. Secretaries of state, members of Congress, presidents of banks, collectors of customs, and governors of states all appeared to be committing fraud, treason, and other crimes. He watched those who had been patriots during the Revolution become "political *prostitutes*, who hang out their infamous traffic, and for some price or other, are always ready for villainy."[63]

Visions of utopia were finally destroyed by political vituperation. The bickering, slander, hatred, deceit, and general degeneration which he now believed characterized the United States shook his hopes and plans for the future. America, divinely favored, provided with a specially created, corruption-free continent, on which a decade earlier he had believed the hopes of all mankind rested, was on the verge of degeneration into complete degradation:

> From the date of Adam, to this moment, no country was ever so infested with corrupt and wicked men, as the United States. Imported "patriots", bankrupt speculators, rich bankrupts, "patriotic" atheists, and other similar characters, are spread over the United States without number, deceiving the people with lies, gaining their confidence, corrupting their principles, and debauching their morals. We see now in our new Republic, the *decrepitude* of Vice; and a free government hastening to ruin, with a rapidity without example.[64]

And the political atmosphere in the United States grew even hotter. Relations with England had improved since 1794 and 1795, but those with France had become strained. As president, Adams sent a diplomatic team to Paris, where they received what amounted to a request for a bribe from Tallyrand, the French minister. This event, known as the XYZ Affair after the three unnamed emissaries from Tallyrand, drew a storm of indignation and protest.[65] This situation aggravated a growing polarization of American politics and intensified the distinction between two types of political preferences. The adoption of the Constitution, Hamilton's economic program, and Jay's Treaty had been issues around which two groups had organized themselves into relatively stable coalitions.[66] Those who called themselves Republicans favored a decentralized system of government and extension of the suffrage. The Federalists, with whom Webster sided, favored a more centralized form and opposed suffrage extensions.[67]

As the nation edged closer to war, Noah Webster became frantic. America's situation seemed serious and alarming; all efforts must be made to stem the overwhelming torrent of foreign influence. The growing French influence especially threatened the subversion of all government, order, peace, and happiness.[68] America seemed to have gone completely crazy: "No people on earth were ever guilty of so many wild and silly projects," he said, "as the Americans." If things continued, "we should be judged worthy of a mad-house and strait-jackets." The world seemed to Noah Webster to be spinning out of control, on the verge of complete chaos. Even the plan to remove the seat of government from New York to the mud flats of the Potomac seemed absurd. He denounced it as "one of the wildest projects that ever entered the head of insanity itself."[69]

The only area that still appeared relatively sane was New England. It seemed a bastion of stability where the people were "firmly attached to the *religious, moral,* and *political* institutions from which we have hitherto derived our private blessings and political prosperity."[70] He had once criticized New England's schools for their rigidity, but now valued their discipline. They were institutions "where the teacher has his pupils under such subordination, that they pass hours almost without a whisper or a smile; and where they are instructed and compelled to be respectful to superiors."[71]

Webster's opinions made him the subject of much personal invective. Two leading editors, Thomas Greenleaf and Benjamin Franklin Bache, led the attack. "Dunghill cock of faction" and "pusillanimous, half-begotten, self-dubbed patriot" were two of the kinder phrases they hurled at him; "most learned stultus," "self-exalted pedagogue," "quack," "mortal and incurable lunatic," were less kind. William Cobbett, an English writer who became famous as "Peter Porcupine," editor of *Porcupine's Gazette* in Philadelphia, accused him of being a monarchist. "Wonderful Noah! amazing prophet!" he said, "prophetical, political, and dictatorial newsman," "spiteful viper" and "base creature." "Rancorous villain," "contemptible creature," "political hypocrite," "demagogue coxcomb," "this prostitute wretch," "disappointed pedant," and "a most gross caluminator, a great fool, and a barefaced liar" were other tags Cobbett had for him.[72]

This abuse splintered Webster's decorum. His own journalistic and deferential principles had precluded character assassination, and while his political invective sometimes reached hysterical heights, he had always used general terms. Personalized venom, he believed, led only to a habit of disrespect for all characters, and thus weakened the entire Republic. Yet he could no longer contain himself. He attacked Cobbett as an *"arch butcher of reputation,*" popular only with "the dupes of British influence and with the coffee house dram and beer drinkers."[73]

The deterioration of Webster's relationship with Joel Barlow reveals the stress Webster was experiencing and illustrates how the events of the world affected his personal life. They had met in 1774, and for most of the years since Barlow had been his closest and most trusted friend. But in the late 1780s Barlow traveled to France and became a strong supporter of the Jacobin faction. In one of the strongest revolutionary statements made by any American in the eighteenth century, *Advice to the Privileged Orders* (1792), Barlow endorsed all revolutions, attacked organized Christianity, and expressed deistic principles.[74]

Webster saw Barlow's advocacy of worldwide revolution as a classic example of the work of Jacobinism. French principles worked in darkness like a vicious mole, corrupting even the strongest men, he believed. They were a "Pandora's box of evils which are let loose upon the world to curse mankind," and Barlow was proof that no person was safe from their influence. Ideas, he felt, were even more dangerous than "war, famine, and pestilence":

> A manly enemy in war disdains to assail his foe without giving him a chance to defend himself, but the French policy creeps in the darkness of midnight into the hearts of the country, secretly undermining all political confidence, and arms neighbor against neighbor. Men never know when they are safe; all is jealousy and apprehension. Men whose labor and prudence have accumulated a little property know not when they shall be robbed of it.[75]

Webster felt so strongly about these dangers that he published the letter in the *Commercial Advertiser*, denouncing Barlow as a "fanatic" who had been "warped" by his passions.[76]

By the spring of 1798 Noah Webster had clearly reached a state of intense anxiety. To say that he criticized the dissolution of primary ties and the extension of human freedom is an understatement. At times he became nearly hysterical. He also experienced tension in his personal life and relationships, as his clash with Barlow indicated. In addition, strong personal abuse had been published in the opposition press, and no one came to his defense. Only James Kent and a handful of physicians visited him at his home two miles outside the city. He seemed to have no effect on the public displays of passion, and he undoubtedly felt rather helpless in the face of the course of national and world events. Feelings of alienation, hostility, personal helplessness, and diminishing self-confidence often pave the way for emotional trauma. All of these were apparent in Webster's work, and this combination led to mental and emotional disintegration.

The situation was intolerable for Webster, and everything came to a climax in the spring of 1798. Hamilton and Adams strongly disagreed over American policies toward France and national defense. Webster sided temporarily with Hamilton against his old friend John Adams, and criticism of the editor and his papers increased. Webster had been ill frequently during the previous five years, and in fact had collapsed twice because of the physical strain. The combination of grueling work, public attacks on his character, and disillusionment with America in general and her leaders in particular, in addition to his fear of the spread of French ideas, resulted in mental and physical exhaustion. The breaks with personal friends like Adams and Barlow were especially difficult to handle. His eyes, said a friend, were "lined with red ferret"; the "absurdities of man" finally got the best of him.[77]

Escape from the center of controversy was "essential to my happiness, if not to my life," Webster told a friend. He was a beaten, dispirited man, in even worse condition than he had been during that long-ago winter in Goshen. "I found in more instances than one that my best endeavors to please those whose esteem I valued gave offense," he wrote; "to a gentleman of my education and standing in society this treatment became intolerable."[78] His motives, he believed, were the purest; he could not understand why they seemed to be consistently misinterpreted in the worst possible way. By late March he had lost his will to continue, and relinquished editorial control of his papers. On 1 April 1798, he left New York and the center of power and activity and fled to the safe environs of solidly Federalist Connecticut, to "seek peace and quietness in more private occupations."[79]

Not long after his return to New Haven, Webster was invited to give a Fourth of July oration. That day was an important one in 1798, celebrated all over the country with patriotic gatherings amidst rampant war fever.[80] By July, Webster had found time to think about the problems he saw around him, about their development and possible solutions. His own experiences during the last two decades had been bound closely to those of the nation at large, and Webster took the opportunity to summarize and analyze them. The idealistic democrat of the early 1780s as well as the "true republican" of 1793, had vanished; in his place stood a man concerned with what he thought was social and moral degeneration.

Echoing his essays of the previous decade, Webster rehashed much of what he had said in favor of the American Revolution, with some important points left out. Looking back at the 1770s, he saw the Revolution as a result of England's attempt to legislate laws for the colonies without their consent. He said nothing about the internal conflicts which he himself had spoken of in the early 1780s. His need for identification with that cause had long since disappeared beneath a variety of other problems and concerns. In his own mind, the Revolution had already been transformed into a mere fight for independence, not for the rights of man or for "power to the people." No attempt to perfect human society through the use of reason had evidently taken place. Indeed, events had shown that reliance on reason was dangerous and that natural laws did not apply to human society. The fear generated by fifteen years of social upheaval from Middletown to Paris had altered his view of the past and of the world in general.[81]

The American Revolution was now a symbol that could be used to instill the values of order, tranquility, and deference. There had been, he believed, no "popular tumult," no rabble rousing, and no rebellion except against the tyranny of England. All Americans must now fight as they had in 1775, but this time the battle would be against France and anarchy. The spirit of the Revolution, lost in the years after the war, must again be raised and embraced by the whole country: "May the illustrious example of the conductors of the American revolution be sacred to imitation in every period of history!"[82]

Yet the new nation was now on the brink of collapse. The vicious propensities of mankind had been unleashed, had taken up the sword, and were now "stalking over the earth, with giant steps, leveling the mounds which wisdom and policy raised" to restrain them. Webster placed the blame for the growing chaos squarely on the shoulders of man himself. Those who shouted for reason and equality were dividing the country into factions, pitting the physical against the moral forces, encouraging violence and robbery, and in general "dragging from the seats of justice, the wise and the venerable, and replacing them with bullies and coxcombs."[83]

Time and time again throughout his oration, Webster made it quite clear that he believed certain ideas were the root cause of all problems. Economic and political events were manifestations of the deeper, far-reaching effects of ideas. Untried and fallacious theories, half-baked opinions, and illogical, dangerous views, when held by thoughtless and unquestioning people, led to the condemnation or simple ignorance of moral and political laws. False ideas resulted in war, the overthrow of authority, piracy, and the denial of justice. Webster left no room for doubt about to whom and to what he was referring:

> Such are the inevitable consequences of that false philosophy which has been preached in the world of Rousseau, Condorcet, Godwin, and other visionaries, who sit down in their closets to frame systems of government, which are as unfit for practice, as a vessel of paper for the transportation of men on the troubled ocean. In all ages of the world, a political projector or system-monger of popular talents, has been a greater scourge to society than a pestilence.[84]

Near the end, his oration became a frenzied call for order and authority. He issued angry warnings against change in the direction of "lawless democracy" in any area of American life, and especially in her civil institutions. "*Experience* is a safe pilot," he declared, "but *experiment* is a dangerous ocean, full of rocks and shoals."[85]

Thus when Noah Webster stood before the Fourth of July crowd in New Haven in 1798, he was no longer the "true republican" who had arrived in New York five years earlier. America now seemed to be whirling out of control, dissolving amidst the onrush of forces beyond his comprehension. Massive social and political movements seemed to be undermining the deferential pattern of social relationships he deemed necessary for the existence of civilization. The events since the Middletown Convention, symbolized in their extreme by Shays' Rebellion and especially by the French Revolution, frightened him into conclusions far different from those he had held in the 1770s and early 1780s. He no longer believed that the purpose of human government was to enhance freedom, or to ensure equality. Instead, he now believed it provided an important source of authority to restrain human passions, and to restore deferential attitudes and even the primary social bonds broken by the Revolution:

> Let us never forget that the cornerstone of all republican governments is, that the will of every citizen is controlled by the laws or supreme will of the state.[86]

*[The people] would be more free and happy, if all were
deprived of the right of suffrage until they were 45 years
of age, and if no man was eligible to an important office
until he is 50, that is, if all the power of government
were vested in our old men, who have lost their ambitions
chiefly and have learnt wisdom by experience.*
      N. W., 1800

6 *Search*

Noah Webster spent the decade after 1798 amidst the relative calm of Connecticut. There, he hoped, no mobs would threaten his home or shout Jacobinical slogans in the streets. For eighteen months he worked on his *Brief
History of Epidemic and Pestilential Diseases*,[1] a treatise that Benjamin Rush
praised highly and that even today is considered a landmark in its field.[2] In
1800 he began compiling his dictionary, on which he worked almost daily for
the next quarter-century. All his efforts during these years centered on an
intense search for a source of authority that would bring social stability to a
volatile world. In essence, during the years between 1798 and 1800 Noah
Webster espoused Federalist ideology, and worked for Federalist causes, in
an effort to find a mechanism capable of controlling the passions of man.

But life in Connecticut and devotion to Federalist principles led only
to an intensification of his anxieties. Instead of clear, decisive, and satisfying
solutions to social and political problems, he found only ambiguity, complexity, and a bewildering development of ever-shifting social conditions and

political alliances. A careful examination of the milieu in which he operated will reveal the intensity of his frustration. Knowledge of social transformations, the growth of Republican opposition, and the nature of its ideology will provide a sense of the struggle in which Webster found himself engaged. The character of the Federalist group, and the contentiousness of the factions within it, underscore the complexity of the world in which Webster conducted his search for answers. He was deeply disappointed by the disintegration of Federalism between 1798 and 1808.

The Connecticut to which he returned was a conservative state, controlled by a tightly knit oligarchy.[3] Both those who lived during this period and historians writing since agree on this point. "The state of Connecticut has always been governed by an aristocracy, more decisively than the empire of Great Britain . . .," said John Adams. "Half a dozen, or, at most a dozen families, have controlled that country when a colony, as well as since it has been a state."[4] Timothy Dwight noted that the homogeneity of Connecticut society lent itself to oligarchic rule. "The inhabitants of the Connecticut River valley might be said in several respects to possess a common character; and, in all the different states resemble each other more than their fellow citizens, who live on the coast," he stated. "The similarity is derived from their descent, their education, their local circumstances, and their mutual intercourse. In the older settlements most of the inhabitants are natives of this valley, and those who are not, yield to the influence of a character which they continually see all around them."[5] A Republican leader put it this way in 1804: "We have lived in a state which, exhibiting to the world a democratic exterior, has actually practiced within itself all the arts of an organized aristocracy, under the management of the old firm of Moses and Aaron."[6] The standard work on Connecticut around 1800, Richard J. Purcell's *Connecticut in Transition: 1775–1818*, bears this out, as does more recent scholarship.[7] "A more complete interlocking of leaders and families would be hard to picture," Purcell concluded. All authors agree that one party ruled Connecticut until 1818. There were no closely contested elections, "practically no political life in the modern sense," in the decade before 1800.[8] In addition, Purcell says that only about 2 percent of all eligible voters actually exercised their right during the 1790s.[9] Every U.S. senator before 1818 was a Federalist.[10]

Connecticut was for all intents and purposes a closed society, and Webster was a part of the circles of power. His old Yale classmate and lifelong friend, Oliver Wolcott, Jr.,[11] was the third of his family to become governor of the state and eventually presided over the formation of a new Constitution. The upper house of the state legislature was the center of power. It "represented the aristocracy of the state, the leaders in the ruling caste."[12] Its members were men of family, wealth, education, and influence. Many of Webster's closest friends and associates were senators, including his son-in-law, Chauncey Goodrich, a leading Federalist. Another son-in-law, William

Wolcott Ellsworth, also became governor. Thus Webster was an intimate of the most powerful circles of the oligarchy, and it was not unusual for many Ellsworths, Wolcotts, Websters, Trumbulls, Swifts, and Dwights to spend their leisure hours in Webster's New Haven home.[13]

Despite the apparently invincible and entrenched power of Connecticut Federalism, the opposition began organizing their forces two years after Webster arrived. They continued to make progress throughout the decade. Abraham Bishop, one of Webster's Yale classmates, inaugurated the struggle in 1800 with an oration on "The Extent and Power of Political Delusions." Bishop and his colleagues vigorously attacked the oligarchy as undemocratic, and were especially bitter in their denunciation of the influence of the clergy and colleges.[14]

As John R. Howe has noted, Republicans operated within the same general framework of concern over the viability of the republican experiment as their opponents. From the middle of the 1790s on, a spirit of intolerance prevailed in the American political press, in speeches, sermons, and even in the private correspondence of individuals. This sense of crisis, of danger primarily from within, pervaded early national America. No one trusted his political opponents; no genuine debate over substantive issues was possible. Toleration of divergent perspectives did not exist. Federalists perceived Republicans as anarchists and proponents of mob rule, determined to destroy all social bonds. The sense of suspicion was mutual: Jeffersonians thought Federalists were monarchists and aristocrats, bent on destroying the republic.[15]

In essence, Republicans could not escape the assumption that the grand experiment was an extremely fragile and vulnerable one. The historical foundation of this view lay in the traditional republican emphasis on the inevitable decay of government. Belief in the cyclical nature of history heightened a sense of the critical importance of each new event. Howe concluded that the republican framework within which both Republicans and their opponents grew was "peculiarly volatile and crisis-ridden," and offered little margin for error or resilience.[16] Richard Buel found that the main question informing all political discussion throughout the period was the stability of the fragile nation. Public opinion was the key ingredient in all political formulations. Republicans sought stability by adjusting government to fit popular demands, while their adversaries attempted to construct an authority insulated from them. The choice of political affiliation, then, was largely a response to fear. Republicans fought subversion aimed at making their administration impractical.

Opposition ideology in the first years of the century centered on several basic concepts. Republicans essentially sought to build a stable political system by enlarging economic, political, and social opportunities for all those groups that had been excluded from full participation by the ruling elite. They accused the clergy of using their pulpits for the dissemination of political propaganda, and the politicians of soliciting support from the Congregational church. And, of course, they believed the Federalists and Congregationalists guilty of exchanging various favors.[17]

Claiming the role of successors to their patriotic forefathers of the revolutionary era, Connecticut's Republicans advocated extension of the right of suffrage. Federalists, they claimed, desired war with France in order to bring the New World under the influence of Old World aristocracy. Suffrage expansion became their most important and controversial position. Yet they did not seek immediate implementation of universal white male suffrage, but merely believed that property qualifications were immoral and dangerous. All those who served in the militia or paid taxes should be allowed to participate in the political process. Since Connecticut was an undistricted state, Republicans sought to divide it into representative districts.[18] Federalists, of course, responded that even this advance would mean certain Republican victory and the end of civilized life.

As Republican organization matured, their competitiveness drew increasingly larger percentages of the population into political battles. Their first candidates for governor and lieutenant governor appeared in 1801. The following year saw 8.2 percent of those eligible turn out to vote, and Republicans gained control of fifty-five seats in the state legislature. In 1803 they held a festival to celebrate their new influence and spread their ideas to an even wider public. The race for governor that year was the closest ever: the Federalist candidate outpolled his rival by a relatively small 2 to 1 margin. The Federalist plurality shrank again the next year, when seventy-eight Republicans won legislative seats. This so alarmed the Federalists that they called for a special convention to write a new Constitution; this idea became their primary concern, along with the suffrage problem, after 1804. The elections of 1805 and 1806, fought over the two issues, recorded the heaviest vote tallies ever, and the latter was the closest contest over the governor's post before the new, more democratically oriented Constitution was implemented.[19]

Federalist response to this development was sharp and aimed at putting elective offices out of the reach of the "rabble." In 1800 voting for representative and state officers was by secret ballot. Yet this secrecy was subject to a moderator's right to inspect folded ballots to prevent stuffing. Nominations of local officials and national congressmen took place by voice vote in an open meeting, attended by all freemen. Republicans charged that such meetings were openly monitored by ministers, deacons, justices, and other Federalist functionaries, and that nominations of persons not in their favor required a boldness only possible when an individual was politically and financially independent, which few Republicans were.[20]

Yet even this system of control was not enough security for the oligarchy. They forced a "stand-up law" through the state legislature in 1801. Now each freemen's meeting would be presided over by an assistant justice, senior constable, or other person selected by a majority of the local justices and constables, nearly all of whom were Federalists. In short, there was no chance that a Republican could become moderator of a freemen's meeting. As before, any freeman could nominate a candidate: but voters had to stand or raise their hand to cast their ballot. In addition, an individual was required to secure the written approval of a majority of the civil authorities of the community to become able to vote. Any freeman known to be "walking scandalously"—guilty of a scandalous offense—could be disfranchised.[21]

As the stronghold of Federalism, Connecticut typified its sociological characteristics. Patterns of political allegiance were complex and even bewildering in early national America, yet they did exist and, as David Hackett Fischer indicates, can be outlined.[22] The most important factor in Federalist influence was the existence of entrenched and established elites. The clash between Federalist and Republican often boiled down to a clash between past attainment and future aspirations. Groups like the Wolcotts and Goodrichs in Connecticut, and the Ameses, Cabots, and Adamses in Massachusetts sought to protect their stability, status, and achievements from the rising generations of newcomers.[23]

Occupational, geographic, demographic, and ethnic differences also divided the two groups. Older, more powerful occupations—lawyers, large merchants, college teachers, parsons, and often, though not always, physicians—tended to be filled with Federalists. Artisans, craftsmen, small shopkeepers, and self-sufficient farmers leaned toward the opposition. Webster's Connecticut River valley, "the most staunchly Federalist region" in the country, according to Fischer, was much like the north shore of Massachusetts and other strongly Federalist areas. Mature in their social development, static in economic and demographic growth patterns, they also had homogeneous populations and were politically ingrown. Wherever new populations entered, competition in all fields intensified, and political dissent appeared. Social differentiation and change brought tensions that weakened habits of deference and generated rivalry and party development.[24] Connecticut was not only the most Federalist state between 1790 and 1810, but the slowest growing as well; her population grew 6 percent in the first decade of the U.S. census, and only 4 percent in the second.[25]

Ethnicity and religious factors also corresponded to political allegiances. The Irish, just beginning to pour into northern cities, voted solidly Republican, and Federalists feared their potential power. The Germans of Maryland and Pennsylvania began to swing toward Jefferson in 1800, as did the smaller number of free Negroes, despite the fact that he was a slaveholder. Federalists drew support in Anglo and Dutch areas. The resonance between religious and political values was expecially strong in New England, where Congregationalism and Federalism were inextricably related. "That conservative Congregationalists were Federalists is not surprising," writes James Banner. "The two ideologies, one political, the other religious, contained great similarities: they extolled stability and uniformity, and they both assumed the imminent ruin of western institutions."[26] In Webster's state, "up to 1815 one might write with a greater degree of truth than epigrams generally bear, that Connecticut's preachers were politicians, and her politicians preachers."[27]

Yet Federalist unity was not strong enough to avoid important divisions within the ranks. Indeed, persistent divisions intensified and multiplied their fears of Republican successes. At the same time that Webster fled to Connecticut, a serious split developed between the followers of Alexander Hamilton and those of John Adams. A number of issues served as points of contention. Hamilton's group included Theodore Sedgwick, William Cobbett, Jonathan Dayton, Oliver Wolcott, William Duane, Timothy Pickering, Gouverneur Morris, C. C. Pinckney, William McHenry, John Carroll, Robert Goodloe Harper, Fisher Ames, George Cabot, and others. They favored economic diversification and increased and improved trade with England, as well as closer political ties with the former mother country. In the late 1790s these High Federalists, led by three cabinet members (Pickering, McHenry, and Wolcott), attempted to maneuver Adams into developing a standing army, and opposed the President's reopening negotiations with France after the XYZ Affair.[28]

The Adams Federalists, with whom Webster usually sided, sought to avoid war with France and opposed the High Federalist program of military development and preparation. Elbridge Gerry, Judge Walker, Benjamin Stoddert, Joseph Lyman, Harrison Gray Otis, Arthur Fenner, Samuel Chase, and Samuel Smith, among others, attempted to develop a moderate program.[29]

After 1801, as Republicans grew stronger in all areas, Federalist divisions became even more complicated. David Hackett Fischer has found a distinct generational conflict; older members, Ames and Sedgwick, for example, opposed the incorporation of campaign organizations and activities such as party tickets, propagandizing, and so forth. Some even dropped out of politics altogether. Younger men like Harrison Gray Otis and Josiah Quincy saw themselves as professional politicians and therefore sought to utilize all the new techniques to expand their influence and control the mob by leading it, not rejecting it.[30]

Federalism also encompassed many groups that found politics generally abhorrent, but nevertheless lent their support at crucial times while maintaining their critical distance. Several groups of New England clergy fall into this category. Hopkinsians and Edwardeans of central and southern Massachusetts, along with orthodox Calvinist ministers from the western counties, vacillated between support and hostility. The Church, after all, was not as influential as it had been, or would like to have been, and clergy often perceived the Federalist party as their principal rivals in the battle for men's minds. Politicians expressed the same values, addressed the same problems, and even recruited the same types of individuals.[31] Indeed, as James Banner has pointed out, the New England clergy had done an effective job of teaching men to think in terms of the evil nature of man, human depravity, and the need for redemption, and to speak in the jeremiad style. They had succeeded so well that Federalist orators employed the basic intellectual, emotional, and rhetorical framework of Calvinist theology. Politicians played the role of secular preachers.[32]

Literary figures, especially those gathered around the *Monthly Anthology and Boston Review* and Joseph Dennie's *Port Folio*, formed a second group of marginal Federalists. They had no formal role in the party, but participated and withdrew from politics as the situation changed. Joseph Stevens Buckminster, John Thornton Kirkland, Samuel Cooper Thacher, and others had no faith in political activity and often disparaged the work of Otis, Quincy, and their friends. The anthologists believed that further democratization of American culture, in the form of the debasement of humane letters, would add to the disintegration of civilization as a whole. They distrusted even Federalist politicians, and often wrote virulent attacks on them.[33]

In one of the more bizarre episodes in Federalist annals, the anthologists waged full-scale war against Noah Webster. His lexicographic and philological work challenged the authority of Samuel Johnson, their traditional hero, and Webster's linguistic reforms smacked of cultural subversion. While the anthologists accused Webster of speculative reasoning and revolutionary innovations in language (quite the opposite of his intentions), John Gardner criticized Webster's work as a formalization of one dialect of English. "Let, then, the projected volume of *foul* and *unclean* things, bear his own christian name, and be called *Noah's Ark*," he wrote. To Gardner, Webster's effort, in and of itself, and regardless of his intentions, had the same effect as Federalist political agitation: it brought about social, cultural, and political change.[34]

Despite these varied perspectives and sociocultural differences, Federalists shared a certain ideology. Webster may have had differences with Wolcott, Pickering, Gardner, or Sedgwick over a certain issue; but all experienced a search for some means of holding their apparently disintegrating society together. All sought to restore proper habits of deference among the American people.

As Linda Kerber has pointed out, Federalists believed that their world was quickly dissolving. Their writings reveal a profound fear of the future.[35] Europe was torn by unparalleled revolution and war that threatened to spread to America in the very ships that brought emigrants from its terror. Population pressures increased dramatically, thereby intensifying the same pressure that had prohibited Webster from following in his father's footsteps. Now, new waves of youths sought alternatives through education, as he had done in the 1770s.[36] With the end of British rule, American settlement west of the Appalachians began in earnest. This trend seemed to undermine the political power of New England in national circles. Patriarchal authority continued to disappear at home, while the gradual widening of suffrage, new campaign techniques, and democratic, participatory ideology, as well as challenges to religious institutions, seemed to undercut every possibility of stabilization.[37] James Banner indicates that Federalism offered a kind of reassurance for those cut off from the securities of the past.[38] Opposition rhetoric stressed social mobility, economic opportunity, and individual self-reliance, especially in Connecticut, where the Republican party drew its support from newcomers and all those who had been excluded from economic and political advancement by the oligarchy.[39] Federalists, especially after 1800, emphasized the reverse: stability, tradition, dependence on authority and order. They shared a "mental association with established authority and an affinity for the fixed and traditional." The average Federalist, whether a leader of the party or an ordinary voter, was an "insider" who enjoyed association with, and identified with, men who customarily exerted personal and political power. Regardless of the individual's social and political standing within his specific community, "he esteemed his 'betters,' his 'elders,' his 'forbear,' and whether from self-interest, long custom, or anxiety, set great store by the dependability of fixed relationships."[40] Anything that offered a chance to stop the changes that to them seemed to threaten the very existence of civilization drew their support. They advocated a stronger, more centralized government, a more powerful executive branch, the Alien and Sedition Acts, and an independent Senate and judiciary.

Their view of the world centered on the belief that mankind was inherently depraved. "The most ferocious of all animals . . . is man," said Fisher Ames.[41] The people, wrote Uriah Tracy, "are vicious, and love vicious men for their leaders."[42] Webster's political hero, John Adams, believed that man was "so corrupt, so indolent, so selfish and jealous, that he is never good but through necessity."[43] The New England clergy, led by Timothy Dwight, Jedediah Morse, and David Tappan, delivered weekly jeremiads against man's pride, avarice, dissipation, idleness, sensuality, and impiety.[44]

Webster often articulated this deeply negative evaluation of the nature of man. "As to mankind," he wrote to Rush, "I believe the mass of them to be *copax rationis*. They are ignorant, or what is worse, governed by prejudices and authority—and the authority of men who flatter them instead of boldly telling them the truth."[45] Novels and other forms of modern literature enfeebled rather than strengthened man's already weak mind.[46]

Webster's view of man appeared in a new edition of his humorous anthology, *The Prompter*, published in 1803. The difference between it and the 1791 version is striking. The original had become an early American classic. During the 1790s its thirty editions provided standard fare in taverns and roadhouses. Selections were reprinted in newspapers all over the country.[47] But the new edition contained nineteen additional essays, and whatever humor Webster had intended was buried beneath overwhelming bitterness and fear. Most of the new stories were vehement attacks on democrats and popular government, with titles like "Pride," "Prejudice," "Popular Discontent," "Popular Delusion," "The Counsels of Old Men Despised," and "Envy, Hatred, and Revenge." "A Gillotin" [sic], the most effective of the new articles, was downright lurid in its depiction of man as beast. Obviously inspired by the revolution in France, it graphically detailed the implications of the current political trend as Webster saw it. He feared that "that terrible instrument of death, that chops off heads, as a butcher's cleaver severs a joint of mutton!" would be used in America.[48]

Man was a savage. Discipline and government were the only things which kept the "wild beast" from becoming the servant of his passions. Man was restrained only by the fear of the dungeon and the gallows, like a tiger enclosed in a cage. Human beings invented bows and arrows, darts, guns, and all kinds of instruments of pain and torture to use on their neighbors; they systematically planned and fought long and bloody wars to subdue or exterminate whole nations. The "lust for prey," once unleashed, could never be satiated. All of this lay in store for America if it continued in its present direction.[49]

Subversion and conspiracy appeared everywhere. Both parties shared what Richard Hofstadter called the "paranoid style" of American political turmoil and uncertainty. These beliefs often called for life and death struggles against specific and symbolic enemies.[50] James Banner points out that one remarkable continuous thread in the political rhetoric of New England between the 1770s and the early 1800s was the recourse to conspiratorial explanations. Yet a distinctly different kind of fear marks the later period. The revolutionaries saw danger from the monarch and his court, while most of the Federalists' bogeymen were American. While some of the plots they described involved direct foreign influence, most seemed to come from within the breast of wicked and degenerate Americans. After 1795 a whole host of conspiracies plagued the minds of New England Federalists. Aaron Burr's threat of secession was only the largest and most notable among many attempts to rig elections, undermine government, destroy tradition and religion, and make secret agreements with France.

Most widespread was the belief that an organized, secret revolutionary movement known as the Bavarian Illuminati had active support in America.[51] John Robison, a professor of natural philosophy at Edinburgh, had written an intriguing book in which he theorized that the French Revolution was only one manifestation of a gigantic plan to destroy "ALL RELIGIOUS ESTABLISHMENTS," and to overturn "ALL EXISTING GOVERNMENTS OF EUROPE." The plan, according to Robison, was the product of a group of masons in Bavaria. Quite a few New England clergymen evidently believed that Robison had really uncovered a worldwide conspiracy. Timothy Dwight, spiritual leader of Connecticut and president of Yale College, was convinced that the Jeffersonians were at least friends of the Illuminati, if not outright members. His brother Theodore agreed.[52]

Fears of other subversive activity abounded. Towns with fifteen or sixteen professed supporters of the French Revolution were said to be infiltrated, Jacobinized, or revolutionized.[53] Thomas Paine's *Age of Reason* was available in cheap editions and was even occasionally distributed free of charge, which added to the anxiety of many.[54] When a new Connecticut constitution was proposed in 1804, the outcry against it grew to near-hysterical heights.[55] David Daggett led the attack on the proposition by calling it a "mischievous and alarming project" and a Jacobinical plot.[56]

Noah Webster was as frightened as anyone. There seemed to be an organized movement under way to overthrow the government and replace it with one based on French principles. The method being used was the spreading of lies, deceit, and misrepresentation, and the victims always turned out to be Federalists. The true leadership of the country was being undermined; the chief voices of subversion were Greenleaf's *New Daily Advertiser* in New York, and Connecticut's *New London Bee*. They engaged in slanderous attacks on the government, reprinting the words of its critics from Maine to Georgia. The conspiracy seemed to be well organized and to control many presses.[57]

Webster was beginning to think about the meaning of words, and his fears led to the formulation of a definition of "Jacobinism." "It consists in an opposition to established government and institutions, and an attempt to overthrow them," he wrote, "by private accusations or by violent and illegal means." It was founded on no clear principles; all who opposed legitimate authority, from Tom Paine to the lowliest newspaper editor, were one and the same in the eyes of Webster. All were dupes of revolutionaries.[58]

Webster the historian traced Jacobinism back through time. It now seemed that conspiracies—defined broadly as self-pride, the inability to understand another point of view, and the urge to impose one's viewpoint on others—had always existed. He saw it at work in the Garden of Eden, in Cain and Abel, and throughout all of biblical and recorded history. Its center was now in Paris. "The whole story of the fall of man, whether literally true, or an allegory designed to represent the beginning and progress of evil in the human heart," he believed, "is a sample of Jacobinism."[59]

It also seemed as though the American people were on the verge of succumbing to the lure of Jacobinism. The revolutionary schemes of the 1770s and 1780s had been "too visionary," and the wild hopes for the future (which of course he had shared) had been too sanguine.[60] The willingness to believe in them was still prevalent, and therein lay great danger. The people, he feared, were being enticed by "visionary theories, or the mad projects of designing men." They must be awakened.[61]

Jacobins spoke of the equality of all men, an idea rejected by Federalists. This concept must be opposed wherever it was found, for as Fisher Ames said, "little whirlwinds of dry leaves and dirt portend a hurricane."[62] Instead, order, deference, and equality must be stressed. "In all societies some must be uppermost," said one editor, for "the levellers only change and pervert the natural order of things."[63] "Each American should learn his proper place," said another, "and should busy himself keeping in it."[64]

Hierarchical social relationships provided one means of securing order and authority, as well as insuring domestic tranquillity. "The doctrine of *equality*," said Webster, was "fallacious." Elijah Parish preached that "order is the glory of the universe. The excellence of creation results from the subordination of the parts to the whole. In civil government, the people obey. The magistrates rule, order and security follow."[65] That all men had an equal right to life and the purchase of property Webster would not deny. But if equality meant that all men were equal in talent, distinction, influence, or power, then men were definitely *"not* equal." He would have felt right at home in the Adams-Jefferson correspondence after 1812. They agreed with Webster's belief that age, talents, virtue, and public services carried with them just claims to distinction, influence, and authority.[66]

To many Federalists, democracy meant unlimited suffrage, corrupt electioneering, and a general degradation of all civilized values.[67] In short, democracy meant disorder, and they were strongly opposed to it. "There is in all popular governments," said one New Englander, "a natural tendency, to a state of things, which constitutes tyranny." Democracy made government "a despotism beyond rule."[68]

Webster firmly rejected the concept of universal white male suffrage. "No government, in which the right of suffrage is founded on *population* can be durable," he wrote to Wolcott, "and the cheapness of that right will greatly accelerate the destruction of ours."[69] In his most sustained examination of the question, he denied that the sovereignty of the government and its laws was derived from the people; that state or federal officers were servants of the people; or that legislators were responsible to their constituents. Extension of the suffrage would not guarantee free elections or a pure administration. Instead, it merely accelerated the growth of corruption by multiplying the number of corruptible electors and reducing the price of the necessary bribes.[70] Suffrage should be based on property, and only those who were fatherly figures of authority could really be trusted:

> It would be better for the people, they would be more free and happy, if all were deprived of the right of suffrage until they were 45 years of age, and if no man was eligible to an important office until he is 50, that is, if all the power of government were vested in our old men, who have lost their ambitions chiefly and have learnt wisdom by experience.[71]

Webster's most famous attack on the extension of the suffrage came in a speech before the Connecticut Assembly in 1802. While part of the American Navy lay at Philadelphia, some of the crew were invited to a freemen's meeting ashore. They attended and were given strict instructions by a local party on how they should vote. They followed them dutifully. Not long afterward, claimed Webster, the same seamen were returning up the Delaware River from a cruise when they saw a school of porpoises swimming toward Philadelphia. "One of them asked the other where are those porpoises going," he recounted. "Why, damn it, replied the other, to a freemen's meeting to vote for ———."[72] The story was picked up and printed in several Republican newspapers, and for months afterwards Connecticut's Jeffersonians gleefully referred to themselves as "porpoises."[73]

Political parties were as odious as suffrage extension. Suspicion and distrust of parties was nothing new. Before 1820 fear of extraconstitutional organizations was widespread. British radicals, led by Trenchard and Gordon, had denounced them throughout the century. Alexander Hamilton, James Madison, George Washington, Thomas Jefferson, and most of the other political leaders of the late eighteenth century criticized their development. John Adams believed that parties "destroyed all sense and understanding, all equity and humanity, all memory and regard to truth, all virtue, honor, decorum, and veracity."[74]

His viewpoint was a representative one, no more hysterical in tone than those expressed by hundreds of others. To Webster, political parties were a form of subversion. They now appeared to be stronger and more threatening than they had been in the 1790s. Naturally, he was especially afraid of the Republican party. Centered in Virginia, it had members from Maine to Georgia. They corresponded regularly, planned specific campaigns, had "secret agents or delegates" who traveled to the seats of governments to spy on everyone, published subversive pamphlets, influenced voters, and in general destroyed all good order.[75] Their views were "opposed to everything that can render this country great and respectable." The Sedition Act should be used to punish them, and all aliens who were Republicans should be exported. If they were not, America faced "national degradation."[76]

A proposal by one Connecticut resident to celebrate a local Republican victory in 1803 brought forth his wrath. It was a scheme directly subversive of all freedom of election because it attempted to influence electors. He even threatened legal action, claiming that such events violated the spirit and letter of the Constitution.[77] When the opposition in Connecticut did manage to begin an organization, Webster saw it as a "violation of our ancient fundamental laws: and a flagrant violation of the right of suffrage." Their only aim was to "subvert the liberties of the people."[78]

Instead of enlisting under the banner of a party, men should investigate the character and ideas of each candidate and evaluate the effects of his election on the good of the nation. "If the charm of names cannot be dissolved, our condition is hopeless."[79] Indeed, the whole idea of men following leaders and parties, along with the use of patronage and campaigning for votes, seemed to be a *"perversion"* of the true principles of an elective government.[80]

Anxiety over political development conjured up fears of Napoleonic repression. Words like "tyranny," "despotism," and "oppression" appeared in the Federalists' predictions of the future. "Liberty is no longer the question," said Fisher Ames in 1804; instead, "to mitigate the rigors of despotism is all that is left to us."[81] Republicans, believed Webster, were all "Deists, atheists, adulterers, and profligate men" who, if elected, would bring either monarchism or anarchy.[82] The civil commotion of the Union would in turn lead to civil war and dictatorship.[83]

Yet the Republican victory in 1800 and Jefferson's ascension to power convinced him that the younger Federalists were correct; the only way of controlling parties was to organize against them and utilize their tactics. Harrison Gray Otis and others tried to overcome their antipathy toward parties, and on at least one occasion Webster agreed with them. The right of suffrage, if used correctly, could preserve order and stability by voting Republicans out of power.[84] At one point he even helped draw up a list of candidates for office. He justified his attempt to entice others to vote for Oliver Wolcott, David Daggett, William Hillhouse, Chauncey and Elizur Goodrich, Stephen T. Hosmer, Simeon Baldwin, as well as other relatives and other Federalists. It was a defensive move, he said, one that should be used against those who already practiced it.[85] There was no reason, he said in 1807, why honest, independent men could not find a middle ground between the self-interest of Hamilton and the wild democracy of Jefferson. The Federalists' loss of power was so serious that something must be done. Yet they should not attempt to win by yielding entirely to popular opinion, but by using political campaigns to control it. The people could be gradually weaned from their most foolish schemes and brought back into the fold. Good men must not "lose their weight or character for if they do not lead the people, fools and knaves will."[86]

This attempt to control political parties included control of newspapers. In an obvious reference to his own experiences, he noted that those who spoke out against slander in the press often found themselves the object of the same abuse. The press debased the public mind, discouraged virtue, and in general created some social schisms and widened others. It was a source of "unrelenting passions, and irreconcilable factions."[87] Laws must be passed to exercise a restraining power over such occurrences.[88]

Wise, experienced John Adams epitomized the type of leader envisioned by New England Federalists. Webster supported his candidacy again in 1800. The two were similar in age, background, and political philosophy. Adams's career had rendered him highly worthy of public confidence; he had exhibited a clear concern for the public interest, not just for himself. Webster believed that his theoretical writings had proved Adams sound in mind as well as in action. Jefferson, on the other hand, was a foolish vision-ary.[89]

More importantly, Webster believed that Adams's break with Hamilton had proven him a firm but fair ruler, the kind America needed. He now looked back and saw the incident as an example of how the president had suppressed faction. His efforts to defeat the High Federalists were evidences of his firmness and independence, which rendered him doubly worthy of public confidence.[90]

Adams symbolized stability and righteousness, honesty and sincerity. In 1800 he was threatened by both Hamilton and Jefferson; Webster defended his fellow New Englander against subversion from both sides. Hamilton circulated a letter among his supporters attacking Adams for disregarding the advice of his Cabinet. Sending William Vans Murray to France had damaged the nation's honor and credibility abroad, claimed the former secretary, as had the pardoning of John Fries and the President's non-enforcement of the Alien laws. Several of the Adams group responded by indicating that they thought that Hamilton was responsible for the recently authorized army and the Alien and Sedition Acts, which they thought were the Federalist Party's greatest political liabilities.[91] In an effort to help elect Adams, Webster published a long and strenuous denunciation of Hamilton. The New Yorker had publicly acknowledged his private intrigues with the wife of another man and had thus degraded himself beyond repair. Unfit for office and even unfit to be listened to, Hamilton had stooped to the point of scandalizing not only himself but an entire family in order to clear himself of charges which no one had believed in the first place. Adams, of course, had no such moral flaws. In addition, Hamilton had attempted to manipulate the Cabinet members among his followers: Wolcott, McHenry, and Pickering. Finally, Webster flatly stated that if Jefferson were elected, Hamilton would be responsible.[92]

But if Hamilton was dangerous and unfit for office, the election of Jefferson was downright frightening. Webster attacked the Virginian in harsh terms. He was an infidel, unqualified for public office, and "nothing but the madness of party could ever have held up Mr. Jefferson as a candidate." Both individuals elected to the Presidency before him were sound, practical men with sufficient experience to insure their capacity to govern the country. Jefferson was a silly philosopher who wasted his time dabbling in useless metaphysics. He had "very little sound philosophy, and still less practical knowledge." His *Notes on Virginia*, charged Webster, was full of factual errors and foolish principles. Jefferson had merely adopted the wildest French theories of philosophy and government. His work could not compare favorably with Webster's own *Brief History* or Adams's *Discourses*. More importantly, Webster feared Jefferson because those who had opposed the work of Washington and Adams considered him their candidate. As far as Webster was concerned, this fact alone was enough to disqualify him from any office. The greatest condemnation he could heap upon Jefferson was that "the *French wish him elected.*"[93]

Webster refrained from commenting on the Virginian after his election, but resumed his attacks in the fall of 1801. At first he advocated a calm acquiescence to Jeffersonian rule, or so he told James Madison. He was resolved to allow the new president's policies to have full effect before denouncing him.[94] When they did he reacted strongly. One of Jefferson's first moves was the replacement of the New Haven port collector, an avid Federalist. His choice was elderly, feeble Samuel Bishop, a man who knew little about collecting revenues but was a firm Republican. In addition, the man's son was none other than Abraham Bishop, Webster's old classmate and archenemy. The younger Bishop soon inherited the post.[95] This was the type of appointment and maneuver Webster had expected, and he quickly denounced it as government by money and favor. It was an example of the failure of representative government. Webster was convinced Jefferson had used flattery and promises of patronage to secure his election.[96]

The Bishop affair seemed representative of Jefferson's appointments. In an obvious reference to Albert Gallatin, he accused the president of placing "*foreigners*" in positions of power.[97] Most of his appointments seemed to be based not on merit, but on political preferences, and Webster felt that this did great harm to all American governments.[98] Moreover, he criticized his moral judgment. The Republican appointees, it seemed, openly reviled religion, marriage, and all that was good. They were all men who "live in the habitual indulgence of the most detestable vices, as adultery and lewdness." It was as if Jefferson deliberately picked out the worst criminals he could find, and sent them into Connecticut. They openly violated laws, destroyed the peace, and committed atrocious crimes.[99]

The most vicious comments Webster saved for the personal character of Thomas Jefferson. By 1801 he had become the symbol for all of the political and social changes then in progress, not only for Webster but for many others as well.[100] Timothy Pickering, Elijah Parish, Fisher Ames, Harrison Gray Otis, and their colleagues accused him of being corrupt, deceitful, hypocritical, and of having virtually every moral flaw imaginable. To them the Virginian was an anti-Christ: Jereboam, Absalom, and Beelzebub rolled into one.[101] One Federalist orator even called him a "mean-spirited, low-lived fellow" who was "half-Injun, half-nigger, half-Frenchman." Anyone who voted for him, he continued, "ought to be deemed guilty of treason."[102] Webster believed that he was generally a "wretched man: ambitious, totally corrupt even in his personal life, and interested only in his personal gain at the expense of the best interests of the general public.[103]

Webster shared many of the political and social anxieties common to his class and circles in Connecticut, and the dissonance that lay beneath them extended into his sense of the world as a whole. He felt keenly alienated not only from the seemingly chaotic developments in American life, but even from many Federalists. He had sharp political disagreements with even his closest friends, Timothy Pickering and Oliver Wolcott. Ironically, he may have been a relatively popular figure, at least among those who could vote. The town of New Haven elected him to the city council in 1799 and several times thereafter. He was elected justice of the peace yearly between 1801 and 1810, and served as a member of the state legislature intermittently between 1800 and 1807. Even though he served when chosen, he had little enthusiasm for public office, prefering to write pamphlets and work on his dictionary.

His lack of financial stability explains at least part of his personal unhappiness. He held no steady job after 1798, existing on the rather small revenues from his schoolbooks. While his speller sold about 200,000 copies annually, his share of the profits had been reduced significantly by the sale in the 1780s of the rights to the royalties.[104] After 1800 the Webster family struggled along, eating little and counting every penny.[105] Time after time Webster was forced to ask friends for loans or to attempt to sell copies of his books by subscription, years ahead of actual publication. In 1803, for example, he begged Oliver Wolcott, whose business was thriving, to help him out.[106]

A clear correlation existed in Webster's mind between his intellectual activities and his financial problems. His books, with the exception of his speller, did not sell in large quantities, and he felt that no one agreed with him about anything, or cared what he had to say. His feeling of isolation and alienation from those with whom he shared common ideological ground was profound. "Either from the structure of my mind, or from my modes of investigation, I am led very often to differ in opinion from many of my respectable fellow citizens," he said, "and differences of opinion is now a crime not easily overlooked or forgiven." No one seemed to have confidence in him, and his influence and reputation appeared to decay because of his political essays.[107]

His mistake, he felt, was that he could not restrain himself from criticizing those who deserved it. The human mind felt discomfort when its errors were pointed out, and he knew he had exposed the folly of many men in positions of power. He believed that he had done so in the best interests of the country, and thus he refused to stop being critical. "No task is more delicate and hazardous than that of criticism and censure," he remarked. Yet if no one pointed out errors, wrongs would not be corrected, nor peace, tranquillity or authority restored. It was the duty of each citizen to criticize public policy. Without an honest and candid discussion the best course of procedure would not be found.[108]

But perhaps the most important reason for Webster's unhappiness after 1800, underlying his personal sense of failure and alienation, was his inability to cope with the general trend of events in the nation at large. The sense of change and doom exhibited by Webster and the Federalists was at times overwhelming, and the existence of divisions and petty, often vicious quarrels within their own ranks intensified their despair. Some of the older New Englanders simply gave up and retired from participation in public affairs.[109] In their attempts to check the erosion of the deferential world, they grasped at any means they could think of to ensure stability and shore up what they perceived as the crumbling foundations of American society. Yet nothing seemed to work. While Adams was in office, a man like Webster could advocate the attitude that "the Executive can do no wrong."[110] After 1801, with Beelzebub in the White House, that option was impossible.

The only way to avoid a calamity, felt Webster and the Federalists, was for the people to submit their hearts and minds to some sort of authority. "The very essence of civil liberty consists in the entire subjection of every citizen to the laws and constitution," he said in 1803. The *"monstrous absurdity"* of dissent, turmoil, and party politics must end. The effort "to make rulers servants, and the citizens masters" must be halted.[111] Yet that obviously was not happening. The year after Webster spoke these lines Jefferson was reelected. As early as 1802, the lexicographer felt that he should "withdraw myself from every public concern, and confine my attention to private affairs and the education of my children."[112] Between 1804 and 1807 he made very few public appearances and said very little about national events.

*Real religion, which implies a habitual sense of the divine
presence, and a fear of offending the Supreme Being,
subdues and controls all the turbulent passions; and
nothing is seen in the Christian, but meekness,
forbearance, and kindness, accompanied by a serenity of
mind and a desire to please, as uniform as they are
cheering to families and friends.*
    N. W., 1809

7 *Submission*

In 1808 Noah Webster turned from politics to religion and found an answer
to all problems: belief in an omnipotent God. A descendant of Puritans, he
reverted to a system of values and a world-view not unlike those of the
generation of John Webster. Yet his emotional conversion in the spring of
that year was motivated by factors that were very much products of his own
time. He had experienced intense anxiety over past and contemporary national events; the failure of Federalism as a viable means of controlling social
trends and providing public leadership was quite evident. The negative view
of human nature and need for strong authority he had affirmed since the
1790s had readied him for acceptance of evangelical Protestantism. A crisis
in his personal relationships with his own family added to his preparation
and brought home to him in personal terms the erosion of patriarchal influence throughout America. Altogether those factors provided an emotional
matrix that made his conversion possible. The result was a psychological and
intellectual acceptance of and the submission to authority that stemmed from

a deep need within him and led to profound alterations of his views on every subject.

After his conversion Webster believed that religion provided the only valid basis for social stability, and in this he was not alone. Many old Federalists like John Jay, Stephen Van Rensselaer, Timothy Dwight, John Cotton Smith, and Elias Boudinot voiced the same conclusion. Known to historians as members of the religious benevolence movement, they perceived themselves as moral stewards for the entire nation.[1] In fact, they wished nothing less than a return to what they dreamed had been the political and social status quo of the seventeenth century. America must once again become a Closed Christian Utopian Corporate Community.[2] Stability would be achieved through obedience to a narrow group of pious, conservative leaders. Perfection could be gained if all Americans learned the wisdom of the past and submitted to their superiors. As "their brother's keepers," these latter-day Puritans founded several large national organizations with the express purpose of proselytizing the central concepts of God's absolute sovereignty and man's total depravity as a means of securing social tranquillity. The American Education Society, founded in 1815 in Boston, subsidized divinity students, while New York's Home Missionary Society provided funds for ministers to the poor. The American Bible Society distributed millions of free gospels, and the American Tract Society passed out 200 million pamphlets.

The heart of the value system they espoused was a negative evaluation of the basic nature of man. They distrusted all types of social change, and especially democracy, and warned that it could only lead to chaos, tyranny of the majority and eventually to dictatorship. Instead, their own minority of solid Christians should rule. They were hostile to the nation's press and highly critical of the concept of universal white male suffrage. The only viable bases for social organization, they repeated endlessly, were set forth in the Bible. Moreover, they advocated a personality structure and pattern of individual conduct that I have designated the Quiet Christian. All Americans should attempt to live by the word and will of God as interpreted by his disciples, members of evangelical organizations. Men should not argue among themselves over offices or agitate for broad reforms that would weaken social cohesion. Americans should only concern themselves with living good Christian lives in meek, passive ways. As one committee of the American Tract Society stated, the country could not be considered sound or stable until each American citizen professed his "absolute dependence on God" in all areas of political, social, and religious endeavor.[3] Noah Webster became one of the most vocal proponents of these ideas.

Religion had not been central to the life of the young Webster. Indeed, he had developed no strong convictions while growing up in the relatively tolerant atmosphere of Connecticut in the 1760s and 1770s. Yale during his residency had been significantly less orthodox than it became in the 1790s.[4] After his conversion in 1808 he looked back at his early life and noted that while his family had observed the outward forms of piety, he had not understood nor fully absorbed "the doctrines of the Christian religion." At Yale, he had fallen into "vicious company," lost what little concern he had developed, and "contracted a habit of using profane language."[5]

In the years after college Webster embraced a rather open-minded view of religion. As Gary B. Nash has noted, Webster believed in a mild deism that included rejection of the doctrines of regeneration, election, salvation by free grace, atonement, and the divinity of Christ. A broad sort of toleration had been among the principles he had advocated in the 1780s, and he had specifically attacked the narrowmindedness of the early Puritan inhabitants of New England and their descendants.[6] At the same time he had praised the Quakers. In the late 1780s Webster published a new edition of the *New England Primer*.[7] His version differed significantly from the original. The early editions had used the alphabet to introduce a strict, Calvinistic catechism:

A. In Adams Fall
    We sinned all.
B. Thy Life to Mend
    This *Book* [the Bible] Attend.
S. Samuel anoints
    Whom God appoints.[8]

Webster's edition omitted orthodox religious tenets and substituted rather pallid aphorisms:

A. Was an Apple-pie made by the cook.
B. Was a Boy that was fond of his book.
S. Was a Simpleton, ready to cry.[9]

Furthermore, Webster publicly rebuked Timothy Dwight in 1788 for his harsh religious convictions. Dwight had evidently gone through a change of heart between his *Conquest of Canaan* (1785), which Webster had praised highly, and his *Triumph of Infidelity* (1788). The latter traced the efforts of Satan throughout history while strongly attacking Hume, Voltaire, paganism, Popery, and eastern mysticism. Webster accused Dwight of being a theological dogmatist who had found the right way to heaven and excluded all other opinions. Webster's own religious views were abundantly clear in his hostile reaction to Dwight's poem. "A man who can group together such men as Shaftesbury, Priestley, Chauncey and Allen and stigmatize these and many of the first philosophers promiscuously as fools and knaves," he said, "can hardly be a candidate for that heaven of love and benevolence which the scripture informs us is prepared for good men."[10] When other newspapers attacked his views, Webster responded with the clearest statement of his religious beliefs before 1808. To say they were unorthodox is an understatement. "I believe that all men are my brethren," he said: "I believe that religion which teaches *God is Love*."[11]

Beginning in 1790, Webster slowly approached an awareness that religious beliefs are connected to other kinds of values and ideals. In thinking about the American experience of the 1780s, he concluded that those areas with well-supported clergy had fewer rebellions and less social unrest than those without. The example which came to his mind was Shays' Rebellion. He noted that in 1785–86 those areas with few or no clergy had been hotbeds of rebellion, while strongly religious areas had suffered less. Opposition to strong religion in Rhode Island, traceable to Roger Williams, had prepared that state for social convulsions. Since the body of the people were unaccustomed to the sobriety and decent deportment necessary in religious worship, he wrote, they became licentious, vulgar, and unable to tell right from wrong.[12] The French Revolution had made him even more aware of the social role of religious belief.

When Webster wrote about religion after his flight from New York in 1798, he seemed somewhat closer to evangelical Christianity. A new edition of *The New England Primer*, published in 1801, restored the original alphabet and contained many harsh stories that described the omnipotence of God and the helplessness of man. "The Dutiful Child's Promises" included a promise to fear God and obey superiors. It also instructed the reader to say: "I will honor those in authority, I will submit to my elders."[13] In 1801 Webster wrote to a friend that he believed in the all-powerful Supreme Being who was the first cause of all things and could cause rain to fall at will. Indeed, he said that "every operation in the universe" could be explained by the "direct exertion of omnipotence."[14] His schoolbooks reflected these views,[15] and he once came very close to making the connection between spiritual and civil tranquillity. "How little of our peace and security depends on Reason and how much on *Religion* and *government*," he remarked, without further elaboration, in 1805.[16]

Specifically, Webster characterized his own beliefs before his conversion in 1808 as "a species of scepticism." He did not doubt that there was a God or that he was perfect and sublime; yet he could not convince himself that the fundamental doctrines of the need for regeneration, election, or salvation by free grace were necessary or even correct. In fact, he believed that even a mere profession of faith was not absolutely necessary for salvation.[17] When he did connect religion and government, he spoke only of a mild form of religiosity. A free government, he remarked in 1802, "must be raised upon the pure maxims, and supported by the undying practice, of that religion, which breathes 'peace on earth, and good will to men.'" Its character would induce "humble pride" and restrain oppression. It would, by itself, "banish tyranny from the earth."[18] Yet it was not central to his political or social thought, and certainly of minor importance to him as an individual. When he was presented with a petition *opposing* a tax on all citizens to support religion, he signed it.[19]

Nevertheless, Webster's sensitivity to the social and political aspects of religion gradually increased before 1808. As early as 1798 a friend had written to him expounding the nonreligious benefits of evangelical Protestantism.[20]

By the spring of 1808, Webster's anxiety over national events had reached a level which evidently surpassed even his fears of 1798. He wrote to a newspaper editor that "no period since the conclusion of the revolutionary war has been more important than the present."[21] He observed the decline of the Federalist group in national affairs. The Embargo seemed to him to be aimed at the destruction of New England, commerce, and civilization itself. Webster long believed and often stated that commerce opened communication, reduced friction between people, and knitted mankind into "one great brethren." He sincerely believed that trade was "the child of peace, the parent of civilization, and the friend of universal liberty."[22] The Embargo threatened all this. It aimed at keeping the United States out of the Napoleonic wars by stopping all commercial interaction with Europe, yet had a disastrous effect on New England merchants. By May the situation appeared desperate.

"The present crisis in this country seems to call for extraordinary attention and perhaps for extraordinary measures," said Webster.[23] The Embargo was to Webster the final failure of the political parties and factions that he had been criticizing for twenty years. The northern commercial states had lost all influence in national circles, and Webster believed that the federal government was run by southern agrarians. Furthermore, it seemed that the best interests of the country as a whole were ignored by both parties, who instead concentrated on winning "temporary triumphs." Only a few politicians benefited from political parties, and the rest of America, Northerners and Southerners, Federalists and Republicans, merchants and farmers, suffered greatly.

The time had come for "the sound friends of the country" in both parties to come together and discuss the situation.[24] Instead of controlling the divisive elements that had concerned him for so long, the Federalists appeared to be on the verge of collapse. In desperation he tried to find some means of controlling the drift of events. He now believed that both parties must be abandoned and that a person unaligned with the main factions must be elected President. He favored George Clinton, then the vice-president under Jefferson, and formerly governor of New York.

As "public spirit," Webster wrote a circular, "To All American Patriots," in the spring of 1808. It indicated his anxiety and emphasis on the need for unity. The essential message was that neither the Republican nor the

Federalist party was aligned with any of the warring European nations, and that both must cease their self-centered manipulations. The last few paragraphs were frantic calls for cooperation and unity:

> Citizens of the northern states, our condition is deplorable and there is no resource but in UNION. This is the only remedy for our political evils; and the remedy must be speedy; we are upon the brink of a precipice. Our party dissensions *must cease*—we MUST UNITE—or our country is doomed to encounter calamities which in prospect, appall the stoutest heart.[25]

Conformity of opinion and obedience to a greater authority was the answer. Once again, as he had since the 1790s, Webster sought to quiet dissent "under a firm, vigorous, administration." Americans must, he believed, array a *"single phalanx of united opinions and united resources against these* [European and domestic] *encroachments."*[26]

Webster's anxiety was increased by events in another area of his life. A small revival supervised by Moses Stuart, who later spent over forty years as professor of sacred literature at Andover, occurred in New Haven in 1807–8.[27] At first, Webster rejected the movement, criticizing it because of its emphasis on the very emotions and passions which he struggled to control. However, in the spring of 1808, just when his anxiety over the Embargo reached its peak, his two eldest daughters and his wife experienced conversions.[28] Webster innately distrusted enthusiastic and evangelical religion, and thus this development caused considerable stress. In reaction, he attempted to convince his family that they should attend the rational, authoritarian, and hierarchically structured Episcopal Church.[29] He was unsuccessful.

Since his marriage in 1789, Webster's family had been the one consistently positive aspect of his life. Now it appeared that a serious deterioration in his most intimate relationships might develop. The pattern of dissolution of parental authority that had been developing throughout the eighteenth century was even more visible in the early part of the nineteenth.[30] "Now, anyone who has been in the United States must have perceived that there is little or no parental control," remarked one visitor. Another believed that American children were absolute masters of their fates. "The authority of the parents is of no restraint at all," he stated.[31] Two recent scholars have concluded that the breakdown of parental authority was so widespread as to be virtually complete. In addition to the pressure of population on land resources, they note that the thrust of the forces of republicanism and democracy unleashed by the Revolution contributed significantly to the trend.[32] The threat to his home life was most serious, and of all his concerns, produced the greatest anxiety. "In this situation," he wrote, "my mind was extremely uneasy."[33]

The conversion itself occurred in the spring of 1808. He admitted that he had "for a number of years just past," become aware of religion and the importance of regulating his own conduct according to certain principles.[34] He reexamined his beliefs early in the year, and even though he still did not believe that a public confession of faith was necessary, he did express a desire to join a church. He applied for a pew in the local Episcopal congregation.[35] It was at this time that his wife and two eldest daughters had their conversions and pressured him to attend Stuart's services.

The culmination of all of these factors and especially his "extreme reluctance against a separation from my dear family in public worship filled [his] mind with unusual solicitude." Under these pressures he once again examined the creeds of the Episcopal and Congregational churches; this time he found fewer differences than he had before. Most of his objections to Moses Stuart's brand of Calvinism were removed after a conversation with the minister. Yet even then he could not make the final decision. The tension increased:

> During this time, my mind became more and more agitated, and in a manner wholly unusual and to me unaccountable. I had short composure, but at all times of the day and in the midst of other occupations I was suddenly seized with impressions, which called my mind irresistibly to religious concerns.[36]

Webster attempted to assuage his troubled mind "by reasoning with myself." It did not work. An emotional conversion was the result:

> The impressions however grew stronger till at length I could not pursue my studies without frequent interruptions. My mind was suddenly arrested, without any previous circumstances of the time to draw it to this subject as it were fastened to the awakening and upon my own conduct. I closed my books, yielded to the influence which could not be resisted or mistaken and was led by a spontaneous impulse to repentance, prayer and entire submission and surrender of myself to my maker and redeemer. My submission appeared to be cheerful and was soon followed by the peace of mind which the world can neither give nor take away.[37]

New England was enveloped after 1800 by the Second Great Awakening, and conversion experiences like Webster's were common. Indeed, evangelical newspapers like the *Massachusetts Missionary Magazine* and the *Connecticut Evangelical Magazine*, published by local or state organizations, were filled with conversion stories. Many were quite similar to Webster's and stressed submission to authority and social control.[38] Webster's account of his experience was published in a widely circulated paper, the *Panoplist*. He also wrote several essays for another, the *Religious Intelligencer*.[39] Timothy

Dwight, leader of the revival, stressed the role of religion in preserving and enforcing social order,[40] and Moses Stuart was his student.[41]

William James, in his seminal work, *The Varieties of Religious Experience*, analyzed several different types of conversions. Webster's was a good example of what James classified as a form of "self-surrender."[42] James indicated that the mind of the candidate is filled with two things. The first is sin, which he defines in psychological terms as a present incompleteness or wrongness. This is the factor that the individual is eager to escape from, and Webster's mind was clearly occupied with several different varieties of incompleteness. One of James's students defines this factor as a feeling of unwholeness and moral imperfection, both of which are apt descriptions of Webster's state of mind. The second factor in the mind of the candidate for self-surrender is the positive ideal which he longs to encompass. National unity, peace, and tranquillity at home and in the nation were the ideals Webster longed for.[43]

Finally, James indicated that there is a third mental area that also may guide an individual toward conversion. It is the elusive memories, emotional residues, and fragmentary beliefs, the half-remembered scars that remain in the mind of every human being. In this paragraph James could be speaking about Webster's experiences with the Middletown Convention, the French Revolution, or his memories of his flight from New York in 1798. James could even be talking about the long-range effects of Webster's Puritan heritage, of growing up in New England and living among the religious beliefs of individuals like Timothy Dwight. These residues are part of our "total mental state," both within the "entire wave of consciousness" and outside it:

> Our whole past store of memories floats beyond this margin, ready at a touch to come in; and the entire mass of residual powers, impulses, and knowledges that constitute our empirical self stretches continuously beyond it. So vaguely drawn are the outlines between what is actual and what is only potential at any moment of our conscious life, that it is always hard to say of certain mental elements whether we are conscious of them or not.[44]

Webster's conversion was clearly one that James would classify as "self-surrender." With it came a deep and enduring belief in moral stewardship. Like his old friends John Jay, president of the American Bible Society, and Stephen Van Rensselaer, president of the American Home Missionary Society, Noah Webster concluded that men were utterly unable to control themselves by their own talents and powers. Each individual must become a Quiet Christian: meek, passive, humble, devout, and submissive. Religious training, said the American Sunday School Union, was an excellent way of keeping youths out of crime and making worthy citizens of them.[45] The Bible, wrote one evangelical, had the same effect as a good police force.[46] One way to stop the destruction of property by mobs, said another, was to encourage reading of the Bible. The ideas it taught acted like "moral police."[47] The leaders of the Missionary Society of Connecticut commanded that all individuals should practice "civil order and . . . subordination," among other "principles and habits . . . which are essential to the welfare of society."[48] Man's "natural pride and opposition to God," believed Noah Webster, was the source of all problems, and was the method by which "multitudes of men, especially the more intelligent and moral part of society are deluded into ruin."[49] During the remainder of his life, Webster advocated principles widely accepted by evangelical Protestants. In doing so he published books and essays designed to spread his concept of the social lessons of the gospel, helped found a college specifically dedicated to this work, and even edited the *Holy Bible* to conform to his values.

After his conversion, Webster consistently emphasized man's "duty" to authority, not his right of freedom. Moral and political corruption would disappear if all followed His word as set forth in the Bible. Peace and tranquillity would reign, and man could finally achieve the "supreme happiness" to which he was entitled in America if all would become Quiet Christians, conforming totally "to God's image."[50]

It was immediately apparent that he had found the only way to control human passions. God the Father was clearly the source of discipline for the American family:

> For in the minds of the best regulated by family discipline, the rules of civility, there will at times break forth sallies of envy, jealousy, petulence, and discontent, which annoy the peace of families and neighborhoods. Nothing seems effectually to restrain such passions but divine grace. The fear of man, and a regard to decorum, will not produce the effect, in minds of a particular structure. But the humbling doctrines of the gospel change the tiger to a lamb. —Real religion, which implies a habitual sense of the divine presence, and a fear of offending the Supreme Being, subdues and controls all the turbulent passions; and nothing is seen in the Christian, but meekness, forbearance, and kindness, accompanied by a serenity of mind and a desire to please, as uniform as they are cheering to families and friends. On this subject I speak with delight for observation.[51]

Webster viewed the human family as a sort of psychological agent of society, transmitting its repressive tendencies and controls to the child through its very structure.

Nations were merely large families, and both social organizations should be run in an authoritarian manner. "No small part of the vices and disorders of society, personal enmities, quarrels and lawsuits originate in the wrong or defective governments of families."[52] The family system was "the origin of nations," and "the subordination of children in families, tends to favor subordination in citizens: respect for parents generates respect for rulers and laws."[53]

Webster detailed the exact attitude that he believed the Quiet Christian should have. Obedience to authority, be it in religion, national affairs, or the human family, was of the utmost importance. A slow, reluctant obedience, accompanied by murmurings of dissatisfaction, was not acceptable "to parents, nor to God." The inferior being in any situation should be ready to comply like a good slave to command: easily and cheerfully. Webster summed up the interrelationships of subordination to the father, to God, and to political rulers quite succinctly:

> The subordination of children to their parents, is the foundation of peace in families; [it] contributes to foster those kindly dispositions, both in parents and children, which are the sources of domestic happiness, and which extend their influence to all social relations in subsequent periods of life.[54]

There could be no doubt that this submission to all authority was the will of God. "This entire subjection to parents [is] expressly enjoined by divine precepts," he said.[55]

As he himself admitted, "my belief is the fruit of some experience and much inquiry."[56] It was clearly an attempt to become a part of a bigger whole outside of himself, to submerge himself in an organic unity in which all questions are answered.[57] It was a source of both inner peace and external tranquillity:

> The soul of man is, I am persuaded, never tranquil, till the will is subdued, and has yielded, with implicit submission, to God's sovereign grace. This submission, however humiliating it may appear to the natural man, is accompanied or followed with unspeakable satisfaction. The most dignified attitude of feeble, sinful man, is that of a penitent at the foot of the cross, imploring pardon from an offended God, and I firmly believe, that every man must be brought to this posture, before he can enjoy any permanent tranquillity of mind in this life, or possess any qualification for the happiness of the next.[58]

From 1808 on Webster described himself as a Calvinist. He prayed three times a day.[59] In short, his view of everything was Christian in its orientation. He had gone through a "regeneration" which he said was "*an entire change of the affections.*"[60] His view of the scriptures, religion, salvation, and God's moral government were very much changed, he said, "and my heart yields with delight and confidence to whatever appears to be the divine will."[61]

He had virtually reverted back to the belief system of the Puritan generation. The Bible provided answers for all questions, guidelines for all behavior.[62] The longer he lived, the stronger became his belief in the correctness of his basic Calvinism. "I am perfectly well satisfied that what is denominated 'modern Calvinism' is the genuine religion preached by Christ and his Apostles," he said in 1835, "and that there is no other genuine religion."[63] The "fear of God" was "the spring, the source of all religion and piety."[64] It would reduce man to a full sense of the feebleness of his powers, and to a sense of his utter depravity.[65]

The duty of men was not to do good to other men, but to love the Almighty. Social and even moral reform came second to worship. God had a right to the love and reverence of the beings he created. Man must respect God first, then be concerned with good works.[66] Morality was only a secondary obligation. Moses had come down from the mountain with two tablets; the first and most important contained man's duties to God, the second his duties to other men.[67]

Revelation was now more important and reliable than man's reason. The latter had been given by the Creator to use, but it was not enough. Man must also rely on the mysterious revelations of God for guidance. Men, and especially young students, must ask the cosmic question: "*Who made me? Why was I made? What is my duty?*" The answers to such questions constituted the whole business of life; yet they could not be reached through man's mind. Instead, revelation alone could furnish correct knowledge.[68]

Americans must accept the Bible as literal truth. The doctrine of the divinity of Christ and all other miracles were true: "God does, at times directly interpose in behalf of those who *ask him in faith.*" He restored health to the sick, sight to the blind, and so on. Christ was God manifest in the flesh. Predestination and election, although beyond human comprehension, were also real.[69]

Such an important work as the Bible must have no flaws, and Webster was convinced that some improvements should be made. As early as 1822, he wrote to Moses Stuart of the need for a new edition.[70] Webster's version of the holy scriptures appeared in 1835. Its importance, he believed, far outweighed his dictionaries. "I consider this emendation of the common version as the most important enterprise of my life," he said just before it was published.[71]

Webster was convinced that there were many parts of the Bible that should be corrected. The vocabulary was restricted, and many words were obsolete. There were grammatical errors. Since the Bible would have a considerable influence on the formation of useful language, its contents should be correct and easy to read. Even more important to Webster was the elimination of what he believed were vulgar phrases, which might hinder the dissemination of its message. The common version contained many impolite words which could not be used in mixed company; many parents, he felt, would not let their children read certain chapters because of vulgarisms. Other young people refused to go to Bible classes in which they were required to read certain passages which made them blush. "To retain such offensive language" would be "injudicious, if not indefensible."[72]

Most of the words and imagery he changed were sexual in nature. Names of the parts of the body were often altered; "breasts" was substituted for "teats," for example. In discussions of birth, "belly" was changed to "born," and "womb" was usually omitted. All references to male genitals were deleted. Another area of concern was terms for excretion and secretion. Webster exercised a complete taboo on "dung," "stink," and "piss." The sexual act itself was severely censored; "fornication" was changed to "lewdness" or "lewd deeds," and "fornicators" became "lewd persons." "Whore" was deleted in every instance.[73] All these terms presumably would undermine the purity of Quiet Christians.

After 1808, Webster's conversion, his belief in the Bible, and evangelical Protestantism all affected his view of American history. If the Bible was literal truth, then of course its story of the origin of man must be correct. Thus when he wrote his *History of the United States* in the 1830s, Webster began with Genesis. Adam and Eve were the first real human beings, and all Americans were descendants of Japeth, one of Noah's three sons. All three had been together at the Tower of Babel, and when God dispersed them, Japeth's descendants migrated to England, then to America.[74]

His account of the Revolution also differed considerably from the view he had espoused before. The role of religion, which he had previously ignored, now took on greater significance. Webster noted that the roots of the Revolution went back to the first generation of settlers. The essential point of contention, from the very beginning, had been religion, not politics or economics. He believed that opposition to the English church naturally fostered an enmity to monarchy, and this had developed into outright opposition.[75] Furthermore, Webster stressed the religiosity of the colonists. At each point in his narrative of the events before and during the war, Webster carefully noted that the colonists always sought divine blessings and the aid of Christ in making decisions.[76] When Cornwallis surrendered, Congress reacted by proceeding to the nearest church to "make public acknowledgment of gratitude to Heaven for the singular event."[77]

Alterations in his view of history coincided with changes in his political and social thought. The laws of Moses provided an adequate foundation for all social regulation.[78] God had "a right to give laws to man for his government."[79] On this question as on all others, men must not perplex their minds with abstruse reasonings on subjects beyond mortal comprehension.[80] The "adaptation of the law of God to human society," both in temporal and spiritual things was "absolutely necessary."[81] He was now convinced that *"the fear of God"* was *"the beginning of wisdom; the foundation on which the whole system stands."* The "social benefits of Christianity" were no less "obvious than the spiritual."[82] Without it there could be "no effectual restraint on all the evil propensities of mankind, of lust, ambition, anger, and revenge."[83] Disobedience to divine law was the "cause of almost all the sufferings of mankind." Conformity to it in society brought peace, prosperity and happiness. If men were wretched, it was because they rejected the government of God. The fact that men have not obeyed God's precepts was in his mind "the most prominent cause of all political evils."[84]

The impact of the conversion on Webster's social concepts is indicated by his use of the phrase "sheet anchor." In the 1780s he had said that the rights of man, equal distribution of property, and so forth were America's sheet anchor. In the 1790s and early 1800s it had been the Constitution.[85] After his conversion he stated that "I consider the Christian religion as our sheet anchor during our political storms."[86]

The teachings of Christ formed the moral basis for the Quiet Christian's life. In 1823 Webster wrote an essay of instructions to young men about to enter college. It was a specific example of how the Quiet Christian should live. Good breeding and close attention to virtue and complementary habits were guides to the selection of friends, and of course evangelical Protestantism was central to the development of good character. "Never maintain a familiar intercourse with the profane, the lewd, the intemperate, the gamester, or the scoffer at religion," he warned. The common civilities of life should be extended towards these people, but beyond that "nothing is required of men who reverence the divine precepts, and who desire to keep themselves *unspotted from the world.*"[87]

After 1808 his heroes were the very people whom he had chastised as bigots in the 1780s. The Quiet Christians would do well to model themselves after the original pious and devout settlers of New England. They had lived every detail of their lives by the Bible and had managed to avoid crime, vice, and corrupt amusements. The regularity of their worship, their simple rituals, their industry and plain clothes all made them seem saintly. The nineteenth century could learn much from the seventeenth.[88]

"The Bible must be considered as the great source of all the truth by which men are to be guided in government," he said, "as well as in all social transactions."[89] He looked to the past and found that civil liberty originated with Christianity. The Reformation was the birth of natural rights, and civil liberty "has been gradually advancing and improving, as genuine Christianity has prevailed."[90] The Puritans now seemed like the first true republicans, and "their liberal and wise institutions . . . have been the foundation of our republican governments." He was careful to point out that their mode of government had been transcribed literally from the scriptures.[91]

Education also took on a new significance in this light. After trying to utilize schools to encourage progressive social change in the 1770s and 1780s, Webster's concern with education slowly disappeared around the turn of the century. It was of relatively little importance to him even after his conversion, and in fact he mentioned it only rarely. The reason for his loss of interest was quite clear: it was of no use to control human passions, and, in fact, a little education could even be dangerous. "Knowledge, learning, [and] talents are not necessarily connected with sound moral and political principles," he said, and universal education would not "insure unbiased elections, or an upright administration." Indeed, "eminent abilities, accompanied with depravity of heart," he thought in 1814, "render the possessor tenfold more dangerous in a community."[92]

Yet just after that statement his views on education took another, more drastic, turn. In 1812 he moved to Amherst, Massachusetts, where he remained for ten years. There he became the primary force behind the founding of Amherst College.[93] He also began to think about the role of education in society and its possible use as a tool of social control, as well as in the propagation of evangelical Protestantism.[94] The duty of the new college, he said in 1817, would be to inculcate certain doctrines, including the sound precepts of morality and evangelical piety. The students who passed through his school would become obedient and passive, the epitome of the Quiet Christian.[95] "I believe more than is commonly believed may be done in this way toward correcting the vices and disorders of society."[96] From Amherst the entire world could be pacified through missionaries: future Americans would find satisfaction in knowing that their fathers had gone out from Amherst to Africa and Siberia to convert entire kingdoms to Christ. Lovers of peace and security who realized the influence of Christianity in civilizing savages and in "restraining the disorders of civilized society" must lend their support to the new college. Amherst would spread evangelical Protestantism because it was the only reliable social cement. Only the Bible could convert swords to plowshares and spears into pruning hooks. "The gospel only can supersede the necessity of bolts and bars" or could "dispeople the state prison and the penitentiary!"[97]

Finally, Webster detailed the kind of education that Amherst would provide for all good Quiet Christians. Its main emphasis would not be on science, literature, or philosophy, or even on vocational training, but on moral reform. Each individual would try to model himself on God, the only perfect being. Reading would be confined to those books that helped build moral character. Plays, novels, poetry, romance, and any other forms of human expression not directly linked to emotional and intellectual repression or obedience would be avoided. Most important of all, each student would be taught to respect his elders and live by the ten commandments. All important knowledge would be gleaned from the *Holy Bible*.[98]

After 1808, Webster found the answers to all questions in the Bible and evangelical Protestantism. William James said that a man is "converted" when religious ideas, previously peripheral in his consciousness, take a central place, and when religious beliefs form the core of his view of the world.[99] This is an apt description of Webster's thinking. His conversion was a product of his entire personality and life experiences; it dominated his view of everything. Most importantly, he applied evangelical Christian principles of behavior to all areas of life. If Americans were all Quiet Christians, he believed, there could be no political divisiveness, no economic chaos, no social upheaval. All would be serenity and tranquillity, especially if everyone thought the same way he did.

*"It is obvious to my mind, that popular errors proceeding
from a misunderstanding of words are among the
efficient causes of our political disorders."*
    N.W., 1839

8 *Control*

"I finished writing my Dictionary in January, 1825," Noah Webster once recalled. It was a solemn moment:

> When I had come to the last word, I was seized with a trembling
> which made it somewhat difficult to hold my pen steady for writing.
> The cause seems to have been the thought that I might not then live
> to finish the work, or the thought that I was so near the end of my
> labors. But I summoned the strength to finish the last word, and then
> walking about the room a few minutes I recovered.[1]

So ended a quarter-century of constant, daily labor. The finished
product was, by all standards, a monumental achievement. With 70,000 entries, all written out by his own hand, it was indeed a massive work, the last
major dictionary ever compiled by a single individual.[2] It has become, in the
form of its successors, an integral part of American culture. As early as the

mid-nineteenth century the name "Webster" had become synonymous with "dictionary."[3]

Webster's definitions of words, both in his private correspondence and in the work itself, as well as his etymology, clearly reflect Quiet Christian values. If all Americans would only see the world through the eyes and mind of Noah Webster as set forth in his dictionary, Christian peace and tranquility would reign.

Like religion, language took on great importance in the early republic. Noah Webster was not alone in his concern over definitions; in fact, a heated public debate arose over certain key words and the whole problem of defining terms. Thomas Jefferson's inaugural statement that all Americans were both Federalists and Republicans fell hard on sensitive ears and sparked nationwide arguments. Both sides of the political spectrum participated, and the question spread to editorials from New England to South Carolina.

Thomas Green Fessenden's attitude epitomized that of others. "We believe that words are things," he said. "If false, they give a wrong direction to the public mind, and are of consequence to the physical community."[4] High emotion infused terms like *Federalist* and *Republican*; *Jacobin*, *democrat*, and *republic* were approached with extreme care, for they seemed to sum up all the social and political problems of the day. Lexicography became a national issue, and all spokesmen carefully worded their conclusions.

Rufus King, one of Webster's staunchest supporters, summed up the attitude of Washington Irving, Alexander Hamilton, John Quincy Adams, and most Federalists. "Words without meaning, or with wrong meaning have especially of late years done great harm," he said. "Liberty, Love of Country, Federalism, Republicanism, Democracy, Jacobin, Glory, Philosophy and Honor are words in the mouth of everyone and used without precision by anyone; the abuse of words is as pernicious as the abuse of things."[5] Noah Webster spent the better part of three decades attempting to come to grips with the meaning of words, and thereby understand and order a confusing and chaotic world.

Virtually everyone believes that the *American Dictionary of the English Language* was a nationalistic tract. Webster was a great patriot, a founding father at least as nationalistic as his more famous distant cousin, Daniel. Indeed, so pervasive is this belief that many historians, like Oscar Handlin and John D. Hicks, discuss the work in the context of rising nationalism without really stating that it was thus motivated.[6] They write as if Webster's nationalism were common knowledge and as if there were no other possible explanation. Charles Beard called the dictionary a high note of American nationalism.[7] Merle Curti and his associates believed it was a patriotic effort.[8] Two more historians believed that in compiling his dictionary Webster "wanted to complete our independence."[9] Even Lawrence J. Friedman, who correctly notes Webster's alienation, portrays the dictionary as a patriotic work.[10] Those who have concentrated specifically on Webster or the dictionary itself have been even more adamant in their conclusions. Homer D. Babbidge represents the attitude and method employed by most commenters: he consistently confused Webster's nationalistic statements in the 1780s with his later work, as if nothing occurred between 1783 and 1841.[11] Perhaps the clearest example of this approach is the analysis presented by David Littlejohn. Webster's activity and thoughts, he said, were dominated by the need for "an independent, manly, *national* American spirit." Littlejohn followed this statement with the "unshackle your chains" statement taken from the *American Magazine*, published in 1788.[12] Webster's biographer, Harry R. Warfel, in 1936 spent several pages explaining Webster's "inner drive of patriotism."[13]

Nationalism is a simple explanation for what was in fact the product of a complex interaction of an individual and the society in which he lived. When the work is considered within the context of Noah Webster's life, it becomes apparent that it was stimulated by much more than just patriotism. That was undoubtedly an important factor in his early conceptions of the work, and his desire to compile a scholarly dictionary superior to any in existence probably helped keep him going.

Yet the *American Dictionary* was the product of an entire lifetime. As such it reflected the events and inheritances of that human life, and contained all the biases, concerns, and ideals of an individual. Indeed, it was an extension of his whole personality. It reflects much about the man and his times, although one must read it carefully to understand the tale it tells. Webster's main concern while writing and publishing it was not to celebrate American life or to expand independence. Instead, he sought to counteract social disruption and reestablish the deferential world-order that he believed was disintegrating.

Although he had contemplated the need for a new dictionary as early as the 1780s,[14] Webster did not begin the tedious task until 1800.[15] It was not an easy assignment, and in fact, there were many obstacles which had to be overcome. As Linda Kerber has pointed out, even staunch Federalists like Josiah Quincy, who ostensibly shared his views on politics and society, publicly criticized his work. They saw linguistic reform as another source of discord, undermining the very order that Webster was trying to strengthen.[16] In 1822 a comic opera, Samuel Woodworth's *Deed of Gift*, mocked Webster's work when a lead character uttered definitions and pronunciations in a pretentious and haughty manner.[17] Even Webster's close friends, including John Quincy Adams,[18] James Kent,[19] John Jay,[20] and his brother-in-law, Thomas Dawes,[21] continually discouraged him over the entire twenty-five years. Webster was also in constant need of financial support, and was often forced to solicit funds from friends and strangers.[22] In 1812, he moved from New Haven to Amherst in order to take advantage of the lower cost of living.[23] In addition, the physical aspects of writing hundreds of thousands of words often brought great discomfort.[24] He occasionally complained of exhaustion;

while in the final stages of preparation he told his daughter that his labors were severe enough to produce constant pain and soreness in his hand.[25]

It is natural to draw links between Webster's early work and his *American Dictionary*. And, of course, he encouraged this in the seemingly nationalistic title of his most famous work. He noted that the chief glory of a nation arose from its authors and purposefully stated that he believed American writers were equal in skill and brilliance to Englishmen. He even named those on this side of the Atlantic whom he considered comparable to the best of Europe. Franklin, Washington, Adams, Jay, Madison, Marshall, Dwight, Trumbull, and Irving were his favorites. Today we have forgotten many of the others he named, such as Ames, Cleaveland, Hare, and Walsh.

Perhaps as an indication of what was to come, Webster did not mention an internationally famous American who was also the symbol of all that he loathed: Thomas Jefferson. Thomas Paine and all other earlier American celebrators of democracy and freedom were also neglected. As George Krapp, the most respected twentieth-century student of the development of the English language, has noted, merely naming Franklin, Washington, and others as authorities "is quite a different matter from the narrow patriotic zeal which was rampant in the years immediately following the Revolution."[26]

In addition, Webster himself indicated that his views had changed immensely. "It is not only important, but, in a degree necessary," he said in the opening pages, "that the people of this country, should have an *American Dictionary* of the English language." Notice that he did not advocate the development of a new language, or even a new dialect, separate and distinct from that spoken in England. Instead, he perceived himself to be writing merely an *American* dictionary of the English language, which is of course a very different thing from creating a whole new language. And he further explained his position, noting that the body of the language was basically the same as that of England. He added a significant statement: "it is desirable to perpetuate that sameness."[27]

Thus, the end product of Webster's toils was anything but a new "American tongue." He included only about fifty Americanisms, a fact which prompted H. L. Mencken to label Webster a defective observer of his own country.[28] The lexicographer's nationalism had in fact reached a low point in 1814, when he helped draft the first circular calling for the Hartford Convention.[29] In that year, he also denounced the Constitution as naive and wildly democratic, ridiculed the concept of universal white male suffrage, and called for division of the union into three separate countries.[30]

The *American Dictionary* was perfectly acceptable in England. The first edition of 2,500 copies was quickly followed by an English edition of 3,000, and one major student of lexicography has noted that Webster's crowning achievement was quite suitable for use in America and England.[31] Indeed, his dictionary was received more warmly across the Atlantic than in the United States. Warfel stated that "soon Webster became the standard in England."[32] When his publisher went bankrupt, copies of the English edition were sold without change in America.[33]

Other incidents indicate that his dictionary was not a nationalistic tract. In the 1830s he stated his position in explicit terms. "Our language is the *English* and it is desirable that the language of the United States and Great Britain should continue to be the same," he told an acquaintance, "except so far as local circumstances, laws and institutions shall require a few peculiarities in each country."[34] When the second American edition was published in 1841, he sent a copy to Queen Victoria. Significantly, he told the person carrying it to her that "our common language is one of the ties that bind the two nations together; I hope the works I have executed will manifest to the British nation that the Americans are not willing to suffer it to degenerate on this side of the Atlantic."[35] Half a century earlier he had despised England and all that it stood for. Now he told the queen that he hoped his dictionary might furnish evidence that the "genuine descendants of English ancestors born on the west of the Atlantic, have not forgotten either the land or the language of their fathers."[36]

In attempting to understand the *American Dictionary* in its entirety, it must be remembered that Webster's view of language was dualistic. It was, of course, to be studied for its own sake, but it was also something much more. Language, he believed, influenced opinion and behavior. If people believed that all men were in fact "equal," they would act in certain ways, probably in different ways than if they believed that men were not necessarily "equal." Thus, language was something that could be used as a means to a greater end. It could be changed, altered, and manipulated, and in so doing, one could affect millions of people. Although he never explicitly said so, Webster believed this from the very beginning of his work. It is implicit in his early attempts to forge an "American tongue" as a means of encouraging independence from a vile and corrupt England, and to further his utopian dreams. Even in 1788, he could conceptualize the use of language in purifying society. In that year, he called for studies which would "show how far truth and accuracy of thinking are concerned in a clear understanding of words." Language should be studied "if it can be proved that *mere use of words* has led nations into error, and still continues the delusion."[37] As early as 1790 he was actively engaged in manipulation of language as a means of influencing opinion and behavior. He had just completed another book, he told a friend. "I have introduced into it some definitions, relative to the slave trade," he said, "calculated to impress upon young minds the detestableness of the trade."[38]

Webster made his intentions in the dictionary quite clear. The values expressed within the work were his. "In many cases, I have given brief sentences of my own," he declared, "and often presenting some important maxim or sentiment in religion, morality, law or civil policy."[39] To his daughter, Emily, he confessed that he had used the definitions in his work in less than scholarly, objective ways. "I suppose you must have noticed that I have not forgotten my own country and friends," he told her.[40]

Another significant indication of the framework within which Webster wrote was his work in etymology. The pronunciation and spelling of words, as well as his criticism of Samuel Johnson and other lexicographers, is not central to an understanding of his work, and has been dealt with adequately elsewhere.[41] His etymology has been analyzed by others, but never accounted for within the context of his larger concerns. Yet it was, in Webster's own mind, an integral and very important part of his work. In relation to the rest of his life, it reveals much about how he operated.

Noah Webster's etymological work has been heavily criticized by nearly all students of the subject. His method was quite simple: walking around his circular table he examined each of the dictionaries of twenty languages for external similarities. If the number of letters and basic structure of a word in one language was similar to that of another, he assumed that they carried the same meaning or meant something quite similar. One etymologist, Mitford Mathews,[42] has lamented that this severely limited the usefulness of his work; others have been less kind. The most recent and thorough student of lexicography, Joseph Friend, said Webster was "confused [in] the jungle of historical and comparative linguistics," and called his etymology "wild."[43] His derivations were "often as ingenious as they were wildly wrong."[44] Charlton Laird studied Webster's use of Anglo-Saxon as a test of his knowledge of language and concluded that the lexicographer had no detailed understanding of it. He also believed that Webster's etymology was quite inferior to that of his contemporary, Thomas Jefferson. Laird pointed out that those who revised Webster's work shortly after his death "felt obliged quietly to remove great numbers of [his] etymological surmises."[45] One of the most famous modern students of the language, George Philip Krapp, believed that the dictionary was "only partially successful," and that it was "in parts executed with an inadequate scholarship and with a stubbornness of personal conviction that seriously impaired the noble design." Specifically, Krapp said that "in etymology Webster was least successful and most ambitious."[46] Sir James Murray believed that Webster "had the notion that derivations can be elaborated from one's own consciousness."[47]

Etymologists have noted that the framework within which Webster tried to work was simply incorrect. Friend said that his basic understanding of the principles of comparative and historical linguistics was "gravely defective" and "insufficient,"[48] while others have called his work in this area "simple fantasy."[49] H. L. Mencken remarked that Webster showed little understanding "of the basic 'direction of genius' of the English language":

> One always sees in him . . . the teacher rather than the scientific inquirer; the ardor of his desire to expound and instruct was only

matched by his infinite capacity for observing inaccurately, and his profound ignorance of elementary principles.[50]

Krapp agreed with Mencken's portrait of Webster as basically incompetent in the field of etymology:

> Writing, or at least publishing, in the second quarter of the nineteenth century, Webster can scarcely be excused for not knowing that Grimm's *Deutsche Grammatik* was in existence, that the comparative relations of words in languages of the same group are to be determined by the tests of regular phonetic rules or laws, not by casual external similarities or by subtle spiritual interpretations.[51]

Yet Noah Webster believed that his etymology was new, scholarly, and, in fact, the most important part of his work. As Laird correctly notes, of all the causes he supported over his long life, and they were legion, "none was dearer to him than was the pursuit of etymologies, and in nothing so much as in his vast synopsis of 'language affinities' . . . did he repose his hopes for the gratitude and admiration of society."[52] His failure is symbolized by his huge handwritten manuscript study of the relationships of languages, still unpublished, totally ignored by modern etymologists, and now locked away in the New York Public Library.[53]

As early as 1806, Webster had vowed to "make one effort to dissolve the chains of illusions" surrounding the development of language.[54] A year later, he reported that he had begun compilation of the dictionary by concentrating merely on definitions and correcting errors in orthography. This had led him "gradually and almost insensibly" to investigate the origin of the English language. He had been surprised to learn that the path of development of all European languages was a subject virtually unexplored. All other etymologists had "wandered into the field of conjecture, venturing to substitute opinions for evidence."[55] He believed that he had already made many discoveries that penetrated deeply into scholarly knowledge, and would fundamentally revise the conceptualization of mankind's linguistic development.[56] By 1809, he had concluded that language had begun in Asia and migrated outward.[57] At about this time, Webster stopped working on definitions and orthography and spent ten years compiling his synopsis of the affinities of languages.[58] Four years before his death, he still believed that his work was superior to any others and that the work of all other etymologists, "even the German scholars, the most accurate philologists in Europe, appears to be wholly deficient."[59]

In the course of his work, Webster rejected not only the studies of European etymologists, but his own previous theories as well. In his *Dissertations on the English Language*, written in 1789, he had concluded that northern Europe had developed two basic languages, Gothic and Celtic. English was a descendant of the ancient Gothic, as were German, Dutch, Danish, Swedish, and Swiss.[60] Mallet and Pelletier, two leading European etymologists, had concluded that the original stock had been Hebrew, and Webster agreed.[61] His theories in 1828 hardly resembled what he had said in 1789.

Most commenters on Webster's etymology have not attempted to explain his work, but have merely condemned it. Edgerton pointed out that even the relative isolation of American scholarship "hardly excuses such astounding ignorance in Webster."[62] Sledd and Kolb remarked that "for such invincible ignorance, it is best to attempt no excuse."[63] Friend noted that Webster proposed absurd derivations forty years after he should have known better, twenty years after the work of Schlegel had been published, and a dozen years after the works of Jacob Grimm appeared.[64]

On the surface, at least, all of this adds up to a puzzling problem. Given his remark about the inaccuracy of the Germans, it is safe to say that Webster knew of their existence. He either read their work and rejected it, or simply chose to ignore it, believing that they were wrong. Webster was clearly not ignorant, nor was he incompetent. He was aware of the work of others, but chose to follow his own beliefs instead. Why, then, did he spend ten years spinning out fantasy after fantasy based on what he believed was solid concrete evidence?

George Krapp has come close to explaining this situation. In short, it was really spiritual, not phonological, truth in which Webster was primarily interested. He seems to have thought "that the truth of a word, that is the primitive and original radical value of the word, was equivalent to the truth of the idea."[65]

Webster's etymology was simply a literal extrapolation of scriptural truth into another field. Since 1808, he had believed that the Bible was factually correct, and that it must be accepted as such. Without it, there was no basis for civilization itself. Thus, his rejection of European etymologists is no mystery. Their scientific attempts to unravel the development of language led away from the story of the Tower of Babel. They were directly challenging the validity of the Bible, the only rock upon which peace and tranquillity could be secured.

In 1806, as he began his etymological studies, Webster commented specifically on this subject. He believed that etymology illuminated not just the origins of words, but the development of human history as well. The etymology of the European languages "will throw no inconsiderable light on the origin and history of the several nations who people it, and confirm in no small degree, the scriptures' account of the dispersion of men."[66]

In the final analysis, Webster had no choice but to write Christian etymology, regardless of the methodology and insights of all other authors. The only ultimate truth, as Krapp might say, was contained in the scriptures, and it dictated the mere truth of words. Beside Christ, Schlegel and Grimm were insignificant. They challenged the validity of Christianity, and should the authority of the scriptures be demolished, there was simply no hope for mankind. Without literal belief in biblical truth, he said in 1823, "we are cast on the ocean of life, without chart, or compass, or rudder." The "tempestuous sea," Webster's metaphor for the society in which he lived, could only end in "annihilation and despair" if the scriptures were found invalid in any area.[67] Given this mental context, Webster was obviously incapable of seeing the development of language in any framework of explanation other than that set forth in the Bible.

Webster introduced his work with a literal belief in the origin of language according to Genesis. Vocal sounds, he noted, were used to communicate between Adam and Eve. "Hence, we may infer that language was bestowed on Adam, in the same manner as all his other faculties and knowledge, by supernatural power; or in other words, was of divine origin." It is, therefore, "probable that *language* as well as the faculty of speech, was the immediate gift of God."[68] Webster then traced the biblical story of the development of man, which was the basis for all the derivations of the words in the two volumes.[69] As Joseph Friend notes, no amount of hard work, not even the labor of a quarter of a century, could overcome the limitations imposed by this naive scriptural literalism.[70] He accepted without question the story of the Tower of Babel and the confusion of tongues. Before that time all mankind had spoken a common language, which Webster called "Chaldee," and which all modern etymologists agree was a fantasy. When those in Babel were dispersed, they divided into three groups, each led by a son of Noah: Shem, Ham, and Japeth. The last had eventually migrated to northern Europe, and thus all the languages of that area were labeled "Japethic." This development, believed Webster, could be traced through the existence of certain words with similar construction and meaning in various languages. But above all else, the Bible, the basis for all man's knowledge in other fields, was also the key to etymology.

One example of Webster's etymology will illustrate both his change in viewpoint over time and his cast of mind. In 1789 he had remarked that the word "God" had come from the concept "good," and that His nature was the explanation of the derivation.[71] In 1828, he specifically rejected that idea. Instead, he noted that "Supreme Being" was taken from "supremacy or power." Thus, "God" was "equivalent to lord or ruler, from some root signifying to press or exert force."[72]

Webster believed that the misunderstanding of words led to social and political upheaval. Words should not be used vaguely. "There is one remarkable circumstance in our own history which seems to have escaped observation," he noted in 1838, "which is, the mischievous effect of the indefinite application of terms." The evils proceeding from the improper understanding of words were enormous, at least in his mind. It was a problem rarely observed by the mass of men, but one that sometimes led to serious mistakes, both in religion and government. In 1839 he wrote an essay in which he summed up his entire life's work in linguistics, philology, etymology, and lexicography. It was "obvious" to him that "popular errors proceeding from a misunderstanding of words are among the *efficient causes of our political disorders.*"[73]

Webster's keen sensitivity to the use and effect of the definition of words was often exhibited in his correspondence. His firm belief that the definitions of words affected human behavior appeared time and time again throughout the course of his life. Moreover, his discussions of the true meanings of words clearly record his conscious manipulation of definitions in ways that he hoped would influence events. Indeed, the thought processes that led to specific definitions of key words can clearly be seen. They reveal that Webster's strong social and political values and his longing for public submission to authority and for social tranquillity dictated what he believed should be the correct understanding of important words.

He believed that an inaccurate understanding of the word "pension" had been partially responsible for social discord in the 1780s. Congress had granted a pension to officers who had served in the continental army. Many had protested, and the convention held in Middletown had called for its repeal. This unrest had distressed Webster. It had been "a remarkable, but an unfortunate instance of the use of the word, in a sense so indefinite that the people at large made no distinction between *pensions* granted as a provision for old officers, and *pensions* granted for the purpose of bribery for favor and support." Obviously Webster thought that the half-pay for officers was the first type of pension, while to the convention it was the second. In his dictionary he was careful to say that it meant "to grant an annual allowance from the public treasury to a person for past services." No example of the misunderstanding of words, he thought, was as clear as that surrounding the phrase "union of church and state." He understood the aversion of many Americans to the unification of ecclesiastical and civil authority because of the European experience. Along with many others, Webster had spoken in favor of their separation in the 1780s. But times had changed, and by 1838 his conception of that relationship had also changed. Now the union of the two meant that "all laws must have *religion for their basis.*" In this sense, there clearly was a strong need for a "union of civil and ecclesiastical powers; in support of the laws and institutions."[74] This union was the seedbed of Quiet Christians and the heart of his concept of social relations.

Jacobinism, democrat, and *republican* were important words that Webster's biases led him to define in significant ways. The first, he said in 1799, was not merely the philosophy of a French political faction. It was instead "an opposition to established government and institutions, and an attempt to overthrow them, by private accusations or by violent or illegal means."[75] *Democrat* was "synonymous with the word Jacobian in France." Democratic organizations arose from the attempt to "control our government by private associations." By 1800 the word signified "a person who attempts an undue opposition to or influence over government by means of private clubs, secret intrigues, or by public popular meetings which are extraneous to the Constitution."[76] *Republicans*, on the other hand, were "friends of our Representative Governments, who believe that no influence whatever should be exercised in a state which is directly authorized by and developed by legislation."[77] Similar definitions appeared in his dictionary.

A key word, the definition of which he believed could directly influence behavior, was *free*. Most Americans really believed that all men were free to act according to their own will. The belief that this abstract condition was natural and was a basic part of American life was widely upheld, or so thought Noah Webster. It was absurd, and in fact "contributed to the popular licentiousness, which often disturbs the public peace, and even threatens extensive evils in this country." A misunderstanding of *free* threatened the very permanency of government because it led people to believe that somehow individuals were "*above* the constitutional authorities."[78] It was also simply incorrect. Instead, all individuals, from the time of their birth, were subject to the commands of their parents, of God, and of the government of the country in which they lived.[79] There would be far fewer problems in society, believed Noah Webster, if all Americans understood that "*No person is born free*, in the general acception of the word *free*."[80]

Equality and *equal* were also key terms. "Nothing can be more obvious than that by the appointment of the creator, in the constitution of man and of human society," he wrote a few months before his death, "the conditions of men must be different and *unequal*."[81] The common American belief that all men must be equal in conditions in which they lived was totally incorrect. The Declaration of Independence was wrong when it began by affirming as a self-evident truth that "all men are born *equal*." That was the work of the infamous idealist Thomas Jefferson, and as a universal proposition could not be possible. In their intellectual and physical powers men were born *unequal*, and hence inequality was a basic part of human life. Webster said that most of the men of the earlier generation had believed that each person was born with an "equal natural right to liberty and protection," something far different from total equality, a belief that led to agitation over the right of suffrage.[82] The founders had believed in equality of opportunity, with which Webster had no argument. "But *equality of condition* is a very different thing and dependent on circumstances over which government and laws have no control."[83]

Most importantly, when people expected equality of condition, it led inevitably to opposition to authority, chaos, and ultimately anarchy. Misunderstanding of the words "*free* and *equal*" led "the more ignorant and turbulent part of the community" to become "emboldened" and to "take the law into their own hands, or to trample both constitution and law under their feet."[84] The very concept of equality of condition could lead only to disaster:

it is not for the interest and safety of society that all men should be equal. Perfect equality, if such a state could be supposed practicable, would render due subordination impossible, and dissolve society. All men in a community are equally entitled to protection, and the secure enjoyment of their rights. . . . Superiority in natural and acquired endowment, and in authority derived from the laws, is essential to the existence of social order, and of personal safety.[85]

In his dictionary, Webster listed nineteen definitions of the words *equal* and *equality*. He conspicuously did not celebrate equality among men.

Webster's belief in Quiet Christian behavior appears throughout the work. The reader is constantly reminded of his divinely directed role in life and the values by which he lives. The fear of God, absolute and rigid controller of all things, the depravity of man, and the character traits of meekness, humility, passivity, and wholehearted submission to proper authority are consistently supported in the definitions of hundreds and perhaps thousands of words. This was done in two basic ways: either through specific definitions of words indicating correct behavior, or through the use of quotations illustrating the meaning of the word. "Author," for instance, was defined as "One who produces, creates, or brings into being." Webster could have stopped there, with an objective statement, as other lexicographers did. Instead, he added "as, God is the *author* of the Universe," thus reminding the reader of his own relative meaninglessness.[86]

Ironically, Webster managed to inject his authoritarian desires into even the most intimate of human relationships. The verb form of *love* was "a sense to be pleased with," to which he added a significant set of examples of its usage, again designed to instruct the Quiet Christian:

The Christian *loves* his Bible. In short, we *love* whatever gives us pleasure and delight, whether animal or intellectual; and if our hearts are right, we *love* God above all things, as the sum of all excellence and all the attributes which can communicate happiness to intelligent beings. In other words, the Christian *loves* God with the love of complacency in his attributes, the love of benevolence towards the interests of his kingdom, and the love of gratitude for favors received.

The noun form of *love* was used in a similar way. Webster gave another example of the role of religion in forming deferential, Quiet Christian personalities and behavior:

The *love* of God is the first duty of man and this springs from just views of his attributes or excellencies of character, which afford the highest delight to the sanctified heart. Esteem and reverence constitute ingredients in this affection, and a fear of offending him is the inseparable effect.

Webster's disgust with politicians is evident in his dictionary. He defined them as men "of artifice or deep contrivance" rather than as people engaged in the government or management of affairs. The adjective form of *politician* meant "cunning; using artifice." His own longing for a return to some former time before the rise of democratic politics was indicated in his definition of *polity*. He quoted Ezra Stiles, who said "were the whole Christian world to revert back to the original model, how far more simple, uniform and beautiful would the church appear, and how far more agreeable to the ecclesiastical *polity* instituted by the holy apostles."

Laws were "the *laws* which enjoin the duties of piety and morality, and prescribed by God and found in the Scriptures." Under *submission* Webster again indicates that the Quiet Christian should be full of *resignation*, meaning "entire and cheerful *submission* to the will of God [which] is a christian duty of prime excellence." The only individual who could be "esteemed really and permanently *happy*" is the one "who enjoys a peace of mind in the favor of God," not unlike the mental tranquillity he had found in 1808. Defining *improve*, he commands that "it is the duty . . . of a good man to *improve* in grace and piety." He tells us that "the distribution of the Scriptures may be the instrument of a vastly extensive reformation in morals and religion." Webster's view of the family appears in his definition of *marriage* as "instituted by God himself, for the sexes, for promoting domestic felicity and for securing the maintenance and education of children." The helplessness of a man is indicated when he tells us under *meritorious* that "we rely for salvation on the *meritorious* obedience and suffering of Christ."

The dictionary is saturated with commands to be meek and passive. Even a few examples will suffice as a general indication of the flavor of the work. "Good breeding forbids us to use *offensive* words." "A man is profane when he takes the name of God in vain, or treats sacred things with abuse and irreverence." "*Perfect rectitude* belongs only to the Supreme Being." The more nearly the "rectitude of men approaches to the standard of divine law, the more exalted and dignified is their character. Want of *rectitude* is not only sinful, but debasing." *Freedom* is defined in one sense as "violation of the rules of decorum," while Webster warns us to "beware of what are called innocent *freedoms*." Webster's denial of freedom and advocacy of submission to authority is consistent. *Freedom* in another sense is defined as "license."

Duty is a key concept, and in defining it Webster commands us to obey virtually any authority:

> That which a person owes to another; that which a person is bound, by any natural, moral or legal obligation, to pay, do or perform. Obe-

dience to princes, magistrates and the laws is the *duty* of every citizen and subject; obedience, respect and kindness to parents are the *duties* of children; fidelity to friends is a *duty*; reverence, obedience and prayer to God are indisputable *duties*; the government and religious instruction of children are *duties* of parents which they cannot neglect without guilt.

Submission was synonymous with "obedience," and "*submission* of children to their parents is an indispensable duty." *Government* meant "control; restraint." In this definition he added that "children are often ruined by a neglect of *government* in parents." Under *inferior* Webster commands us to "pay due respect to those who are superior in station, and due civility to those who are *inferior*."

Liberty is one of the most revealing terms in the *American Dictionary*. His first definition was simply "freedom from restraint." To this, however, he added some significant distinctions. Most important were the two types of liberty John Winthrop had spoken of in 1645. *Natural liberty* meant the "power of acting as one thinks fit, without any restraint or control, except from the laws of nature." Like Winthrop, he emphasized that this condition was impractical and was always "abridged by the establishment of government." He was not speaking of the Lockean notion of a government as liberty. *Civil liberty*, on the other hand, was the liberty "of men in a state of society" in which natural liberty was "abridged and restrained," not to enhance cooperation or the distribution of goods, but for "the safety and interest of the society, state or nation." Civil liberty, he believed, was "secured by established laws, which restrain every man from injuring or controlling others." He was undoubtedly thinking of the turmoil since the 1780s when he noted that "the restraints of law are essential to civil liberty."

That Christianity was the only basis for civilization was clear in Webster's mind. "Moral law" prescribed to men "their duties to God," which were to be realized before their duties "to each other." In addition, "the moral law is summarily contained in the decalogue or ten commandments," and was written by the finger of God on two tablets of stone, and "delivered to Moses on Mount Sinai."

Perhaps the most revealing and significant definition in the entire two-volume work was that of *education*. This small paragraph in many ways summed up much of Webster's life. Education had always been of major concern to him, not only for its own sake, but as a means of inculcating values of one sort or another. In the early 1780s, it had been an instrument of increasing both cultural independence from England and progressive social change. Indeed, these two motivations were behind his first attempt to systematically Americanize the schools. After 1808, Noah Webster had seen schools as institutions for producing Quiet Christians, as a means of insuring social tranquillity by teaching a specific form of behavior. Through them, discipline could be instilled and the unruly passions of men checked and limited. His definition of education did not stress the increase of learning, of understanding, or comprehending the world. Value-laden words emphasizing this side of education appear only twice: "enlighten the understanding," and "arts and science." On the other hand, terms emphasizing authoritarian control appear nine times in the space of three sentences: "formation of manners," "discipline," "correct the temper," "form the manners and habits of youth," "fit them for usefulness in their future stations," "manners," "religious *education*," "immense responsibility," "duties." And this is not counting the use of "instruction," a term he chose instead of "learning," or other less authority-laden terms:

> The bringing up, as of a child: instruction; formation of manners. Education comprehends all that series of instruction and discipline which is intended to enlighten the understanding, correct the temper, and form the manners and habits of youth, and fit them for usefulness in their future stations; to give children a good *education* in manners, arts and sciences, is important; to give them a religious *education* is indispensable; and an immense responsibility rests on parents and guardians who neglect their duties.

Finally, notice that an education in manners, arts, and science is merely "important." A religious education, with all its overtones of the Quiet Christian, is "indispensable."

One last definition demonstrates the interrelationship between religion, politics, behavior, and language that existed in the lexicographer's mind. Under *reason*, he quotes an author who said, "God brings good out of evil, and therefore it were but *reason* we should trust God to govern his own world." Implicit is the notion that man should follow God's law, not his own reason. Thus, reason was used to advocate its opposite.

Webster's social and religious views permeated every area of his dictionary, including the dedication. One might expect a man who labored for twenty-five years on a single work to acknowledge the role played by those who surrounded him. Webster did not do so in his long introduction. Modern scholars usually mention the work of those who came before them or others in the field. But, of course, Noah Webster could not do that. No one else had followed, and in fact others working in the field directly challenged the assumptions that he built his work on. If Webster had been a strong nationalist, as most historians have said, one might expect long paeans to American freedom, celebrations of the heroes of the Revolution, or perhaps a smattering of other spread-eagle statements. None appeared. Instead, the completion of this lifetime effort was ascribed to the Supreme Power who controlled all things. The *American Dictionary* was a product of the religious benevolence movement of the early nineteenth century, whose major concern was social control, not of the nationalistic fervor of the late eighteenth century. It was dedicated to God:

> To the great and benevolent Being, who during the preparation of this work, has sustained a feeble constitution, amidst obstacles and toils, disappointments, infirmities and depression; who has twice borne me and my manuscripts in safety across the Atlantic, and given me strength and resolution to bring the work to a close, I would present the tribute of my most grateful acknowledgements.[87]

I would, if necessary, become a troglodyte and live in a cave in winter, rather than be under the tyranny of our desperate rulers.
        N. W., 1836

9 Resignation

By the end of his life Noah Webster was aware that as he had experienced much, his basic beliefs and values had endured enormous alterations. "Sir, I have been all my life changing my opinions," he quoted his old friend Benjamin Franklin as saying. "Now at seventy-six years of age," added Webster, "I can say the same thing." The young Noah Webster had believed in a rosy future for America. Her people were bound for utopia, to build a temple of freedom on a divinely favored continent. His efforts in behalf of the improvement of the human condition on all levels reflected the general optimism of the revolutionary era. Moral reform, complete religious toleration, equal distribution of property, and the abolition of slavery were the ideals he espoused. Yet his positive belief in the perfectibility of mankind had been shattered by a long series of events and changes. The central transformation in his life was his acceptance of a profoundly negative view of human nature which dominated his analysis of every subject. The famous lexicographer died a pessimistic authoritarian, concerned with limiting human freedom whenever possible, not expanding it. "I began life, as other young men do, full of confidence in my own opinions, many of which I afterwards found to be visionary and deceptive. . . . To err is the lot of humanity."[1] Noah Webster's long journey ended in disillusionment, bitterness, and despair.

Yet the last few years of his life were among the most productive. He not only issued a slightly revised *American Dictionary*, which took several years to re-edit, but at the age of seventy-seven he published his version of the *Holy Bible* and an explanation of his reasons for changing the King James version. Webster's correspondence was voluminous, as were his articles and letters, covering a wide variety of topics, to newspaper editors. In 1834 he published his main contribution to the evangelical Protestant movement, *Value of the Bible*. Three years later he summarized his life's study in linguistics under the title *Observations on Language* . . . A few weeks before his death in May of 1843 he issued a *Collection of Essays*, including some recently written pieces as well as essays from the turn of the century.[2]

Almost until the end, Webster tried to make his opinions well known in hopes of changing the general trend of events. His last important essay on national affairs, published in 1837, was one of the most controversial. It was a cynical attack on democracy, the Constitution, and the American people in general. Reprinted by a Democratic newspaper, "The Voice of Wisdom" was labeled the last gasp of Federalism. "Since I have taken pains to write," he said unashamedly, "I wish to have my views . . . left to the world as a memorial of my efforts to serve my country; an enduring testimony of my abhorrence to corrupt principles."[3]

The views Webster expressed during his last decade were diametrically opposed to those he had held in his youth. He was convinced that man was innately evil, depraved, and incapable of governing himself.[4] Reason was an imperfect guide on any issue; man must look to God and his revelations for answers to any and all questions.[5] It followed that popular sovereignty and other democratic ideals were absurd.[6] The people must be saved from themselves,[7] for attempts at self-control could lead only to "furious and implacable despotisms."[8]

All of these beliefs added up to a profound pessimism. "We are indeed an erring nation," he stated.[9] The obsession with physical comforts, social status, and the worship of progress, defined as increasing material prosperity and wealth, had destroyed the utopian possibilities of the American experiment. Morality and religion were completely neglected in the world characterized by what Marvin Meyers has called the "venturous conservative."[10] This was the cause of all the nation's ills. Americans had *"forsaken God, and he has forsaken us."*[11] The natural order of things had been destroyed by the revolutions of the previous century and by the vast social changes they had engendered; they could not be reestablished. Political and social disorders, symbolized by the agitation of the abolitionists and of those who opposed them, added to the general turmoil. "It is questionable whether all the wisdom and talents which can be brought to counteract their influence, will be sufficient to arrest the progress of our political disorders," he said.[12] American society and behavior failed to live up to his youthful ideal. "I now give up all expectation or hope."[13]

His rejection of democracy was total. "If I could be certain that Vermont would remain firm to the old Federalist principles, I should be tempted to remove into that state, to be freed from our democracy," he wrote at the age of seventy-eight. "As to the cold of winters, I would, if necessary, become a troglodyte and live in a cave in winter, rather than be under the tyranny of our desperate rulers. . . . We deserve all our public evils. We are a degenerate and wicked people."[14]

"And I quit the contest forever." With these words, written to his daughter in 1840, the eighty-one-year-old Webster finally gave up his attempt to guide the American people toward the path of righteousness. For six decades he had observed closely the flow of national events and voiced his opinions on virtually every subject of importance. The final step in his long journey was the presidential campaign of 1840. Both Whig and Democratic candidates portrayed themselves as common men, espousing every idea the old lexicographer found frightening. To Webster it was final proof that Americans would never realize their need for dependence on God and his apostles:

> But the Log cabin—oh how our country is degraded, when even men of respectability resort to such means to secure an election! I struggled, in the days of Washington, to sustain good principles—but since Jefferson's principles have prostrated the popular respect for sound principles, further efforts would be useless.[15]

Anxiety over the course of American society and deep doubts about the nature of man were not limited to Webster's mind. Social pessimism was widespread, and while no historian has attempted to measure its extent or strength, evidence suggests an important segment of early nineteenth-century American society shared Webster's fears. Broad social movements with millions of adherents reflected a profound fear and need for social control. Webster's authoritarian God was worshipped by hundreds of thousands of those who followed the teachings of conservative evangelicals like Lyman Beecher.[16] The American Temperance Society, founded in 1826 during the fiftieth anniversary of the Declaration, believed that widespread use of alcohol, especially by the lower classes, undermined the order of both church and state.[17] Political rhetoric during this period was saturated with stark contrasts between the morality of the past and the iniquity of the present, and thus politicians capitalized on anxiety and attempted to turn it into votes.[18] Like Webster, Horace Mann, Edward Everett, and others tried to use mass education as a means of controlling social and political behavior.[19] Mann's work, as symbolized by his fifth and twelfth reports as secretary of the Massachusetts Board of Education, was an effort, as one recent historian has put it, to "housebreak the masses."[20] In their attempts to combat crime, poverty, unrest, and all the other ills that seemed to be emerging from the disintegration of the deferential order of the eighteenth century, Americans created an incredible number of asylums: almshouses, prisons, houses of refuge, mental hospitals, and other institutions of confinement. Americans came to the conclusion, according to a recent study, that "to comprehend and control abnormal behavior promised to be the first step in establishing a new system for stabilizing the community, for binding citizens together."[21] The thought of freeing slaves evoked even deeper fears of further degeneration and violent demonstrations against change.[22] Politicians developed structured parties designed to contain disruptive issues.[23] The return of Lafayette in 1825 after a forty-year absence gave rise to a torrential outpouring over an alleged retreat from the grandeur and honor of the revolutionary era.[24] Nostalgia for the past and fear of the present found its way into art and popular music. The values of home, family, and nature, highly characteristic of songs like "Woodman, Spare That Tree," "The Old Arm Chair," and "The Old Oaken Bucket," were clearly reactions to rapid change, as were the cataclysmic paintings of Benjamin West, Asher B. Durand, Washington Allston, and others.[25] Indeed, Webster's cries for social control were echoed in various ways across the country.

Noah Webster spent his final years amidst the peace and tranquillity of his family. He had led a long life of anxiety and excitement, sorrow and joy. After 1840 he largely ignored the currents of national events and retreated into a private world. He wrote no more angry polemics; his only projects were a slightly revised edition of his dictionary and an anthology of widely diverse essays. The elder of a political and social group now long gone spent his time amusing his grandchildren and their children. They lived in a world far different from the one into which he was born, a world unlike anything he had imagined in his youthful dreams: he ignored it.

In 1842 the Webster family gathered to celebrate (three years late) the golden wedding anniversary of Noah and Rebecca Webster. For the occasion thirty-five children, grandchildren, and great-grandchildren came to New Haven to sing songs and pray. In keeping with his long-held piety, Webster presented each family member with a handsomely bound, autographed copy of his edition of the *Holy Bible*.[26]

In May of the following year Noah Webster contracted a terminal illness. As he lay slowly dying in his study, many who thought highly of the old revolutionary and who shared his belief in evangelical Protestantism came to pay their respects. Moses Stuart, who thirty-five years earlier had guided Webster through his conversion, now a famous professor of sacred literature, came from Massachusetts. The president of Yale and numerous members of the faculty made frequent visits.

Noah Webster's final thoughts summed up much of his long journey. He had struggled to guide his country down the path of righteousness and civilized behavior, and to restore the deferential world of the eighteenth century. He had failed, but in the course of his failure he had found his own solution to problems national and personal. "I'm ready to go; my work is all done, I know in whom I have believed," he said shortly before he died. America might destroy itself and burn in the eternal flames; the Quiet Christian would not. Noah Webster said, "I am entirely submissive to the will of heaven."[27]

Notes

Abbreviations

ACL   Amherst College Library. Special Collections.

CHS   Connecticut Historical Society Library. Webster Family Papers.

HSP   Historical Society of Pennsylvania. Archives.

NYHS   New York Historical Society. Webster Papers. Archives.

NYPL   New York Public Library. Manuscripts and Archives. The Papers of Noah
        Webster.

PM   John Pierpont Morgan Library. Archives.

Yale   Yale University. Sterling Memorial Library. Webster Family Papers.

Introduction
    1. "To the Editor of the Palladium," 7 February 1835, in Harry R. Warfel,ed.,
The Letters of Noah Webster (New York: Library Publishers, 1953), p. 446.
    2. Chauncey A. Goodrich, "Life and Writings of Noah Webster . . . " *American
Literary Magazine* (1848): (5)–32; [William C. Fowler], "Memoir," in *A Dictionary of the
English Language*, revised edition (New York: Huntington and Savage, 1845).

3. Horace E. Scudder, *Noah Webster* (Boston: Houghton Mifflin Co., 1883). For a full list of accounts of Webster's life, see Edwin H. Carpenter, Jr., *A Bibliography of the Writings of Noah Webster* (New York: New York Public Library, 1958), pp. 594–600.

4. Emily Ellsworth Fowler Ford, *Notes on the Life of Noah Webster*, 2 vols. (New York: [Privately printed], 1912). Hereafter cited as Ford, *Notes*.

5. Ervin C. Shoemaker, *Noah Webster, Pioneer of Learning* (New York: Columbia University Press, 1936).

6. Harry R. Warfel, *Noah Webster: Schoolmaster to America* (New York: Macmillan, 1936).

7. Gary R. Coll, "Noah Webster: Journalist, 1783–1803" (Ph.D. diss., Southern Illinois University, 1971); Dennis Patrick Rusche, "An Empire of Reason: A Study of the Writings of Noah Webster" (Ph.D. diss., University of Iowa, 1975).

8. John R. Howe, Jr., *The Changing Political Thought of John Adams* (Princeton, N.J.: Princeton University Press, 1966); Eric Foner, *Tom Paine and Revolutionary America* (New York: Oxford University Press, 1976); Kathryn Kish Sklar, *Catharine Beecher: A Study in American Domesticity* (New Haven: Yale University Press, 1973); Michael Paul Rogin, *Fathers and Children: Andrew Jackson and the Subjugation of the American Indian* (New York: Alfred A. Knopf, 1975); and Richard Lebeaux, *Young Man Thoreau* (Amherst: University of Massachusetts Press, 1977).

9. Letter to Thomas Jefferson, 1790, in Carpenter, *Bibliography*, p. 268.

Chapter 1

1. The material on Webster's family background and most of the information on his early years is drawn from secondary sources, since no primary material from the years before he went to Yale survives. The earliest full-length biography, Horace E. Scudder's *Noah Webster* (Boston: Houghton Mifflin Co., 1883), is virtually useless. A few items of information appear in Harry R. Warfel, Noah Webster: Schoolmaster to America (New York: Macmillan, 1936), and in Emily E. F. Ford, *Notes on the Life of Noah Webster* (New York: [privately printed], 1912). Most helpful for the Webster family is Noah Webster, *Webster Genealogy* (Brooklyn, N.Y.: [privately printed], 1876).

2. Webster, *Genealogy*.

3. Ibid., and Warfel, *Webster*, chapter 1.

4. Ibid., and William H. Hall, *West Hartford* (Hartford: James A. Reid, 1930). Florence S. Marcy Crofut, *Guide to the History and the Historic Sites of Connecticut*, 2 vols. (New Haven: Yale University Press, 1937).

5. The five children were Mercy (born 8 November 1749); Abram or Abraham (17 September 1751); Jerusha (22 January 1756); Noah (16 October 1758); Charles (2 September 1762). Ford, *Notes*, 1:10.

6. Lloyd de Mause, ed., *The History of Childhood* (New York: Harper and Row, 1975), contains essays on childhood in widely ranging geographical areas and chronological periods, as well as additional bibliography.

7. John F. Walzer, "A Period of Ambivalence: Eighteenth-Century American Childhood," in de Mause, *Childhood*, pp. 351–82, and N. Ray Hiner, "Adolescence in Eighteenth-Century America," *History of Childhood Quarterly* 3 (1975): 253–80.

8. Walzer, "Ambivalence," pp. 358–65.

9. Ibid., pp. 360–63.

10. Ibid., pp. 369–70.

11. Ibid., pp. 371–73.

12. The impact of population pressures on land and in turn on intrafamily relationships is a central concern and important insight of the "new social history." See especially Philip J. Greven, *Four Generations: Population, Land, and Family in Colonial Andover, Massachusetts* (Ithaca: Cornell University Press, 1970); Kenneth Lockridge, *A New England Town: The First Hundred Years* (New York: W. W. Norton, 1970); "The

Population of Dedham, Massachusetts, 1636–1736," *Economic History Review*, 2d ser. 59 (1966): 339–41; and "Land, Population and the Evolution of New England Society, 1630–1790, and an Afterthought," in *Colonial America: Essays in Politics and Social Development*, ed. Stanley Katz (Boston: Little, Brown, 1971), pp. 466–91; James A. Henretta, *The Evolution of American Society, 1700–1815: An Interdisciplinary Analysis* (Lexington: D. C. Heath, 1973); Daniel Scott Smith, "The Demographic History of Colonial New England," *Journal of Economic History* 32 (1972): 184–213; Edward Cook, "Changing Values and Behavior in Dedham, Massachusetts, 1700–1775," *William and Mary Quarterly*, 3d ser. 27 (1970): 578–80; and Jack P. Greene, "Autonomy and Stability: New England and the British Colonial Experience in Early Modern America," *Journal of Social History* 7 (1974): 187–92; Richard Bushman, *From Puritan to Yankee: Character and the Social Order in Connecticut, 1690–1765* (Cambridge: Harvard University Press, 1967).

13. Greven, *Generations*.

14. Hiner, "Adolescence," passim.

15. Walzer, "Ambivalence," p. 362.

16. Ibid.

17. Otto Zeichner, *Connecticut's Years of Controversy, 1750–1776* (Chapel Hill: University of North Carolina Press, 1949), p. 144, came to this conclusion about Webster's home state nearly twenty years before the new types of studies appeared.

18. Nathan Perkins, *A Half-Century Sermon* (Hartford: n.p., 1822).

19. [New York] *Daily Advertiser*, 5 September 1788.

20. Max Weber, *The Protestant Ethic and the Spirit of Capitalism* (New York: Scribner's, 1958). For extended commentary on Weber's work see Robert W. Green, ed., *Protestantism, Capitalism, and Social Science: The Weber Thesis Controversy*, 2d ed. (Lexington: D.C. Heath, 1973).

21. Edmund S. Morgan, "The Puritan Ethic and the American Revolution," *William and Mary Quarterly*, 3d ser. 24 (1967): 3–43.

22. Benjamin Franklin, *Autobiography and other Writings*, edited with an Introduction by Russel B. Nye (Boston: Riverside Press of Houghton Mifflin Co., 1958).

23. See chapter 5.

24. Letter to Henry Barnard, 10 March 1840, New York Historical Society Archives, Webster Papers.

25. Bushman, *Yankee*, passim. See also Alan Heimart's discussion of antiauthoritarianism in *Religion and the American Mind: From the Great Awakening to the Revolution* (Cambridge: Harvard University Press, 1966).

26. Bushman, *Yankee*.

27. Ibid.

28. Morgan, *Connecticut*, p. 41.

29. Ibid., p. 44.

30. See Abraham to Noah Webster, 21 April 1797, Ford, *Notes*, 1: 411.

31. Crofut, *Guide*, notes that Perkins, minister of the Fourth Church of Hartford for over sixty-six years, prepared many area youths for college. See also Matthew Spinka, *A History of the First Church of Christ Congregational, West Hartford, Connecticut* (Hartford: Hartford Seminary Foundation, n.d.).

32. [Noah Webster], "Memoir of Noah Webster," Yale University Archives, Webster Family Papers, Box 1. The memoir is autobiographical in nature and was probably an attempt to organize the beginning of a full-scale work. Webster evidently based it on his collection of his own writings, for it is quite accurate when checked against other sources. In fact, he included several letters within the body of the memoir itself. The New York Public Library collection, now ten boxes altogether, was his private collection and several of the letters quoted in part or in full in the memoir can be found there. The memoir is unsigned and in the third person, but it is in Webster's hand.

33. David F. Allmendinger, Jr., *Paupers and Scholars: The Transformation of Student Life in Nineteenth-Century New England* (New York: St. Martin's Press, 1975), illustrates this trend and indicates that it began in the 1760s.

34. The most recent and by far the most scholarly treatment of Yale is Brooks Mather Kelley, *Yale: A History* (New Haven: Yale University Press, 1974).

35. On the Enlightenment, see Daniel Boorstin, *The Lost World of Thomas Jefferson* (New York: Henry Holt, 1948); Herbert Schneider, *The History of American Philosophy* (New York: Columbia University Press, 1963); Charles A. Barker, *American Convictions: Cycles of Public Thought, 1600–1850* (Philadelphia: Lippincott, 1973); Merle Curti, *The Growth of American Thought* (New York: Harper and Row, 1964); Gordon S. Wood, ed., *The Rising Glory of America* (New York: George Braziller, 1971); Joseph Ellis, "Habits of Mind and an American Enlightenment," *American Quarterly* 28 (1976): 150–64; and Donald H. Meyer, *Democratic Enlightenment* (New York: Basic Books, 1976). Henry May, *The Enlightenment in America* (New York: Oxford University Press, 1976), distinguishes four different phases of the Enlightenment: Moderate, Skeptical, Radical, and Didactic. Using May's categories, we can say that Yale exposed Webster to the Moderate Enlightenment of Newton, Locke, Montesquieu, and others; its basic characteristic was a fondness for order, balance, and intelligence in all endeavors.

36. Carpenter, *Bibliography*, lists all of Webster's scientific writings.

37. This paper was published in the *New York Magazine and Literary Repository* 1 (1790): 338–40, 383–84.

38. Gordon S. Wood, *The Creation of the American Republic, 1776–1787* (Chapel Hill: University of North Carolina Press, 1969), and Bernard Bailyn, *The Ideological Origins of the American Revolution* (Cambridge: Belknap Press of Harvard University Press, 1967), both stress the utopian thrust of revolutionary ideology.

39. On the European image of America, see Michael Kraus, "America and the Utopian Ideal in the Eighteenth Century," *Mississippi Valley Historical Review* 22 (1936): 487–504, and Howard Mumford Jones, *O Strange New World: American Culture, The Formative Years* (New York: Viking Press, 1964).

40. May, *Enlightenment in America*, and Meyer, *Democratic Enlightenment*.

41. On the agrarian tradition in America, see Leo Marx, *The Machine in the Garden: Technology and the Pastoral Ideal in America* (New York: Oxford University Press, 1964); Henry Nash Smith, *Virgin Land: The American West as Symbol and Myth* (Cambridge: Harvard University Press, 1950); Marvin Meyers, *The Jacksonian Persuasion: Politics and Belief* (Stanford: Stanford University Press, 1957); and John William Ward, *Andrew Jackson: Symbol for an Age* (New York: Oxford University Press, 1955).

42. Wood, *Creation*; Robert Hay, "George Washington: American Moses," *American Quarterly* 21 (1969): 780–91.

43. Koch, *Enlightenment*, and Wood, *Glory*.

44. Kelley, *Yale*, p. 85.

45. Ibid., p. 84.

46. Ibid. See also David Potter, "Nathan Hale and the Ideal of American Union," *Connecticut Antiquarian* 6 (1954): 23.

47. Ford, *Notes*, 1: 18.

48. Kelley, *Yale*, p. 85.

49. Ibid., p. 87, and [Webster], "Memoir," p. 4.

50. Ford, *Notes*, 1: 20–21.

51. Ibid., pp. 27–28.

52. Kelley, *Yale*, p. 85.

53. James Woodress, *A Yankee's Odyssey: The Life of Joel Barlow* (Philadelphia: Lippincott, 1958), pp. 44–45.

54. "Confessions of Causing a Disturbance in Chapel, Signed by 25 Students," Bieneke Rare Book and Manuscript Library, New Haven, Connecticut, Manuscript

Vault, Section 17. This was signed by members of the class of 1778, including Webster, Wolcott, and Meigs.

55. Josiah Meigs to Noah Webster, 20 August 1779, NYPL, Box 2.

56. [Webster], "Memoir," p. 4.

57. Ford, *Notes*, 1: 39.

58. [Webster], "Memoir," p. 5.

59. [Noah Webster], *Diary*, 14 April 1790, NYPL, Box 10.

60. See letters from Abraham to Noah Webster, Ford, *Notes*, 1 and 2.

61. [Webster], "Memoir," pp. 6–7.

62. *Gazette of The United States*, 9 January 1790. Webster's own copy of this essay is marked "Written in the winter of 1779–1780." See Carpenter, *Bibliography*, p. 443.

63. *Gazette of The United States*, 19 January 1790.

64. Ibid., 13 January 1790.

65. Ibid., 16 January 1790.

66. Warfel, *Webster*, and [Webster], "Memoir."

67. [Webster], "Memoir," p. 6.

68. Ibid.

69. *Connecticut Courant*, 1 June 1781.

70. [Webster], "Memoir," p. 6.

71. Webster's diary reveals his early social life.

72. Joel Benton, "An Unwritten Chapter in Noah Webster's Life . . . " *Magazine of American History* 10 (July 1883): 52–56.

73. Hiner, "Adolescence," fully illustrates the striking similarities in the characteristics of this stage of life in Webster's day and twentieth-century America. According to Hiner, the difficulties were clearly rooted in the social transformations outlined by Greven, et al. Webster may be seen as a concretely human example of the effects of these tendencies in the life of an individual. Adolescence is a historically controversial issue; for bibliography, see John and Virginia Demos, "Adolescence in Historical Perspective," in *The Family in Social-Historical Perspective*, ed. Michael Gordon (New York: St. Martin's Press, 1973), and Hiner's footnotes.

74. [Webster], "Memoir," p. 7. Compare the vividness of this passage with the relatively drab style of the rest of the manuscript and Webster's diary after 1800. A word must be said at this point about the use of psychology in this study. Attempts to wed psychology and history or biography have proliferated in this century, especially since Erik Erikson published his landmark *Young Man Luther: A Study in Psychoanalysis and History* (New York: W. W. Norton, 1958). During the past twenty years numerous scholars have discussed "psychohistory" at length in all its various forms. The most extensive bibliography is Faye Sinofsky, John J. Fitzpatrick, Louis W. Potts, and Lloyd de Mause, "A Bibliography of Psychohistory," *History of Childhood Quarterly* 2 (1975): 517–62. Cushing Strout, "The Uses and Abuses of Psychology in American History," *American Quarterly* 28 (1976): 324–42, presents a useful analysis of efforts in subjects similar to my study.

The most widely held and often repeated criticism of the use of psychology in historical studies is that scholars often seem more concerned with psychological theory than with the figures to whom it is applied, as Norman Kiell, ed., *Psychological Studies of Famous Americans: The Civil War Era* (New York: Twayne, 1964), has indicated. Indeed, as Anthony Storr said in *The Dynamics of Creation* (New York: Atheneum, 1972), p. xii, attempts to explain human actions in the light of specific theories or schemes often turn out to be "procrustean" efforts to "fit obstinate facts into a bed of psychoanalytic theory which is both too short and too narrow to accommodate them." Thus historians who begin attempting to further understand their subjects through the use of psychology often seem to end up obfuscating, even distorting, their lives, actions, and motivations.

Yet no biographer can safely ignore the real insights psychology can bring to a historical figure. This study seeks to avoid these pitfalls by utilizing diverse psychological theories as tools of analysis to illuminate certain developments, to clarify their meaning and impact. Instead of forcing the figure of Noah Webster into a strict systematic interpretation, I hope to apply the ideas developed by scholars flexibly, always with the greater understanding of the life of one individual in mind. For example, the concept of an identity crisis formulated by Erik Erikson helps make the events of 1781–82 and shortly thereafter more understandable. Yet Erikson believes that the identity crisis is only one stage in an epigenetic life-cycle shared by virtually all human beings. He has sketched out additional stages of development, none of which add useful perspectives for this particular study, though they might for others.

Furthermore, the various ideas I have found helpful are consistent in their overall perception of individual psychological and emotional growth and development. The work of ego-psychologists (like Erik Erikson, Erich Fromm, Karen Horney, and others), share an emphasis on social and cultural influences, rather than innate biological drives. They also stress the years between late childhood and adulthood, rather than early childhood.

Chapter 2

1. Letter to George Washington, 18 December 1785, NYPL, Box 1.

2. Historians writing since 1945 have been largely divided over these two interpretive viewpoints on the Revolution. For a full analysis of the historiography of this period, see George Athan Billias, "The Revolutionary Era: Reinterpretations and Revisions," in Billias and Gerald N. Grob, *American History: Retrospect and Prospect* (New York: Free Press, 1971).

3. Merrill Jensen, *The New Nation: A History of the United States During the Confederation, 1781–1789* (New York: Alfred A. Knopf, 1965).

4. Bushman, *Yankee*, and Richard D. Brown, *Modernization: The Transformation of American Life, 1600–1865* (New York: Hill and Wang, 1976). Chapter 5, "Revolutionary Consequences: The Modernization of Personality and Society," is especially relevant. Even his father recognized this difference in attitudes. See letters in Ford, *Notes*, 1, and NYPL, Box 2.

5. Edwin G. Burrows and Michael Wallace, "The American Revolution: The Ideology and Psychology of National Liberation," *Perspectives in American History* 6 (1972): 303.

6. Quoted ibid., p. 292.

7. Noah Webster, *A grammatical institute of the English language, comprising an easy, concise, and systematic method of education, designed for the use of English schools in America. In three parts. Part I* (Hartford: Hudson and Goodwin, 1783), p. 14; New York *Packet*, 31 January 1782.

8. New York *Packet*, 31 January 1782.

9. Burrows and Wallace, "Revolution," p. 265. Lockridge, *Hundred Years*, and Greven, *Andover*, have both commented on the preparatory role that the disintegration of parental authority within families may have played in the coming of the Revolution. See especially Jack P. Greene, "Autonomy and Stability: New England and the British Colonial Experience in Early Modern America," *Journal of Social History* 7 (1974): 171–94.

10. At least one historian believes that the entire Whig system of thought may have rested on this point. See Bailyn, *Origins*, p. 47.

11. Ibid., p. 67.

12. See especially Pauline Maier, *From Resistance to Revolution: Colonial Radicals and the Development of American Opposition to Britain, 1765–1776.* New York: Alfred A. Knopf, 1972.

13. New York *Packet*, 31 January 1782. Winthrop Jordan links the antiauthoritar-

ian perspective to Thomas Paine's essay and the response to it in "Familial Politics: Thomas Paine and The Killing of the King, 1776," *Journal of American History* 61 (1974): 294–308.

14. The role of the English radicals in American revolutionary thought has drawn increasing attention from historians in recent years. See Bailyn, *Origins*; Wood, *Creation*; Maier, *Resistance*; Caroline Robbins, *Eighteenth-Century Commonwealthman* (Cambridge: Harvard University Press, 1959); and Staughton Lynd, *Intellectual Origins of American Radicalism* (New York: Vintage Books, 1968).

15. [Webster], "Memoir," p. 12. On the influence of Rousseau in America, see May, *Enlightenment in America*, pp. 165–78, and Paul Merrill Spurlin, *Rousseau in America, 1760–1809* (University: University of Alabama Press, 1969).

16. Noah Webster, *Sketches of American Policy* (Hartford: Hudson and Goodwin, 1785), p. 2.

17. Richard Price to Noah Webster, 29 August 1785, NYPL, Box 2.

18. Noah Webster, *A grammatical institute of the English language, comprising, an easy, concise, systematic method of education, designed for the use of English schools in America. In three parts. Part III* (Hartford: Barlow and Babcock, 1785), p. 1.

19. Quoted in R. N. Stromberg, "History in the Eighteenth Century," *Journal of the History of Ideas* 12 (1951): 295–304. Also helpful is Stow Persons, "The Cyclical Theory of History in Eighteenth Century America," *American Quarterly* 6 (1954): 147–68.

20. New York *Packet*, 7 February 1782.

21. *Freeman's Chronicle*, 27 October 1783.

22. Ibid., 10 November 1783.

23. On ascetic revolutionaries as a personality type, see Michael Walzer, *The Revolution of the Saints: A Study in the Origins of Radical Politics* (Cambridge: Harvard University Press, 1965). Pauline Maier, "Coming to Terms with Samuel Adams," *American Historical Review* 81 (1976): 12–37, and Morgan, "Puritan Ethic," describe Webster's contemporaries in similar terms. Bruce Mazlish's study of revolutionary leadership, *The Revolutionary Ascetic: Evolution of a Type* (New York: Basic Books, 1976), concentrates on non-Americans.

24. Frederic M. Litto, "Addison's Cato in the Colonies," *William and Mary Quarterly*, 3d ser. 23 (1966): 431–49.

25. Shoemaker, *Bibliography*.

26. *Freeman's Chronicle*, 10 November 1783.

27. Ibid.

28. Webster, *Sketches*, p. 18.

29. Ibid., p. 25.

30. Ibid., p. 25–26.

31. Ibid., p. 20.

32. Ibid.

33. *Freeman's Chronicle*, 3 November 1783.

34. Ibid., 10 November 1783.

35. Ibid., 3 November 1783.

36. Ibid., p. 6.

37. Ibid.

38. Quoted in Wood, *Creation*, p. 166.

39. *Freeman's Chronicle*, 10 November 1783.

40. See Wood, *Creation*; Bailyn, *Origins*; and Jensen, *Nation*.

41. Webster, *Sketches*, p. 45.

42. Ibid., p. 10.

43. Ibid., p. 46.

44. Ibid., p. 11.

45. Benjamin T. Spencer, *The Quest for Nationality* (Syracuse: Syracuse University Press, 1957), and J. Meredith Neil, *Toward a National Taste: America's Quest for Aesthetic Independence* (Honolulu: University of Hawaii Press, 1975).

46. Robert Coram, "Political Inquiries, etc.," in *Essays on Education in the Early Republic*, ed. Frederick Rudolph (Cambridge: Harvard University Press, 1965), pp. 79–145.

47. *Connecticut Courant*, 22 January 1784.

48. [Webster], "Memoir," p. 9.

49. Ibid.

50. Bob Eddy, "The *Courant* Took A Chance," *The Quill* 52 (1964): 12.

51. Webster, *Institute*, part 1: [3], 5.

52. See Warfel, *Webster*, for the sales figures and the 1936 incident. One of the two editions currently available is printed for the Noah Webster Foundation, West Hartford, Connecticut, by Connecticut Printers, Inc., and is only available through that organization. The other is Noah Webster, *Noah Webster's Spelling Book*, introduction by Henry Steele Commager (New York: Columbia University, 1962). *Books in Print* lists this edition as suitable for children over four years old, and so it may still be in use.

53. Letter to John Canfield, 6 January 1783, Warfel, *Letters*, p. 4.

54. Webster, *Institute*, part 1: 1–14.

55. Ibid., pp. 13–14.

56. To Canfield, p. 4.

57. "Memorial to the Legislature of New York," Warfel, *Letters*, p. 5.

58. Ibid., p. 6.

59. Webster, *Institute*, part 1: 118–19.

60. Noah Webster, *A grammatical institute of the English language; comprising an easy, concise, and systematic method of education, designed for the use of English schools in America: In three parts. Part II* (Hartford: Hudson and Goodwin, 1784).

61. Webster, *Institute*, part 3: [1].

62. Ibid., especially p. [iii].

Chapter 3

1. *Diary*, 1784–85, NYPL. For the Wits, see Leon Howard, *The Connecticut Wits* (Chicago: University of Chicago Press, 1943).

2. Historians of the Confederation have been divided into two groups. Noah Webster would undoubtably agree with John Fiske, *The Critical Period of American History, 1783–1789* (New York: Appleton, 1888), who viewed it as an era of chaos and collapse which led to stabilization under the new Constitution. Merrill Jensen, in *The Articles of Confederation* (Madison: University of Wisconsin Press, 1966), and in *The New Nation*, sees the Confederation government as the embodiment of the Declaration of Independence spirit overthrown in a counter-revolution led by aristocrats.

3. Jensen, *Nation*.

4. Ibid., p. 70.

5. Ibid.

6. Quoted in Collier, *Connecticut*, p. 216. This is the best secondary account of the commutation crisis in New England.

7. Ibid.

8. Ibid., p. 212

9. Quoted in Louie May Miner, *Our Rude Forefathers: American Political Verse, 1783–1788* (Cedar Rapids, Iowa: Torch Press, 1937).

10. Collier, *Connecticut*.

11. Letter To His Excellency George Washington, Esq., 18 December 1785, NYPL, Box 1.

12. *Diary*, 29 March 1784.

13. *Connecticut Courant*, 23 September 1783. See also 9 September 1783.

14. Ibid., 30 September 1783 and 14 January 1784. See also *Diary*, 17 December 1784.

15. To Samuel Adams, 24 March 1784, in Warfel, *Letters*, p. 7.

16. *Connecticut Courant*, 14 October and 26 August 1783; 13 January 1784.

17. Ibid., 23 September 1783. See also 9 September 1783.

18. Ibid., 20 April 1784

19. Webster, *Sketches*, p. 34.

20. *Connecticut Courant*, 26 September 1783.

21. Ibid.

22. Forest McDonald and Ellen Shapiro McDonald, eds., *Confederation and Constitution, 1781–1789* (New York: Harper and Row, 1968), p. 40; Quoted in Hesketh Pearson, *Tom Paine: Friend of Mankind* (New York: Harper and Brothers, 1937), p. 64; *Connecticut Courant*, 24 February 1784. For Webster's views, see also *Sketches*, pp. 30–31.

23. *Essex Journal*, 14 December 1786. Reprinted in *Noah Webster, A Collection of Essays and Fugitiv [sic] Writings on Moral, Historical, Political, and Literary Subjects* (Boston: J. Thomas and E. T. Andrews, 1790), pp. 119–24. Hereafter cited as Webster, *Essays*. In Henry May's terms, he was clearly more influenced by Radical Enlightenment concepts than those of the Moderate Enlightenment.

24. Webster, *Sketches*, pp. 45–46, 32.

25. Webster, *Sketches*, p. 48

26. Ibid., pp. 41, 48. See also pp. 38–39.

27. Ibid., pp. 33–35. He made no mention of any qualifications for suffrage.

28. To Timothy Pickering, 20 January 1785, in Warfel, *Letters*, p. 44.

29. Gerald W. Johnson, *Mount Vernon* (New York: Random House, 1953).

30. To Noah Webster, 30 July 1785 in John C. Fitzpatrick, ed., *The Writings of George Washington from the Original Manuscript Sources, 1745–1799*, 39 vols. (Washington, D.C.: Government Printing Office, 1931–44), 28: 216.

31. [Webster], "Memoir," and Warfel, *Webster*.

32. A good example of Webster's advertisements for his lectures appeared in the *Massachusetts Centinel*, 12 July 1786. A set of notes taken at his lecture in Philadelphia are in the Archives of the Historical Society of Pennsylvania.

33. In addition to the biographical studies cited in the introduction, see Henry Steele Commager, "Noah Webster, 1758–1958," *Saturday Review*, 10 October 1958.

34. Positive reactions and reviews of his lectures were numerous. See especially the *Maryland Gazette*, 10 January 1786 and *Maryland Journal*, 3 January 1786.

35. Ford, *Notes*, 1: 142–44, 146.

36. Letter to George Washington, 31 March 1786, NYPL, Box 1.

37. Reprinted in Webster, *Essays*.

38. Jensen, *Nation*.

39. Ford, *Notes*, 1: 157

40. Letter to Hudson and Goodwin, 10 September 1786, NYPL, Box 1; see also Letters to Hudson and Goodwin, 9 August and 28 September 1786 in Box 1, as well as Letter to Timothy Pickering, 15 September 1786, in Massachusetts Historical Society *Proceedings*, p. 126.

41. Webster, *Essays*, p. 130.

42. Letter to Hudson and Goodwin, 28 September 1786, NYPL, Box 1.

43. Webster, *Essays*, p. 130.

44. *New Haven Gazette*, 14 December 1786. Reprinted in Webster, *Essays*, p. 153.

45. *Essex Journal*, 13 September 1786. Reprinted in Webster, *Essays*.

46. *Connecticut Courant*, 20 November 1786.

47. Letter to Hudson and Goodwin, 26 July 1786, Pierpont Morgan Library.

48. His depression was quite clear in a series of articles entitled "Remarks on the Manners, Government, and Debt of the United States," in the *Pennsylvania Packet*, 15, 17, 19, and 21 February 1787. Reprinted in Webster, *Essays*.

49. Webster, *Essays*, pp. 99, 103, 100–101.

50. See *Diary*, Summer 1787.

51. *Pennsylvania Gazette*, 25 April 1787.

52. See *Diary*, Summer 1787.

53. [Webster], "Memoir," p. 18. Webster included the entire letter in this document.

54. Saul K. Padover, *To Secure These Blessings* (New York: Washington Square Press, 1962), p. 499.

55. [Webster], "Memoir," p. 18.

56. [Noah Webster], *An examination into the leading principles of the Federal Constitution proposed by the late Convention held at Philadelphia. With answers to the principal objections that have been raised against the system. By a citizen of America* (Philadelphia: Pritchard and Hall, 1787).

57. Ibid., pp. 6, 43, 7, 23, 40.

58. Ibid., p. 43.

59. *American Museum*, October 1787.

60. [Webster], *Examination*, p. 47.

61. Ibid., pp. 28–29, 34, 19, 8, 23.

62. *American Museum*, October 1787.

Chapter 4

1. Ford, *Notes*, 1: 176–77. Benjamin Rush wanted Webster to call it the "Monthly Asylum." The first issue was dated December 1787.

2. *American Magazine*, December 1787, p. 9; January 1788, p. 76; March 1788, p. 204.

3. The best source of information concerning opposition to the Constitution is Jackson Turner Main, *The Anti-Federalists: Critics of the Constitution, 1781–1788* (Chapel Hill: University of North Carolina Press, 1961).

4. As Main points out, at this time a "federal" government was one in which the sovereignty remained in the federated units. A "national" government was one in which the central authority was supreme, and in which the states had only limited powers. Thus the Anti-Federalists were in fact Federalists, and the federalists were opposed to a "federal" system. Ibid., p. 120.

5. *Diary*, 11, 13, and 14 April 1787.

6. Gordon S. Wood notes that this disillusion was widespread: "because the Revolution represented much more than a colonial rebellion, represented in fact a utopian effort to reform the character of American society and to establish truly free governments, men in the 1780s could actually believe that it was failing. Nothing more vividly indicates the intensity of Americans' Revolutionary expectations than the depth of their disillusionment in the eighties." Wood, *Creation*, p. 395.

7. *American Magazine*, February 1788, pp. 95, 139.

8. Ibid., December 1787, pp. 13–14.

9. Ibid., January 1788, p. 75; December 1787, p. 10.

10. Ibid., March 1788, p. 204; January 1788, p. 75.

11. Frederick Rudolph, ed., *Essays on Education in the Early Republic* (Cambridge: Harvard University Press, 1965); May, *Enlightenment in America*.

12. *American Magazine*, May 1788, p. 374; December 1787, p. 23.

13. Ibid., March 1788, p. 213; April 1788, p. 311; February 1788, pp. 159–60.

14. On education in the 1780s, see Rudolph, *Essays*; Lawrence A. Cremin, *American Education: The Colonial Experience, 1607–1783* (New York: Harper and Row, 1970); Wilson Smith, ed., *Theories of Education in Early America, 1655–1819* (Indianapolis: Bobbs-Merrill, 1973); Eleanor Flexner, *Century of Struggle* (Cambridge: Harvard University Press, 1950), and Joan Hoff Wilson, "The Illusion of Change: Women and the American Revolution" in *The American Revolution: Explorations in the History of American Radicalism*, ed. Alfred Young (De Kalb: Northern Illinois University Press, 1976).

15. *American Magazine*, May 1788, pp. 367–68; March 1788, p. 246.

16. *American Magazine*, May 1788, p. 368.

17. Ford, *Notes*, 2: 461–65; Warfel, *Webster*, pp. 185–86.

18. Ford, *Notes*, 1 and 2; NYPL, Box 1, 2, and 10; Yale.

19. Timothy Pickering to Noah Webster, 4 July 1786, Ford, *Notes*, 1: 102.

20. Ebenezer Hazard to Jeremy Belknap, 5 March 1788, Massachusetts Historical Society *Collections*, 5th ser. vol. 3, part 2: 230.

21. Quoted in Warfel, *Webster*, p. 189.

22. James Greenleaf to Noah Webster, 19 January 1788, Ford, *Notes*, 1: 185–88.

23. To Rebecca Greenleaf, 11 January 1788, Warfel, *Letters*, p. 73.

24. Hazard to Belknap, 13 January 1789, *Collections*, p. 94.

25. Warfel, *Webster*, p. 189.

26. Hazard to Belknap, 4 February 1789, *Collections*, p. 101.

27. Hazard to Belknap, 13 January 1789, ibid., p. 94.

28. To James Greenleaf, 16 May 1789, Ford, *Notes*, 2: 409.

29. Letters to James Greenleaf, 1 February and 6 June 1789, HSP.

30. Letter to James Greenleaf, 12 August 1789, NYPL, Box 1. See also Letters to Greenleaf on 15 February and 20 September 1789 on the same subject.

31. Warfel, *Webster*, p. 196.

32. Emily Scholten (4 August 1790), Frances Juliana (5 February 1793), Harriet (6 April 1797), Mary (7 January 1799), William Greenleaf (15 September 1801), Eliza (21 December 1803), Louisa (2 April 1808), and Henry Bradford (who died shortly after his birth on 20 November 1806). Warfel, *Webster*, p. 298.

33. Warfel, *Webster*.

34. For example, see *Warfel*, Webster, p. 419, and several letters in NYPL, Boxes 1 and 2.

35. Letter to W. W. Ellsworth and Emily Ellsworth, 6 March 1819, CHS, details the death of Mary Webster Cobb and plans for raising the child.

36. Quoted in Warfel, *Webster*, p. 328.

37. Ibid., p. 417

38. Webster's family was of such importance in his life and development that an extended analysis of intrafamily relationships is certainly called for, and would doubtless yield important insights. Unfortunately, the dozens of letters between Noah Webster and his family contain only minute details of daily life: weather, travel plans, food, descriptions of sightseeing trips, changes in personal health, neighborhood gossip, and so forth. All that can be gleaned about attitudes toward each other is quoted here, with the exception of the warm salutations in the letters. See Letter to Dear Sister, April 6 1797; Letters to Eliza, Harriet, Emily, and Rebecca Webster, At Sea, 1824, 10, 12, and 21 July 1824, 19 August 1824, 14, 17 December 1830, 4, 9 January 1831, NYPL; Letters to William Greenleaf Webster, 1836–37, NYPL; Letters to Emily, Julia, Rebecca, and Harriet Webster, 7 September 1824, 3 April and 20 June 1838; Rebecca Webster to Noah Webster, 23 June–11 October 1824, Box 1.

39. Quoted in Carpenter, *Bibliography*, p. 268.

40. Noah Webster, *Dissertations on the English language: with notes, historical and*

critical. *To which is added, by way of appendix, an essay on a reformed mode of spelling, with Dr. Franklin's arguments on that subject* (Boston: Isaiah Thomas and Company, 1789).

41. Ford, *Notes*, 1: 100.

42. Webster, *Dissertations*, p. [vii].

43. Ibid., p. 25.

44. Ibid., pp. [iii–vii].

45. Ibid., pp. 316–41.

46. Ibid., pp. 340–41.

47. Ibid., pp. 46–47.

48. Ibid., pp. 19–21.

49. Ibid., pp. 397.

50. Ibid., pp. 405–6.

51. Letter to Timothy Pickering, 25 May 1786, in Warfel, *Letters*, pp. 51–52.

52. Ford, *Notes*, 2: 455–57.

53. See Webster, *Dissertations*, pp. 391–94. Also Noah Webster, *The American Spelling Book: containing an easy STANDARD PRONUNCIATION. Being the FIRST PART of a Grammatical Institute of the English Language* (Boston: Thomas and Andrews, 1789), p. x.

54. Webster, *Essays*, p. xi.

55. "The Patriot, no. 3," *Connecticut Courant*, 2 May 1791. Reprinted in Warfel, *Letters*, pp. 95–96. See also *Courant*, 18 April 1791.

56. "The Patriot," *Connecticut Courant*, 2 January 1792. This was part of a long series of articles urging economic improvements. For Webster's equally nationalistic views on economics in the 1780s see "On a Discrimination between the Original Holders and the Purchasers of the Certificates of the United States," reprinted in Webster, *Essays*. See also his articles in the *Pennsylvania Gazette*, 21 March and December 1787, and "To the Public," 8 May 1788, Warfel, *Letters*, pp. 62–67.

57. See comments at bottom of Webster's copy of his article in the *Freeman's Chronicle*, 27 October 1783, Yale.

58. [New Haven, Connecticut] *American Mercury*, 2 January 1790.

59. *American Magazine*, September 1788, p. 751.

60. Letter to Benjamin Rush, 29 December 1788, in Ford, *Notes*, 1: 274.

61. Letter To Benjamin Rush, 4 December 1789, HSP.

62. Webster, *Essays*, p. 365.

63. Recent studies of early antislavery movements are David Brion Davis, *The Problem of Slavery in Western Culture* (Ithaca: Cornell University Press, 1966); Davis, *The Problem of Slavery in the Age of Revolution, 1770–1823* (Ithaca: Cornell University Press, 1975), and Winthrop D. Jordan, *White Over Black: American Attitudes Toward the Negro, 1550–1812,* (Chapel Hill: University of North Carolina Press, 1968).

64. Webster, *Essays*, pp. 367–68.

65. Noah Webster, *The Little Reader's Assistant* (Hartford: Elisha Babcock, 1790).

66. Quoted in Carpenter, *Bibliography*, p. 192.

67. Webster, *Assistant*, pp. 41–42.

68. Noah Webster, *Effects of Slavery, on Morals and Industry* (Hartford: Hudson and Goodwin, 1793), p. 5.

69. Ibid., p. 12.

70. Ibid., p. 14.

71. Ibid., p. 18.

72. Ibid., pp. 50–56, 22–24, 43.

73. Ibid., pp. 38, 37.

74. "To the Inhabitants of Hartford," September 1792, in Warfel, *Letters*, pp. 105–6. See also *Connecticut Courant*, 12 December 1791.

75. *Connecticut Courant*, 5 and 26 September 1791.

76. Letter to James Greenleaf, 6 June 1789, HSP.

77. Letter to James Greenleaf, 24 June 1793, HSP.

Chapter 5

1. I am indebted here to Erich Fromm, *Escape from Freedom* (New York: Farrar and Rinehart, 1941).

2. The historical literature on the 1790s is massive. The most thorough annotated bibliographies are Jacob E. Cooke, "The Federalist Age: A Reappraisal" in Billias and Grob, *American History;* and Shaw Livermore, Jr., "The Early National Period, 1789–1823," in *The Reinterpretation of American History and Culture,* ed. William H. Cartwright and Richard L. Watson, Jr. (Washington, D.C.: National Council for the Social Studies, 1973), pp. 297–308.

3. William Alfred Bryan, *George Washington in American Literature* (New York: Columbia University Press, 1952); Robert Hay, "George Washington: American Moses," *American Quarterly* 21 (1969): 780–91.

4. Rush Welter, "Reason, Revolutionary and Otherwise: The Enlightenment in America," *Reviews in American History* 5 (1977): 321–25.

5. An analysis of recent work in this area and its relationship to Fischer's thesis is contained in Richard M. Rollins, "New Perspectives on Early National America" (unpublished, 1977).

6. David Hackett Fischer, "America: A Social History. Volume I. The Main Lines of the Subject, 1650–1975" (unpublished, 1974), chap. 2: 19–21.

7. Ibid., passim.

8. Ford, *Notes,* 1: 364–77.

9. "True Republicanism," *Connecticut Courant,* 12 August 1793. For Webster's views on the issue of neutrality at this time, see "Address from the Inhabitants of this City (Hartford), to the President of the United States," ibid., 19 August 1793.

10. Webster, *Morals,* pp. 13–15.

11. This is noted by many historians, including May, *Enlightenment,* and Meyer, *Democratic Enlightenment.*

12. *Connecticut Courant,* 27 July, 5 August 1793.

13. *Greenleaf's New York Journal,* 28 August 1793. See also the essays by Marshall Smelser, listed below.

14. For a study of the Genet mission, see Harry Ammon, *The Genet Mission* (New York: W. W. Norton, 1973).

15. Eugene Perry Link, *The Democratic-Republican Societies, 1790–1800* (New York: Columbia University Press, 1942).

16. *National Gazette,* 10 July 1793.

17. Warfel, *Webster,* p. 220

18. Ammon, *Genet,* p. 118.

19. Webster was so upset over the incident that he made out several affidavits concerning the event. See letter to Oliver Wolcott, Jr., Wolcott Papers, Connecticut Historical Society, volume 8, no. 42. Another is deposited in the Webster Papers, New York Public Library. A third, probably a copy of the one in the Connecticut Historical Society, appears in [Webster], "Memoir," p. 26. See also Ford, *Notes,* 1: 368–69.

20. *American Minerva,* 2 May 1794.

21. Ibid., 6 May 1794.

22. Ibid., 2 May 1794.

23. Ibid., 10 April 1794.

24. To Timothy Pickering, 8 January 1794, Ford, *Notes,* 1: 381.

25. To Oliver Wolcott, 3 May 1794, Ford, *Notes,* 1: 382.

26. Ibid.

27. *American Minerva,* 3 November, 31 October 1794.

28. *The Revolution in France considered in respect to its progress and effects. By an American* (New York: George Bunce and Company, 1794). Reprinted in Noah Webster, *A Collection of Papers on Political, Literary and Moral Subjects* (New York: Webster and Clark, 1843). Cited hereafter as Webster, *Collection*.

29. Ibid., p. 1.

30. Ibid., p. 6.

31. Ibid., p. 21.

32. Ibid., p. 18.

33. Ibid., p. 33.

34. Ibid., p. 12.

35. *Minerva*, 27 January 1797.

36. To Timothy Pickering, 7 July 1797, Ford, *Notes*, 1: 422. See also *Minerva*, 14 August 1797.

37. Webster saw no difference between "faction" and "party." In his first dictionary, published in 1806, he defined "faction" as "a party, tumult, sedition, discord." Webster never accepted the concept of political opposition or organized parties, as others did after 1820. See Richard Hofstadter, *The Idea of a Party System: The Rise of Legitimate Opposition in the United States, 1780–1840* (Berkeley, Los Angeles: University of California Press, 1972).

38. Webster, *Revolution*, pp. 24–39. The most famous attack on the revolution came from Edmund Burke in his *Reflections on the Revolution in France* (London, 1790). Webster and Burke had much in common. Both saw the revolution as a powerful force disrupting all stability, order, and civilization. Its attack on authority was especially feared. Although Webster was at this time less concerned than Burke with organized religion as a tool of social control, both realized its role in restraining the passions of man. Yet there was also a striking difference between the two analyses. Burke was content to point out that the Revolution shattered all the traditions and precedents on which he believed social stability was constructed. Webster agreed, but his emphasis on the revolution as an intellectual movement based on reason went one step farther than Burke.

39. Webster, *Revolution*, p. 41.

40. Ibid., p. 40.

41. Ibid., p. 41.

42. Ibid.,p. 19.

43. Ibid., p. 10.

44. Letter to Oliver Wolcott, 8 March 1795. Wolcott Papers, vol. 6, no. 92, CHS.

45. To Theodore Sedgewick, 2 January 1795, Warfel, *Letters*, p. 125.

46. *American Minerva*, 3 January 1795. See "To the Public," 1 May 1796, Warfel, *Letters*, p. 134; To Oliver Wolcott, 30 July 1795, Ford, *Notes*, 1: 392; Webster, "Vindication . . . " *American Minerva*, 14, 15 May 1795. By 1796–97, Webster had developed a conspiratorial frame of mind, something not uncommon in American history. Conspiracy theories have appeared in virtually every decade of the nation's existence. Two recent studies of this phenomenon are David B. Davis, ed., *The Fear of Conspiracy: Images of Un-American Subversion from the Revolution to the Present* (Ithaca: Cornell University Press, 1971), and Richard O. Curry and Thomas W. Brown, *Conspiracy: The Fear of Subversion in American History* (New York: Holt, Rinehart and Winston, 1972). The best theoretical study of conspiratorial fear is Franz Neumann, *The Democratic and Authoritarian State* (Glencoe, Ill.: Free Press, 1957). Neumann believes that conspiracy theories give a false concreteness to fears and anxieties which often have vague foundations, thus providing specific objects, real or imagined, upon which hatred and resentment of one's self or others may be expended. He also notes that conspiracy theories are often based on some small kernel of truth, and are not always mere figments of the imagination. Neumann's insights seem to be applicable in Webster's case.

47. *Commercial Advertiser*, 9 November 1797.

48. Ibid., 6 December 1797.

49. *Minerva*, 15 March 1797.

50. To Timothy Pickering, 21 October 1797, Ford, *Notes*, 1: 430–31. See also *Minerva*, 14, 21 September 1796, and To Timothy Pickering, 24 November 1796, Ford, *Notes*, 1: 408.

51. To Timothy Pickering, 8 December 1796, Ford, *Notes*, 1: 409–10.

52. To Timothy Pickering, 24 November 1796, Ford, *Notes*, 1: 408.

53. *Commercial Advertiser*, 22 November 1797.

54. "To the Public," 1 May 1796, Warfel, *Letters*, p. 134; to Oliver Wolcott, 30 July 1795, Ford, *Notes*, 1: 392; Webster, "Vindication . . . " *American Minerva*, 14, 15 May 1795.

55. While Webster actually edited only two papers between 1793 and 1798, they appeared under a total of five names. The daily began on 9 December as the *American Minerva*. On 2 May 1796 it became *The Minerva and Mercantile Evening Advertiser*, and changed to *The Commercial Advertiser* on 1 October 1797. He also published a semi-weekly, which went into print on 4 June 1794 as *The Herald: A Gazette for the Country* and changed to *The Spectator* on 1 October 1797. Sidney Kobre, *Development of American Journalism* (Dubuque, Iowa: William C. Brown, 1969), p. 114, notes that Webster's daily had a circulation of 1,700, while the next highest in New York City had a circulation of 1,000. For a column-inch analysis of subject matter, see Gary R. Coll, "Noah Webster: Journalist, 1783–1803" (Ph.D. diss., Southern Illinois University, 1971).

56. To C. I. Volney, 10 July 1796, Warfel, *Letters*, p. 160.

57. *Commercial Advertiser*, 9 November 1797.

58. Affidavit, 13 July 1797, Warfel, *Letters*, p. 160.

59. Letter to Jedediah Morse, 24 July 1797, Yale.

60. *Minerva*, 14 June 1796.

61. Ibid., 7 November 1796.

62. Marshall Smelser has clearly shown how hysterical the rhetoric of the period was in his "The Federalist Period as an Age of Passion," *American Quarterly* 10 (1958): 391–419; "The Jacobin Phrenzy: Federalism and the Menace of Liberty, Equality and Fraternity," *Review of Politics* 13 (1951): 457–82; "The Jacobin Phrenzy: The Menace of Monarchy, Plutocracy and Anglophobia, 1789–1798," *Review of Politics* 21 (1959): 239–58.

63. *Minerva*, 12 July 1797.

64. Ibid.

65. The best study of this episode is Alexander De Conde, *The Quasi-War: The Politics and Diplomacy of the Undeclared War with France, 1797–1801* (New York: Scribner, 1966).

66. Ronald Formisano, "Deferential-Participant Politics: The Early Republic's Political Culture, 1789–1840," *American Political Science Review* 69 (1975): 473–87.

67. This is an oversimplification of specific studies of political development in the period. See chapter 6 for bibliography and a more detailed analysis of early national political ideology and Webster's relationship to it.

68. *Minerva*, 18 August 1797.

69. *Commercial Advertiser*, 7 March 1798.

70. To Timothy Pickering, 12 May 1798, Ford, *Notes*, 1: 462–63.

71. *Minerva*, 27 September 1796.

72. Quoted in Warfel, *Webster*, p. 234.

73. *Minerva*, 22 August 1797.

74. A good introduction to Barlow is Arthur L. Ford, *Joel Barlow* (New York: Twayne, 1971).

75. To Joel Barlow, 16 November 1978, Warfel, *Letters*, pp. 192–93.

76. *Commercial Advertiser*, 16 November 1798. This version is slightly different from the previous citation.

77. Quoted in Warfel, *Webster*, pp. 239–41. Also *Commercial Advertiser*, February and March 1798.

78. To E. Waddington, 6 July 1798, Warfel, *Letters*, pp. 181–82.

79. To Timothy Pickering, 17 July 1798, Ford, *Notes*, 1: 465.

80. On Fourth of July celebrations in 1798, see Friedman, *Inventors*, and Paul C. Nagel, *One Nation Indivisible: The Union in American Thought, 1776–1861* (New York: Oxford University Press, 1965); *This Sacred Trust: American Nationality, 1798–1898* (New York: Oxford University Press, 1971).

81. "An Oration, Pronounced before the citizens of New Haven, on the anniversary of the independence of the United States, July 4, 1798, and published at their request," *Commercial Advertiser*, 24 July 1798.

82. Ibid.

83. Ibid.

84. Ibid.

85. Ibid.

86. Ibid.

Chapter 6

1. Noah Webster, *A Brief History of Epidemic and Pestilential Diseases* . . . , 2 vols. (Hartford: Hudson and Goodwin, 1799).

2. William Osler, "Some Aspects of Medical Bibliography," *Bulletin of the Association of Medical Librarians* 1 (1902): 151–67, calls it the most important work written by a layman in this country. See also Alfred S. Warthin, "Noah Webster as Epidemiologist," *Journal of the American Medical Association* 80 (1923): 755–64; and Charles Edward Amory, *The Conquest of Epidemic Disease: A Chapter in the History of Ideas* (Princeton: Princeton University Press, 1943).

3. Albert E. Van Dusen, "Connecticut History to 1763: A Selective Bibliography" in *Connecticut History* 17 (1975): 49–55. The title is misleading since the essay notes many works which cover the years up to 1818.

4. Quoted in Richard J. Purcell, *Connecticut in Transition, 1775–1818* (Middletown, Conn.: Wesleyan University Press, 1918, 1962), p. x.

5. Quoted in David Hacket Fischer, "The Revolution of American Conservatism," in William Nisbet Chambers, ed., *The American Party Systems* (New York: Oxford University Press, 1967), p. 81.

6. Quoted in Purcell, *Connecticut*, p. 212.

7. See Purcell, *Connecticut*, and Manning J. Dauer, *The Adams Federalists* (Baltimore: Johns Hopkins University Press, 1953).

8. Purcell, *Connecticut*, p. 229.

9. Ibid., p. 147.

10. Ibid., p. xiii.

11. There were two Oliver Wolcotts during this period—Webster's classmate and his father. From here on, the younger will be cited as simply Oliver Wolcott, since the elder played no role in this period of Webster's life.

12. Purcell, *Connecticut*, p. 126.

13. See, for example, an account of a dinner gathering attended by several of the most prominent men in Connecticut in letter to William Webster, 1835, Box 1, CHS.

14. Purcell, *Connecticut*, p. 232.

15. John R. Howe, "Republican Thought and the Political Violence of the 1790s," *American Quarterly* 19 (1967): 147–65.

16. Ibid., p. 165.

17. Purcell, *Connecticut*. See also Paul Goodman, *The Democratic-Republicans of*

Massachusetts: Politics in a Young Republic (Cambridge: Harvard University Press, 1964), pp. 102–3. No similar study of Republicans in Connecticut has appeared, but see Purcell, *Connecticut*, and Dauer, *Adams*, for their ideology.

18. Purcell, *Connecticut*, pp. 221–33.

19. Ibid., pp. 232–76.

20. Ibid., p. 214.

21. Ibid., pp. 214–21.

22. David Hackett Fischer, *The Revolution of American Conservatism: The Federalist Party in the Era of Jeffersonian Democracy* (New York: Harper and Row, 1965).

23. Paul Goodman, "The First American Party System," in Chambers, *American Party Systems*, pp. 65–89; Dauer, *Adams Federalists*; James M. Banner, Jr., *To the Hartford Convention: The Federalists and the Origins of Party Politics in Massachusetts, 1789–1815* (New York: Alfred A. Knopf, 1970); Purcell, *Connecticut*; and Linda Kerber, *Federalists in Dissent: Imagery and Ideology in Jeffersonian America* (Ithaca: Cornell University Press, 1970).

24. Goodman, "First System."

25. Purcell, *Connecticut*, p. 328. See also Banner, *Convention*.

26. Ibid., p. 202.

27. Ibid., p. 326.

28. Dauer, *Adams*, pp. 229–56; Richard H. Kohn, *Eagle and Sword: The Federalists and the Creation of the Military Establishment in America, 1783–1802* (New York: Free Press, 1975); John C. Miller, *The Federalist Era, 1789–1801* (New York: Harper and Row, 1960); Stephen G. Kurtz, *The Presidency of John Adams: The Collapse of Federalism, 1795–1800* (Philadelphia: University of Pennsylvania Press, 1957); Richard Buel, Jr., *Securing the Revolution: Ideology in American Politics, 1789–1815* (Ithaca: Cornell University Press, 1972), pp. 202–13; Morton Godzins, "Political Parties and the Crisis of Succession in the United States: The Case of 1800," in *Political Parties and Political Development*, ed. Joseph La Palombara and Myron Weiner (Princeton: Princeton University Press, 1968).

29. Dauer, *Adams*, pp. 246–58.

30. Fischer, *Revolution*.

31. Banner, *Convention*, pp. 154–200.

32. Banner, *Convention*, pp. 162–63. On the transition from religious preoccupations to political ones, see Edmund S. Morgan, "The American Revolution Considered as an Intellectual Movement," *Paths of American Thought*, ed. Arthur M. Schlesinger, Jr., and Morton G. White (Boston: Little, Brown, and Co., 1963).

33. Banner, *Convention*, pp. 148–50.

34. Quoted in Kerber, *Dissent*, p. 99.

35. Kerber, *Dissent*, passim.

36. Allmendinger, *Paupers*.

37. Fischer, *Revolution*. Scholars have long debated whether political development in early national America was oriented toward local or national issues. An emphasis on local problems, including the question of the disestablishment of the Congregational Church in New England, fits into the framework outlined here. The Church was, for many, an obvious means of restoring deference.

38. Banner, *Convention*, p. 44.

39. Purcell, *Connecticut*.

40. Quoted in Banner, *Convention*, p. 168.

41. Quoted in Miller, *Federalist Era*, p. 110.

42. Quoted in Fischer, *Revolution*, p. 23.

43. Quoted in Charles F. Adams, ed., *The Works of John Adams* (Boston: Little, Brown and Co., 1856), 1: 462.

44. See Miller, *Federalist Era*; Fischer, *Revolution*; and Sydney E. Ahlstrom, *A Religious History of the American People* (New Haven: Yale University Press, 1972).

45. Letter to Benjamin Rush, 15 December 1800, Ford *Notes*, 1: 479.

46. *Commercial Advertiser*, 6, 7 January 1801.

47. See Carpenter, *Bibliography*, for details.

48. Noah Webster, *The Prompter, A Commentary on Common Sayings and Subjects, which are full of Common Sense, The Best Sense in the World. A New Edition, Improved and Enlarged* (New Haven: Joel Walter, 1803), p. 75.

49. Ibid., pp. 78–80.

50. Richard Hofstadter, *The Paranoid Style in American Politics and Other Essays* (New York: Alfred A. Knopf, 1965).

51. Vernon Stauffer, *New England and the Bavarian Illuminati* (New York: Columbia University Press, 1918).

52. John Robison, *Proofs of a Conspiracy Against All . . . The Religions and Governments of Europe* (Edinburgh: William Greech, 1797).

53. For examples of this belief, see the *Connecticut Courant*, 25 February, 22 April, and 3 June 1799.

54. Anson Ely Morse, *The Federalist Party in Massachusetts in 1800* (Princeton: Princeton University Press, 1909), p. 213 ff. Morse also discusses Connecticut.

55. Purcell, *Connecticut*, p. 162.

56. J. Hammond Trumbull, *Historical Notes on the Constitutions of Connecticut, 1639–1818* (Hartford: Case, Lockwood and Brainard Co., 1901), p. 28.

57. *Commercial Advertiser*, 24 July 1799.

58. Ibid., 21 October 1799. See also his letters to Joseph Priestley in Warfel, *Letters*.

59. *Commercial Advertiser*, 23 October 1799. See also 28, 30 October, 1, 4, 6, 8, 11, 19, 21, 23, 27, 30 November, 3, 5, 13 December, and Webster, *Prompter* (1803).

60. Noah Webster, *An Oration, Pronounced before the Citizens of New Haven, on the Anniversary of the Declaration of Independence: July, 1802* (New Haven: William W. Morse, 1802), pp. 24–25.

61. Noah Webster, *An Address to the Freemen of Connecticut* (Hartford: Hudson and Goodwin, 1803), p. 3. Hereafter cited as Webster, *Address* (1803).

62. Quoted in Kerber, *Dissent*, p. 173.

63. [Boston] *Columbian Centinel*, 21 October 1801.

64. Quoted in Banner, *Convention*, p. 54.

65. Ibid., p. 56.

66. Webster, *Oration*, p. 16. See also *Commercial Advertiser*, 28 May 1802.

67. Banner, *Convention*, chap. 1.

68. Quoted ibid., p. 42.

69. Letter to Oliver Wolcott, 16 September 1800, Ford, *Notes*, 1: 504–6.

70. Webster, *Oration* (1802).

71. Letter to Benjamin Rush, 15 December 1800, Ford, *Notes*, 1: 479.

72. Quoted in the *American Mercury*, 2 December 1802.

73. Purcell, *Connecticut*, p. 222.

74. Quoted in Hofstadter, *Idea*, pp. 12–29.

75. Letter to Rufus King, 12 April 1800, Warfel, *Letters*, pp. 216–17.

76. *Commercial Advertiser*, 22 March 1800, and *Boston Gazette*, 13 October 1800.

77. Webster, *Address* (1803), p. 15.

78. Noah Webster, *An Address to the Freemen of Connecticut* (Hartford: Hudson and Goodwin, 1806), p. 5. Hereafter cited as *Address* (1806).

79. Webster, *Miscellaneous*, p. v–vi.

80. Webster, *Oration*, pp. 9–10n.

81. Quoted in Banner, *Convention*, p. 40.

82. [Noah Webster], *A Rod for the Fool's Back* (New Haven: Read and Morse, [1800]), p. 7.

83. *Commercial Advertiser*, 22 April 1800.

84. Webster, *Address* (1806), p. 4.

85. Webster, *Address* (1803).

86. Letter to Rufus King, 6 July 1807, Warfel, *Letters*, pp. 277–78.

87. *Commercial Advertiser*, 8 January 1801.

88. Ibid., 22 March 1800.

89. Ibid., 22 August 1800.

90. *Boston Gazette*, 13 October 1800.

91. Dauer, *Adams*, p. 255, and Buel, *Ideology*, p. 213.

92. [Noah Webster], *A Letter to General Hamilton Occasioned by His Letter to the President*[,] *by a Federalist*, Warfel, *Letters*, pp. 222–26.

93. *Commercial Advertiser*, August 1800.

94. Letter to James Madison, 18 July 1801, Ford, *Notes*, 1: 515–16. See also letter to Oliver Wolcott, 1 October 1801, ibid., p. 481.

95. See Purcell, *Connecticut*, pp. 239–40, and Webster, *Rod*. The latter is a heavily sarcastic, even vitriolic, attack on the younger Bishop.

96. Letter to Benjamin Rush, 11 September 1801, Warfel, *Letters*, pp. 236–37.

97. Letter to James Madison, 18 July 1801, Ford, *Notes*, 1: 515–16.

98. Noah Webster, *Miscellaneous Papers on Political and Commercial Subjects*, American Classics in History and Social Science, no. 19 (New York: Burt Franklin Research and Source Works, 1802), pp. 18, 19, 29.

99. Ibid., p. 56.

100. Merrill D. Peterson, *The Jefferson Image in the American Mind* (New York: Oxford University Press, 1960).

101. Banner, *Hartford*, p. 35.

102. Quoted in Albert Jay Nock, *Jefferson* (New York: Hill and Wang, 1926), p. 141.

103. Webster, *Miscellaneous*, pp. 71, 49.

104. Letter to Joel Barlow, 19 October 1807, Warfel, *Letters*, p. 292.

105. See especially a letter from Rebecca Greenleaf Webster, 5 December 1803, Ford, *Notes*, 2: 533–34.

106. Letter to Oliver Wolcott, 13 April 1803, Ford, *Notes*, 1: 530.

107. Letter to Stephen Twining, 22 January 1802, Ford, *Notes*, 1: 524.

108. Webster, *Miscellaneous*, p. iii.

109. Fischer, *Revolution*, passim.

110. *Boston Gazette*, 13 October 1800.

111. Webster, *Address* (1803). See also Webster, *Oration*.

112. Letter to Stephen Twining, 22 January 1802, Ford, *Notes*, 1: 524.

Chapter 7

1. Several studies of the religious benevolence movement in the early nineteenth century have been written. Most of these stress the social control aspects of the movement, including Clifford S. Griffin, *Their Brother's Keepers: Moral Stewardship in the United States, 1815–1865* (New Brunswick: Rutgers University Press, 1964), and "Religious Benevolence as Social Control, 1815–1860," *Mississippi Valley Historical Review* 64 (1957): 432–44; Stephen E. Berk, *Calvinism Versus Democracy: Timothy Dwight and the Origins of American Evangelical Orthodoxy* (Hamden, Conn.: Archon Books, 1974); M. J. Heale, "Humanitarianism in the Early Republic: The Moral Reformers of New York, 1776–1825," *Journal of American Studies* 2 (1968): 161–75; W. David Lewis, "The Reformers as Conservatives: Protestant Counter-Subversion in the Early Republic," in Stanley Coben and Norman Ratner, eds., *The Development of an American Culture* (Englewood Cliffs, N.J.: Prentice-Hall, 1970); Richard M. Rollins, "Words as Social Control: Noah Webster and the Creation of the *American Dictionary*," *American Quarterly* 27 (1976):

415–30; Raymond A. Mohl, *Poverty in New York, 1783–1825* (New York: Oxford University Press, 1971); Carrol Smith-Rosenberg, *Religion and the Rise of the American City: The New York City Mission Movement, 1812–1870* (Ithaca: Cornell University Press, 1971); David J. Rothman, *The Discovery of the Asylum: Social Order and Disorder in the New Republic* (Boston: Little, Brown and Co., 1971); Evarts B. Greene, "A Puritan Counter-Reformation in America," *Proceedings of the American Antiquarian Society* 41 (1931): 17–46; Dixon Ryan Fox, "The Protestant Counter-Reformation in America," *New York History* 16 (1935): 19–35; Perry Miller, "From the Covenant to the Revival," *The Shaping of American Religion*, ed. J. W. Smith and A. L. Jamison (Princeton: Princeton University Press, 1961); John Boles, *The Great Revival in the South, 1787–1805* (Lexington: University of Kentucky Press, 1972); Richard D. Birdsell, "The Second Great Awakening and the New England Social Order," *Church History* 39 (1970): 345–65; Donald G. Mathews, "The Second Great Awakening as an Organizing Process, 1780–1830: An Hypothesis," *American Quarterly* 21 (1969): 23–43; John L. Thomas, "Romantic Reform in America, 1815–1865," *American Quarterly* 17 (1965): 656–81; Charles I. Foster, "The Urban Missionary Movement, 1814–1837," *Pennsylvania Magazine of History and Biography* 85 (1951): 47–65, and *An Errand of Mercy: The Evangelical United Front, 1790–1837* (Chapel Hill: University of North Carolina Press, 1960); John A. Andrew, III, *Rebuilding the Christian Commonwealth: New England Congregationalists and Foreign Missions, 1800–1830* (Lexington: University of Kentucky Press, 1976); T. Scott Miyakawa, *Protestants and Pioneers: Individualism and Conformity on the American Frontier* (Chicago: University of Chicago Press, 1964); and Jay P. Dolan, *The Immigrant Church: New York's Irish and German Catholics, 1815–1865* (Baltimore: Johns Hopkins University Press, 1975).

Lois W. Banner's "Religious Benevolence as Social Control: A Critique of an Interpretation," *Journal of American History* 60 (1973): 23–41, attempts a complex set of criticisms of the work on the benevolence movement, but ends up strengthening the social-control thesis as a whole. Banner correctly argues that the status-loss thesis apparent in much of the work is too simple, and an inaccurate portrayal of the clergy's concerns—they were in fact much broader and not so personalized as the status-loss thesis would have us believe. This is the central thrust of her essay, and in this she is correct. She also claims that histrians have described the evangelicals as mere seekers after personal power, while in fact their real motives were to save society as a whole. Her view of the historiographical portrait is in itself inaccurate; yet her own viewpoint is much closer to what others have actually said. Banner finds that the idea of benevolence was not new in the early national period, and that it had several eighteenth-century sources in all sections of the country. She points out that the clergy's distaste for politics was based on the belief that it was corrupt and that it undermined national unity, a feeling shared by many political and social leaders. Her analysis of the membership of the societies indicates that they drew support from all Protestant denominations, not just Presbyterians and Congregationalists. This clearly indicates the widespread nature of the fears the movement drew its strength from. That those in the benevolence movement also took part in educational and other reforms only reveals the depth of their concerns for the fragility of American society as a whole and all its institutions. Her belief that benevolent leaders, excluded from politics, "looked toward society to find their solution to the supposed defects inherent in the republican order" (p. 41), fits well with the analyses of many other historians working on benevolence and politics. Finally, Banner's description of the function of the voluntary associations can serve as a nice summary of the view of early national reform developed by a host of recent historians. She notes that they offered "a way of involving citizens with their government and thus insisting that democracy would actually function within the republican framework, of bringing together in harmony people of the various competing classes and sections, and of providing stable organizations and a sense of community within a society in continual flux" (p. 41).

2. Kenneth A. Lockridge, *A New England Town: The First Hundred Years* (New York: Norton, 1970), delineates the fundamentally conservative nature of an early American town and labels them "Closed Christian Corporate Utopian Communities." He states that a basic characteristic was just what Webster was attempting to restore, "obedience to a narrow clique of divinely ordained leaders" (p. 172).

3. Quoted in Griffin, "Control," p. 89.

4. Kelley, *Yale*.

5. Letter to Thomas Dawes, 20 December 1808, Warfel, *Letters*, p. 309.

6. Gary D. Nash, "The American Clergy and the French Revolution," *William and Mary Quarterly*, 3d ser. 22 (1965): 400; Webster, "Remarks on the Manners, Government, and Debt of the United States." This essay was first printed in the *Pennsylvania Packet*, 15, 17, 19, and 21 February 1787. It was reprinted in Webster, *Essays*.

7. *The New England primer, amended and improved. By the author of the grammatical institute embellished with cuts* (New York: J. Patterson, 1789).

8. Paul Leicester Ford, ed., *The New England Primer* (New York: Teachers College, Columbia University, 1962), n.pag.

9. Quoted in Warfel, *Webster*, p. 91.

10. Webster, *American Magazine*, pp. 587–90.

11. [New York] *Daily Advertiser*, 5 September 1788.

12. Webster, "Miscellaneous Remarks on Divisions of Property Government . . . ," *Essays*, p. 335. Dated February 1790.

13. *The New England Primer. Improved and Adapted to the Use of Schools. By Noah Webster, Jun. Esq. Designed as an Introduction to the American Spelling Book. Embellished with Cuts* (Hudson: Ashbel Stoddard, 1801).

14. Letter to Samuel Lathem Mitchill, 2 March 1801, Warfel, *Letters*, pp. 229–30.

15. Noah Webster, *Elements of Useful Knowledge, Volume I. Containing a Historical and Geographical Account of the United States: for the use of Schools* (Hartford: Hudson and Goodwin, 1802), p. [1]; Noah Webster, *Elements of Useful Knowledge, Volume III. Containing a Historical and Geographical Account of the Empires and States of Europe, Asia and Africa . . .* (New Haven: Bronson, Walter and Company, 1806), p. 11. On schoolbooks in the early nineteenth-century see Ruth Miller Elson, *Guardians of Tradition: American Schoolbooks of the Nineteenth Century* (Lincoln: University of Nebraska Press, 1964), and Anne Scott MacLeod, *A Moral Tale: Children's Fiction and American Culture, 1820-1860* (Hamden, Conn.: Archon, 1975).

16. Noah Webster, *An American Selection of Lessons in Reading and Speaking* (Salem, Mass.: Joshua Cushing, 1805), p. 147.

17. To Dawes, p. 311.

18. Noah Webster, *An Oration, Pronounced before the Citizens of New Haven, on the Anniversary of the Declaration of Independence: July, 1802* (New Haven: William W. Morse, 1802).

19. Ford, *Notes*, 1: 527.

20. Benjamin Rush to Noah Webster, 20 July 1798, Ford, *Notes*, 1: 466.

21. *Connecticut Journal*, 7 April 1808.

22. *American Minerva*, 9 December 1793. These ideas appear in nearly everything he wrote between 1781 and 1843.

23. Letter to Oliver Wolcott, Jr., 13 May 1808, Warfel, *Letters*, p. 300.

24. Ibid.

25. "To All American Patriots," May 1808, Warfel, *Letters*, pp. 301–8.

26. *Connecticut Herald Journal*, 17 May 1808.

27. John H. Giltney, "Moses Stuart" (Ph.D. diss., Yale University, 1956).

28. To Dawes, p. 311. See also Noah Webster, *Letter from Noah Webster, Esq., of New Haven, Connecticut, to a Friend in Explanation and Defence of the Distinguishing Doctrines of the Gospel* (New York: J. Seymour, 1809), p. 1. Hereafter cited as Webster, *Doctrine*.

29. To Dawes, p. 312.

30. Burrows and Wallace, "Psychology."

31. Quoted ibid.

32. Ibid.

33. To Dawes, p. 312.

34. To Dawes, p. 310.

35. Ibid.

36. Ibid., p. 312.

37. Ibid., pp. 312–13.

38. Berk, *Calvinism*, passim.

39. For a full listing of Webster's miscellaneous essays, including those in the *Religious Intelligencer*, see Carpenter, *Bibliography*, pp. 433–82.

40. Berk, *Calvinism*, chaps. 1–3.

41. Giltney, "Stuart."

42. William James, *The Varieties of Religious Experience: A Study in Human Nature* (New York: Modern Library, 1902), p. 240.

43. Ibid.

44. Ibid., pp. 206–7.

45. Quoted in Griffin, "Control," p. 91.

46. Ibid.

47. Ibid., p. 95.

48. Quoted in Griffin, *Keepers*, p. 34.

49. To Dawes, p. 314.

50. Webster, *Doctrines*, p. 5.

51. Ibid., p. 22. See also to Thomas Dawes, 23 February 1809, NYPL, Box 1.

52. Noah Webster, *Value of the Bible and Excellence of the Christian Religion: For the Use of Families and Schools* (New Haven: Durrie and Peck, 1834), p. 72. Hereafter cited as Webster, *Value*.

53. Noah Webster, *Instructive and Entertaining Lessons for Youth; with Rules for Reading with Propriety, Illustrated with Examples . . .* (New Haven: S. Babcock and Durrie and Peck, 1835), p. 211, see also p. 106. Hereafter cited as Webster, *Lessons*.

54. Ibid., pp. 219–20.

55. *Commercial Advertiser*, 20 January 1835.

56. To Dawes, 23 February 1809.

57. Erich Fromm, *Psychoanalysis and Religion* (New Haven: Yale University Press, 1950), p. 177.

58. Webster, *Doctrine*, pp. 8, 9. See also to Dawes, 23 February 1809.

59. Ford, *Notes*, 2: 371.

60. Webster, *Doctrine*, p. 8.

61. To Dawes, 20 December 1808, p. 13.

62. Letter to Harriet, 20 December 1841, CHS.

63. Letter to Harriet Webster Fowler, 7 January 1835, Warfel, *Letters*, p. 445. See also Webster, *Doctrines*, p. 10.

64. Webster, *Lessons*, p. 210.

65. To Dawes, 23 February 1809.

66. Ibid.

67. Webster, *Doctrines*, pp. 3, 10. See also Webster, *Value*, pp. 154–55.

68. "Letter to a Young Gentleman Commencing his Education," Webster, *Collection*, p. 295. This essay was first published in 1823.

69. Webster, *Doctrines*, pp. 17, 11, 12, and 19.

70. To Moses Stuart, 23 April 1822, Ford, *Notes*, 2: 186–87.

71. To Messrs Morse, 24 February 1834, Warfel, *Letters*, p. 433.

72. Noah Webster, *The Holy Bible, containing the Old and New Testaments, in the common version. With amendments of the Language* (New Haven: Durrie and Peck, 1833), p. xvi.

73. Ibid., pp. v, xvi, xiv. Allen Walker Read, "Noah Webster as a Euphemist," *Dialect Notes*, 6 (1934): 385–91, and Harry R. Warfel, "The Centenary of Noah Webster's Bible," *New England Quarterly* 8 (1934): 578–82 are interesting secondary commentaries.

74. Noah Webster, *History of the United States; to which is prefixed a brief historical account of our English Ancestors, from the dispersion of Babel, to their migration to America; and of the conquest of South America, by the Spaniards* (New Haven: Durrie and Peck, 1832), p. 9. Hereafter cited as Webster, *History* (1832). See also Noah Webster, *History of the United States* (Cincinnati: Corey, Fairbank and Webster, 1835). Hereafter cited as Webster, *U.S.* See also Webster, *Value*, p. 39.

75. Webster, *History*, p. 197.

76. Ibid., p. 210.

77. Ibid., p. 242.

78. Letter to Harriet, 20 December 1841, CHS.

79. Webster, *Doctrines*, p. 3.

80. Ibid., p. 18.

81. Webster, *Value*, n.pag.

82. To Dawes, 23 February 1809.

83. Webster, *Lessons*, p. 210, also p. 10.

84. Webster, *Value*, pp. 173, 174–75.

85. Webster, "Letter to a young Gentleman . . . ," pp. 300–306.

86. Letter to William Chauncey Fowler, 24 July 1832, Warfel, *Letters*, p. 431.

87. Webster, *Value*, pp. 173–75.

88. Webster, *History*, p. 274. See also "Minutes on Sabbathbreaking," n.d., Pierpont Morgan Library; and Letter to Harriet, 20 December 1841, CHS.

89. Webster, *Value*, p. 177.

90. Webster, *History*, p. 273.

91. Letter to William Chauncey Fowler, 24 July 1832, Warfel, *Letters*, pp. 431–32.

92. Noah Webster, *An Oration Pronounced Before the Knox and Warren Branches of the Washington Benevolent Society, at Amherst, on the Celebration of the Anniversary of the Declaration of Independence, July 4, 1814* (Northampton, Mass.: William Butter, 1814), p. 16.

93. This was the opinion of the original board of directors. Warfel, *Webster*, p. 342.

94. The history of educational ideas and organizations, like that of religion and reform in the early national period, has been largely rewritten in the last two decades. Michael B. Katz and others have recently stressed the role schools played as agents of acculturation and social control. See Michael B. Katz, *The Irony of Early School Reform: Educational Innovation in Mid-Nineteenth-Century Massachusetts* (Cambridge: Harvard University Press, 1973), *Class, Bureaucracy, and Schools: The Illusion of Educational Change in America* (New York: Praeger, 1971), *School Reform: Past and Present* (Boston: Little, Brown, and Co., 1971), and "The Origins of Public Education," *History of Education Quarterly* 16 (1976): pp. 381–407; Diane Ravitch, "The Revisionists Revised: Studies in the Historiography of American Education," *Proceedings of the National Academy of Education* 4 (1977); Carl F. Kaestle, *The Evolution of an Urban School System: New York City, 1750–1850* (Cambridge: Harvard University Press, 1973); William W. Cutler, III, "Status, Values and the Education of the Poor: The Trustees of the New York Public School Society, 1805–1853," *American Quarterly* 24 (1972): 69–85; Raymond A. Mohl, *Poverty in New York, 1783–1825* (New York: Oxford University Press, 1970); Stanley K. Schultz, *The Culture Factory: Boston Public Schools, 1789–1860* (New York: Oxford University

Press, 1973), and Jonathan Messerli, *Horace Mann: A Biography* (New York: Alfred A. Knopf, 1971). Richard Hofstadter, *Academic Freedom in the Age of the College* (Chicago: University of Chicago Press, 1955); Allmendinger, *Paupers and Scholars*; and Steven J. Novak, *The Rights of Youth: American Colleges and Student Revolt, 1798–1815* (Cambridge: Harvard University Press, 1977) reveal the same themes.

95. Noah Webster, "Origin of Amherst College in Massachusetts," Webster, *Collection*, p. 225.

96. Quoted in Warfel, *Webster*, p. 338.

97. Ibid., p. 340.

98. Webster, "Letter to a young Gentleman . . . ," pp. 295–98.

99. James, *Varieties*, p. 162.

Chapter 8

1. Undated quotation in Ford, *Notes*, 1: 293.

2. Robert Keith Leavitt, *Noah's Ark: New England Yankees and the Endless Quest* (Springfield, Mass.: G. and C. Merriam Co., 1947).

3. Scudder, *Webster*.

4. Quoted in Kerber, *Federalists*, p. 195.

5. Ibid., pp. 196–97. See also Robert W. Shoemaker, "'Democracy' and 'Republic' as Understood in Late Eighteenth-Century America," *American Speech* 61 (1966): 83–95.

6. Oscar Handlin, *The History of the United States* (New York: Holt, Rinehart, and Winston, 1967), 1: 393, and John D. Hicks, George E. Mowry, and Robert Burke, *A History of American Democracy*, 3d ed. (Boston: Houghton, Mifflin Company, 1966), p. 185.

7. Charles A. Beard, *The Rise of American Civilization* (New York: Macmillan Co., 1940), p. 766.

8. Merle Curti, Richard H. Shryock, Thomas C. Cochran, and Fred Harvey Harrington, *A History of American Civilization* (New York: Harper and Brothers, 1953), p. 165.

9. John A. Krout and Dixon Ryan Fox, *The Completion of Independence, 1790–1830* (New York: Macmillan, 1944), p. 33.

10. Friedman, *Inventors*, pp. 30–41.

11. Homer D. Babbidge, Jr., ed., *Noah Webster: On Being American, Selected Writings, 1783–1828* (New York: Frederick A. Praeger, 1967).

12. David Littlejohn, *Dr. Johnson and Noah Webster: Two Men and Their Dictionaries* (San Francisco: Book Club of California, 1971), p. 51.

13. Warfel, *Webster*, p. 353. See also Rusche, "Empire of Reason."

14. To Joel Barlow, 12 November 1807, Warfel, *Letters*, p. 298.

15. Ford, *Notes*, 1: 1.

16. Kerber, *Federalists*, pp. 96–103.

17. George Philip Krapp, *The English Language in America* (New York: Frederick Ungar, 1960), p. 336.

18. John Quincy Adams to Noah Webster, 5 November 1806, Ford, *Notes*, 2: 9.

19. James Kent to Noah Webster, 20 March 1810, Ford, *Notes*, 2: 75.

20. John Jay to Noah Webster, 12 January 1811, Ford, *Notes*, 2: 119–20.

21. See for example To Jedediah Morse, 30 July 1806, Warfel, *Letters*, pp. 268–69 and To Joel Barlow, 12 November 1807, Warfel, *Letters*, p. 207.

22. See, for example, Letter to Oliver Wolcott, 13 April 1803, Ford, *Notes*, 1: 530; To John West, 18 August 1807, Warfel, *Letters*, p. 281; To Rufus King, 28 February 1807, ibid., p. 275; To the Friends of Literature . . . 25 February 1807, ibid., pp. 279–80; To Joel Barlow, 12 November 1807 and To Samuel Hopkins, 17 March 1808, CHS; To Josiah Quincy, 12 February 1811, quoted in Scudder, *Webster*, p. 185; To Sir _____, 19 May

1813, NYPL, Box 1; To Samuel L. Mitchill, 12 December 1823. Library of Congress, Miscellaneous Manuscripts Collection.

23. Warfel, *Webster*, p. 323.

24. Letter to William Webster, 27 October 1835, Yale, Box 1; Letter to Horatio Southgate, 26 June 1818, NYPL, Box 1.

25. Letter to Emily Ellsworth, 20 May 1828, CHS.

26. Krapp, *Language*, p. 344.

27. Noah Webster, *An American Dictionary of the English Language* (New York: S. Converse, 1828), p. [iii]. Hereafter cited as *American Dictionary*.

28. H. L. Mencken, *The American Language: An Inquiry into the Development of English in the United States* (New York: Alfred A. Knopf, 1923, 1972), p. 7.

29. From Joseph Lyman, 5 January 1814, Ford, *Notes*, 2: 124. Carpenter, *Bibliography*, p. 363, indicates that Webster was the author of this letter.

30. Noah Webster, *An Oration, Pronounced Before the Knox and Warren Branches of the Washington Benevolence Society, at Amherst . . .* (Northampton, Mass.: William Butler, 1814).

31. George H. McKnight, *The Evolution of the English Language: From Chaucer to the Twentieth Century* (New York: Dover, 1968).

32. Warfel, *Webster*, p. 361.

33. Ibid., p. 365.

34. Letter "from Dr. N. Webster to a gentleman in this town," n.d., Library of Congress, Miscellaneous Manuscripts Collection.

35. Letter to Andrew Stevenson, 22 June 1841, NYPL, Box 1.

36. Letter to Her Majesty, Victoria, Queen of Great Britain, 22 June 1841, NYPL, Box 1.

37. Noah Webster, "A Dissertation Concerning the Influence of Language on Opinions and of Opinions on Language," *American Magazine*, May 1788, p. 399.

38. Letter to J. Pemberton, 15 March 1790, HSP.

39. *American Dictionary*, n.pag.

40. Letter to Emily Ellsworth, 24 February 1829, CHS.

41. See especially Friend, *Development*, and Albert C. Baugh, *A History of the English Language*, 2d ed. (New York: Appleton-Century-Crofts, 1957).

42. Mitford Mathews, *A Survey of English Dictionaries* (London: Oxford University Press, 1933), p. 442.

43. Friend, *Development*, p. 17.

44. Ibid., p. 77.

45. Charlton Laird, "Etymology, Anglo-Saxon, and Noah Webster," *American Speech* 21 (1946): 3–15. Also Thomas Pyles, *The Origins and Development of the English Language* (New York: Harcourt, Brace and World, 1964), p. 68.

46. Krapp, *Language*, pp. 362–63.

47. James A. H. Murray, *The Evolution of English Lexicography* (London: Oxford University Press, 1900), p. 43.

48. Friend, *Development*, p. 76.

49. James A. Sledd and Gwin J. Kolb, *Dr. Johnson's Dictionary: Essays in the Biography of a Book* (Chicago: University of Chicago Press, 1955), p. 197.

50. H. L. Mencken, *Language*, p. 7.

51. Krapp, *Language*, p. 365.

52. Laird, "Etymology," p. 3.

53. NYPL.

54. Webster, *Compendious Dictionary*, p. xxiii.

55. "To the Friends of Literature in the United States," Warfel, *Letters*, p. 272.

56. Letter to Jonas Platt, 24 September 1807, Library of Congress, Miscellaneous Manuscripts Collection.

57. To Thomas Dawes, 25 July 1809.

58. To John Jay, November 1821, Ford, *Notes*, 2: 160–61.

59. Webster, *Observations*, p. 5.

60. Webster, *Dissertations*, p. 54.

61. Ibid., pp. 315–16.

62. Franklin Edgerton, "Notes on Early American Work in Linguistics," *Proceedings of the American Philosophical Society* 87 (1944): 25–34; quoted in Friend, *Development*, p. 77.

63. Sledd and Kolb, *Dictionary*, p. 197.

64. Friend, *Development*, p. 76.

65. Krapp, *Language*, p. 365.

66. Webster, *Compendious Dictionary*, p. xix.

67. Webster, "Young Gentleman," p. 86.

68. To David McClure, 25 October 1836, Warfel, *Letters*, p. 454.

69. *American Dictionary*, p. [viii].

70. Joseph H. Friend, *The Development of American Lexicography, 1798–1864* (Paris: Mouton, 1967), p. 76.

71. Webster, *Dissertations*, p. 399.

72. *American Dictionary*.

73. Noah Webster, *Observations on Language . . .* (New York: S. Babcock, 1839), pp. 31–32. See also Noah Webster, "Discourse delivered before the Connecticut Historical Society on 21 April 1840," CHS, p. 29.

74. *Middletown* [Connecticut] *Constitution*, 5 December 1838.

75. *Commercial Advertiser*, 21 October 1799.

76. To Joseph Priestley, 1800, Warfel, *Letters*, p. 208.

77. Ibid., pp. 207–8.

78. *Middletown Constitution*, 5 December 1838.

79. Webster, "Discourse," p. 29.

80. To Daniel Webster, n.d., Warfel, *Letters*, p. 482.

81. Letter to James Kent, 7 February 1843, NYPL, Box 8.

82. *Commercial Advertiser*, 20 January 1835.

83. Webster, "Discourse," p. 30.

84. *Middletown Constitution*, 5 December 1838.

85. Ibid.

86. The *American Dictionary* was unpaginated, but definitions can be found in their correct alphabetical order.

87. *American Dictionary*, p. [v].

Chapter 9

1. "To the Editor of the Palladium," 17 February 1835, Warfel, *Letters*, p. 446.

2. Webster, *Collection*.

3. Letter to Charles Chauncey, 28 February 1837, Chauncey Family Papers, Box 7, Yale University Library.

4. Noah Webster, *The Teacher: A Supplement to the Elementary Spelling Book* (New Haven: S. Babcock, 1836), p. 59; "A Voice of Wisdom," by "Sidney," *Commercial Advertiser*, 20 November 1837, reprinted as [Noah Webster], *Appeal to Americans* (New York: 1838), pp. 7–8; To William Leete Stone, 29 August 1837, Warfel, *Letters*, pp. 505–6; *Commercial Advertiser*, 20 January 1835.

5. [Webster], "Voice," pp. 3–4, 8; *Middletown Constitution*, 18 April 1838; Noah Webster, *A Manual of Useful Studies . . .* (New Haven: S. Babcock, 1839), p. 70; Webster, *Teacher*, p. 59; *Connecticut Observer*, 11 November 1837.

6. *Gazette*, 11 April 1838.

7. *Commercial Advertiser*, 20 January 1835; To Daniel Webster, 1837, Warfel, *Letters*, pp. 491–92, 486; *Gazette*, 21 March 1838.

8. To W. L. Stone, p. 505.

9. *Gazette*, 23 May 1838.

10. Marvin Meyers, *The Jacksonian Persuasion: Politics and Belief* (Stanford: Stanford University Press, 1957).

11. *Gazette*, 23 May 1838.

12. *Connecticut Observer*, 11 November 1837. See also Letter to William Webster, 23 February 1838, Yale Box 1; Webster, *Observations*, pp. 38–39; Letter to Emily, 6 December 1839, Letters to Emily, 28 June 1837 and 13 April 1842, CHS.

13. *Connecticut Observer*, 11 November 1837; To Thomas Dawes, 1838, CHS.

14. 29 April 1836, quoted in Warfel, *Webster*, p. 423.

15. Letter to Emily, 3 July 1840, CHS.

16. See chap. 7, n. 1 for bibliography.

17. Joseph R. Gusfield, *Symbolic Crusade: Status, Politics and the American Temperance Movement* (Urbana: University of Illinois Press, 1966).

18. Meyers, *Persuasion*; Smith *Virgin Land*; John William Ward, *Andrew Jackson: Symbol For An Age* (New York: Oxford University Press, 1955).

19. See chap. 7, n. 1 for bibliography.

20. Messerli, *Horace Mann*, p. 346.

21. Rothman, *The Discovery of the Asylum*, and other studies listed in chap. 7, n. 1.

22. Leonard L. Richards, *"Gentlemen of Property and Standing": Anti-Abolition Mobs in Jacksonian America* (New York: Oxford University Press, 1970).

23. Hofstadter, *Idea*.

24. Fred Somkin, *The Unquiet Eagle: Memory and Desire in the Idea of American Freedom, 1815–1860* (Ithaca: Cornell University Press, 1967).

25. Douglas T. Miller, *The Birth of Modern America, 1820–1850* (New York: Pegasus, 1970).

26. Eliza Webster Jones, "An Account of the Festival of the Golden Wedding," May 1842, Ford, *Notes*, 2: 359–61.

27. Quoted in Eliza Webster Jones, "Account by Eliza Webster Jones," Ford, *Notes*, 2: 362–71.

Bibliography

Manuscript Collections

American Philosophical Society Library. Philadelphia.

Bienecke Rare Book and Manuscript Library. New Haven, Conn.

Connecticut Historical Society. Hartford. Archives.

Detroit Public Library. Burton Collection.

Dickinson College. Carlisle, Pa. Spahr Library Archives.

Henry E. Huntington Library. Pasadena, Calif. Manuscript Collection.

Historical Society of Pennsylvania. Philadelphia. Archives.

Jervis Public Library. Rome, N.Y.

Library of Congress. Washington, D.C. Manuscripts and Archives. Henry Clay Papers. William Cranch Papers. Jeremiah Evarts Papers. Benjamin Franklin Papers. Thomas Jefferson Papers. James Madison Papers. Miscellaneous Manuscripts Collection. Henry R. Schoolcraft Papers. George Washington Papers.

Maryland Historical Society. Baltimore, Md. Archives.

New York Historical Society. New York City. Miscellaneous Manuscripts. Rufus King Papers.

New York Public Library. New York. Manuscripts and Archives. The Papers of Noah
    Webster.
Pierpont Morgan Library. New York. Archives.
Trinity College Library. Hartford, Conn.
University of Vermont Library.
Yale University. Sterling Memorial Library. Archives and Manuscripts. Webster Family
    Papers.

Webster: Selected Published Works

Webster, Noah. "An Address, delivered at the Laying of the corner stone of the build-
ing now erecting for the Charity Institution in Amherst, August 9, 1820." In *A
Plea for A Miserable World*. Boston: Ezra Lincoln, 1820.
————. *An Address to the Citizens of Connecticut*. N.p.: J. Walters, 1803.
————. *An Address to the Freemen of Connecticut*. Hartford: Hudson and Goodwin, 1803.
————. *An Address, to the Freemen of Connecticut*. Hartford: Hudson and Goodwin, 1806.
————. *An American Dictionary of the English Language*. New York: S. Converse, 1828.
————. *The American Spelling Book: containing an easy STANDARD PRONUNCIATION.
Being the FIRST PART of a GRAMMATICAL INSTITUTE of the English Language*.
Boston: Thomas and Andrews, 1789.
————. *Attention! or, New Thoughts on a Serious Subject; Being an Enquiry into the Excise
Laws of Connecticut; addressed to the freemen of the state. By a Private Citizen*. Hart-
ford: Hudson and Goodwin, 1789.
————. *Biography, for the Use of Schools*. New Haven: Hezekiah Howe, 1830.
————. *A Brief History of Epidemic and Pestilential Diseases . . .* 2 vols. Hartford: Hudson
and Goodwin, 1799.
————. *Circular to the Clergymen or other well-informed Gentlemen in the several towns of
Connecticut*. New Haven: [Broadside], 1798.
————. *A Collection of Essays and Fugitiv* [sic] *Writings on Moral, Historical, Political and
Literary Subjects:* Boston: J. Thomas and E. T. Andrews, 1790.
————. *A Collection of Papers on Political, Literary and Moral Subjects*. New York: Webster
and Clark, 1843.
————. *A Compendious Dictionary of the English Language*. New Haven: Sidney's Press,
1806.
————. "A Dissertation on the Supposed Change in the Temperature of Winters: Read
before the Connecticut Academy of Arts and Sciences." Connecticut Historical
Society.
————. *Dissertations on the English language: with notes, historical and critical. To which is
added, by way of appendix, an essay on a reformed mode of spelling, with Dr. Franklin's
arguments on that subject*. Boston: Isaiah Thomas and Co., 1789.
————. *Effects of Slavery, on Morals and Industry*. Hartford: Hudson and Goodwin, 1793.
————. *The Elementary Spelling Book; Being an Improved American Spelling Book*. Middle-
town, Connecticut: William H. Niles, 1834.
————. *Elements of Useful Knowledge*. Vol. 1. Hartford: Hudson and Goodwin, 1802.
————. *Elements of Useful Knowledge*. Vol. 2. New Haven: Sidney's Press, 1804.
————. *Elements of Useful Knowledge*. Vol. 3. New Haven: Bronson, Walter and Com-
pany, 1806.
————. *An examination into the leading principles of the federal constitution proposed by the
late Convention held at Philadelphia. With answers to the principal objections that have
been raised against the system. By a citizen of America*. Philadelphia: Pritchard and
Hall, 1787.
————. "Experiments Respecting Dew, intended to ascertain whether dew is the descent of vapour during the night, or the perspiration of the earth, or of plants;

or whether it is not the effect of condensation." *Memoirs of the American Academy of Arts and Sciences* 3 (1809): 95–103.

_____. *A grammatical institute of the English language, comprising, an easy, concise, and systematic method of education, designed for the use of English schools in America. In three parts, Part I.* Hartford: Hudson and Goodwin, 1783.

_____. *A grammatical institute, of the English language, comprising, an easy, concise, and systematic method of Education, designed for the use of English schools in America. In three parts. Part II.* Hartford: Hudson and Goodwin, 1784.

_____. *A grammatical institute of the English language, comprising, an easy, concise, and systematic method of education, designed for the use of English schools in America. In three parts. Part III.* Hartford: Barlow and Babcock, 1785.

_____. "The Greeks." *Religious Intelligencer*, 3 January 1824.

_____. *History of the United States; to which is prefixed a brief historical account of our English ancestors, from the dispersion of Babel, to their migration to America; and of the conquest of South America, by the Spaniards.* New Haven: Durrie and Peck, 1832.

_____. *History of the United States.* Cincinnati: Corey, Fairbank and Webster, 1835.

_____. *The Holy Bible, containing the Old and New Testaments, in the common version. With amendments of the Language.* New Haven: Durrie and Peck, 1833.

_____. *Instructive and Entertaining Lessons for Youth: with Rules for Reading with Propriety, Illustrated by Examples. Designed for use in Schools and families.* New Haven: S. Babcock and Durrie and Peck, 1835.

_____. *Letter from Noah Webster, Esq., of New Haven, Connecticut, to a friend, in Explanation and Defence of the Distinguishing Doctrines of the Gospel.* New York: J. Seymour, 1809.

_____. *A Letter to General Hamilton, occasioned by his Letter to President Adams. By a Federalist.* [New York: n.p.], 1800.

_____. *A Letter to the Governors, Instructors and Trustees of the Universities, and other Seminaries of Learning, in the United States, on the Errors of English Grammars.* New York: George P. Hokkins, 1798.

_____. *Letter to a Young Gentleman commencing His Education: to which is Subjoined a Brief History of the United States.* New Haven: Howe and Spaulding, 1823.

_____. *The Little Reader's Assistant.* Hartford: Elisha Babcock, 1790.

_____. *A Manual of Useful Studies: For the Instruction of Young Persons of both Sexes, in Families and Schools.* New Haven: S. Babcock, 1839.

_____. *Miscellaneous Papers, on Political and Commercial Subjects.* American Classics in History and Social Science Series, no. 19. New York: Burt Franklin Research and Source Works, Series 145, 1802.

_____. *Mistakes and Corrections.* New Haven: H. L. Hamlen, 1837.

_____. "Mr. Noah Webster on Raising Potatoes, in a letter to Secretary Samuel L. Mitchill." *Transactions of the Society for the Promotion of Agriculture, Arts and Manufactures* 1 (1798): 90–81. *The New England Primer, Amended and Improved. By the Author of the Grammatical Institute Embellished With Cuts.* New York: J. Patterson, 1789.

_____. *The New England Primer, Amended and Improved. By the Author of the Grammatical Institute Embellished With Cuts.* New York: J. Patterson, 1789.

_____, ed. *The New England Primer.* Hudson, New York: Ashbel Stoddard, 1801.

_____, ed. *The New England Primer, Amended and Improved. By the Author of the Grammatical Institute Embellished With Cuts.* New York: J. Patterson, 1789.

_____. *Noah Webster's Spelling Book.* Introduction by Henry Steele Commager. New York: Columbia University, 1958, 1962.

_____. *Observations on Language, and on the Errors of Class-Books: addressed to the New York Lyceum. Also, Observations on Commerce, addressed to the members of the Mercantile Library Association of New York.* New Haven: S. Babcock, 1839.

———. "On the Decomposition of White Lead Paint." *Memoirs of the Connecticut Academy of Arts and Sciences* 1 (1810): 135–36.

———. "On the Effects of Evergreens on Climate." *Transactions of the Society for the Promotion of Agriculture, Arts and Manufactures* 4 (1799): [51]–52.

———. "On the Theory of Vegetation." *Memoirs of the American Academy of Arts and Sciences* 2 (1793): 178–85.

———. *An Oration, Pronounced before the Citizens of New Haven, on the Anniversary of the Declaration of Independence: July, 1802.* New Haven: William W. Morse, 1802.

———. *An Oration, Pronounced before the Citizens of New Haven on the Anniversary of the Declaration of the Independence of the United States, July 4th, 1798.* New Haven: T. and S. Green, 1798.

———. *An Oration, Pronounced Before the Knox and Warren Branches of the Washington Benevolent Society, at Amherst, on the Celebration of the Declaration of Independence, July 4, 1814.* Northampton, Mass.: William Butler, 1814.

———. "Origin of Mythology." *Memoirs of the Connecticut Academy of Arts and Sciences* 1 (1810): 175–216.

———. *The Prompter; A Commentary on Common Sayings and Subjects, which are full of Common Sense, the Best Sense in the World. A New Edition, improved and Enlarged.* New Haven: Joel Walter, 1803.

———. *The Prompter:; or a Commentary on Common Sayings and Subjects, which are full of Common Sense, the Best Sense in the World.* Hartford: Hudson and Goodwin, 1791.

———. *A Rod for the Fool's Back.* New Haven: Read and Morse, [1800].

———. *The Revolution in France considered in respect to its progress and effects. By an American.* New York: George Bunce and Company, 1794.

———. "A Short View of the Origins and Progress of the Science of Natural Philosophy." *New York Magazine of Literary Repository* 1 (1790): 338–40, 383–84.

———. *Sketches of American Policy.* Hartford: Hudson and Goodwin, 1785.

———. *The Teacher: A Supplement to the elementary spelling book.* New Haven: S. Babcock, 1836.

———. *Value of the Bible and Excellence of the Christian Religion: for the use of families and schools.* New Haven: Durrie and Peck, 1834.

———. "A Voice of Wisdom." N.p., n.d.

———. *Webster Genealogy.* [Compiled and printed for presentation only by Noah Webster.] New Haven: n.p., 1836. Brooklyn, N.Y.: [privately printed], 1876.

Newspapers

American Magazine (New York). December 1787–November 1788.

American Mercury (New Haven). 2 January 1790.

American Minerva (New York). December 1793–May 1796.

American Museum (Philadelphia). October 1787.

Boston Gazette. October 1800.

Columbian Centinel (Boston). 21 October 1801.

Commercial Advertiser (New York). October 1797–May 1843.

Connecticut Courant (New Haven). June 1781–August 1793.

Connecticut Herald (New Haven). January 1806, November 1835–March 1838.

Connecticut Herald and Journal (New Haven). 17 May 1808.

Connecticut Journal and Advertiser (New Haven). April 1808.

Connecticut Observer (Hartford). April 1808.

Daily Advertiser (New York). September 1788.

Essex Journal (Newburyport, Mass.). December 1786.

Freeman's Chronicle (Hartford). September–November 1783.

Gazette of the United States (Philadelphia). 19 January 1790.

Hampshire Gazette (Northampton, Mass.). March–May 1838.

Maryland Gazette (Annapolis). 10 January 1786.
Maryland Journal (Rockville). 1 January 1786.
Massachusetts Centinel (Boston). July 1786.
Middletown Constitution (Middletown, Conn.). April–December 1838.
Minerva and Mercantile Evening Advertiser (New York). May 1796–September 1797.
National Gazette (Philadelphia). July 1793.
New Haven Daily Herald. February 1843.
New York Magazine or Literary Repository. June–July 1790.
New York Packet (Fishkill). January–February 1782.
Panoplist (Worcester, Mass.). July 1809.
Pennsylvania Gazette (Philadelphia). March–April 1787.
Pennsylvania Packet (Philadelphia). February 1787.
Religious Intelligencer (New Haven). September 1835.
Herald: A Gazette for the Country (New York). June 1794–September 1797.
Spectator (New York). October 1797–November 1803.
Vermont Chronicle (St. Johnsbury). April 1840.

Secondary Sources

Adams, Charles F., ed. *The Works of John Adams*. Boston: Little, Brown and Co., 1856.
Ahlstrom, Sydney E. *A Religious History of the American People*. New Haven: Yale University Press, 1972.
Alden, John Richard. *The American Revolution: 1776–1783*. New York: Harper and Row, 1954.
Allen, Frederic Sturges. *Noah Webster's Place Among English Lexicographers*. Springfield: G. and C. Merriam Co., 1909.
Allmendinger, David F., Jr. *Paupers and Scholars: The Transformation of Student Life in Nineteenth-Century New England*. New York: St. Martin's Press, 1975.
Allport, Gordon W. *Personality: A Psychological Interpretation*. New York: Henry Holt and Co., 1937.
Ammon, Harry. *The Genet Mission*. New York: W. W. Norton, 1973.
Amory, Charles Edward. *The Conquest of Epidemic Disease: A Chapter in the History of Ideas*. Princeton: Princeton University Press, 1943.
Andrew, John A., III. *Rebuilding the Christian Commonwealth: New England Congregationalists and Foreign Missions, 1800–1830*. Lexington: University of Kentucky Press, 1976.
Appleby, Joyce. "The New Republican Synthesis and the Changing Political Ideas of John Adams." *American Quarterly* 25 (1973): 578–95.
Babbidge, Homer, ed. *Noah Webster: On Being American, Selected Writings, 1783–1828*. New York: Frederick A. Praeger, 1967.
Bailyn, Bernard. *The Ideological Origins of the American Revolution*. Cambridge: Belknap Press of Harvard University Press, 1967.
———. "Religion and Revolution: Three Biographical Studies." *Perspectives in American History* 4 (1970): 85–172.
Banner, James M., Jr. *To the Hartford Convention: The Federalists and the Origins of Party Politics in Massachusetts, 1789–1815*. New York: Alfred A. Knopf, 1970.
Banner, Lois W. "Religious Benevolence as Social Control: A Critique of an Interpretation." *Journal of American History* 60 (1973): 23–41.
Banning, Lance. "Republican Ideology and the Triumph of the Constitution, 1789 to 1793." *William and Mary Quarterly*, 3d ser. 31 (1974): 167–88.
Barker, Charles A. *American Convictions: Cycles of Public Thought, 1600–1850*. Philadelphia: Lippincott, 1970.
Barlow, Joel. *The Political Writings of Joel Barlow*. New York: Mott and Lyon, 1796.

Barnes, Viola Florence. "Early Suggestions of Forming a National Language Association." *American Speech* 4 (1929): 183–84.

Barzun, Jacques. *Clio and Her Doctors: Psycho-history, Quanto-history and History.* Chicago: University of Chicago Press, 1974.

Baugh, Albert C. *A History of the English Language.* New York: Appleton-Century-Crofts, 1957.

Beard, Charles A. *The Rise of American Civilization.* New York: Macmillan Co., 1940.

Belok, Michael. *Noah Webster Revisited.* Tempe, Ariz.: Bureau of Educational Research and Services, 1973.

Benton, Joel. "An Unwritten Chapter in Noah Webster's Life: Love and the Spelling Book." *Magazine of American History* 10 (July 1883): 52–56.

Bernhard, Winfred E. A. *Fisher Ames: Federalist and Statesman, 1758–1818.* Chapel Hill: University of North Carolina Press, 1965.

Berk, Stephen E. *Calvinism Versus Democracy: Timothy Dwight and the Origins of American Evangelical Orthodoxy.* Hamden, Conn.: Archon Books, 1974.

Billias, George Athan, and Grob, Gerald N. *American History: Retrospect and Prospect.* New York: Free Press, 1971.

Billings, John S. "Literature and Institutions." In *A Century of American Medicine, 1776–1876,* edited by Henry C. Lea, Philadelphia: J. B. Lippincott, 1876.

Birdsell, Richard D. "The Second Great Awakening and the New England Social Order." *Church History* 39 (1970): 345–65.

Bleyer, Willard Grosvenor. *Main Currents in the History of American Journalism.* New York: Houghton Mifflin Co., 1927.

Bodo, John R. *The Protestant Clergy and Public Issues, 1812–1848.* Princeton: Princeton University Press, 1954.

Boles, John. *The Great Revival in the South, 1787–1805.* Lexington: University of Kentucky Press, 1972.

Boorstin, Daniel. *The Lost World of Thomas Jefferson.* New York: Henry Holt, 1948.

Brodie, Fawn. *Thaddeus Stevens, Scourge of the South.* New York: W. W. Norton, 1959.

Brown, Norman O. *Life Against Death: The Psychoanalytical Meaning of History.* New York: Vintage Books, 1959.

Brown, Richard D. *Modernization: The Transformation of American Life, 1600–1865.* New York: Hill and Wang, 1976.

Brown, William Garrett. *The Life of Oliver Ellsworth.* New York: Macmillan Co., 1905.

Bryan, William Alfred. *George Washington in American Literature.* New York: Columbia University Press, 1952.

Buel, Richard, Jr. *Securing the Revolution: Ideology in American Politics, 1789–1815.* Ithaca, N.Y.: Cornell University Press, 1972.

Burns, Edward McNall. *The American Idea of Mission: Concepts of Nation and Identity.* New Brunswick, N.J.: Rutgers University Press, 1957.

Burrows, Edwin G., and Wallace, Michael. "The American Revolution: The Ideology and Psychology of National Liberation." *Perspectives in American History* 6 (1972): 167–306.

Bushman, Richard L. *From Puritan to Yankee: Character and the Social Order in Connecticut, 1690–1765.* Cambridge: Harvard University Press, 1967.

Butterfield, Lyman Henry, ed. *Adams Family Correspondence.* 4 vols. Cambridge: Harvard University Press, 1963.

Calhoun, Daniel H. "From Noah Webster to Chauncey Wright: The Intellectual as Prognostic." *Harvard Educational Review* 36 (1966): 427–46.

Cappon, Lester J., ed. *The Adams-Jefferson Letters.* 2 vols. Chapel Hill: University of North Carolina Press, 1959.

Carpenter, Charles. *History of American Schoolbooks.* Philadelphia: University of Pennsylvania Press, 1963.

Carpenter, Edwin H., Jr., ed. *A Bibliography of the Writings of Noah Webster*. Compiled by Emily Ellsworth Ford Skeel. New York: New York Public Library, 1958.

Chambers, William Nisbet, ed. *The American Party Systems*. New York: Oxford University Press, 1967.

———. *Political Parties in a New Nation: The American Experience, 1776–1809*. New York: Oxford University Press, 1963.

Chapman, Robert W. *Lexicography*. London: Oxford University Press, 1948.

Charles, Joseph. *The Origins of The American Party System*. New York: Harpers, 1956, 1961.

Christensen, Merton A. "Deism in Joel Barlow's Early Work." *American Literature* 27 (1956): 509–20.

Clark, Mary Elizabeth. *Peter Porcupine in America: The Career of William Cobbett, 1792–1800*. Philadelphia: University of Pennsylvania Press, 1939.

Clifton, John L. *Ten Famous American Educators*. Columbus, Ohio: R. G. Adams and Co., 1933.

Cohan, Mary Helen. *Our Own Words*. New York: Alfred A. Knopf, 1974.

Cohen, Sheldon S. "Student Unrest in the Decade Before the American Revolution." *Connecticut Review* 7 (1974): 51–58.

Cole, Charles C., Jr. *The Social Ideas of the Northern Evangelicals*. New York: Columbia University Press, 1954.

Coll, Gary R. "Noah Webster: Journalist, 1783–1803." Ph.D. dissertation, Southern Illinois University, 1971.

Collier, Christopher. *Roger Sherman's Connecticut: Yankee Politics and the American Revolution*. Middletown, Conn.: Wesleyan University Press, 1971.

Commager, Henry Steele. "Noah Webster, 1758–1958." *Saturday Review*, 18 October 1958, pp. 10–11, 66–67.

Connecticut Academy of Arts and Sciences. *Memoirs*. 1810.

Cook, Edward. "Changing Values and Behavior in Dedham, Massachusetts, 1700–1775." *William and Mary Quarterly*, 3d ser. 27 (1970): 546–80.

Cooke, Jacob E. "The Federalist Age: A Reappraisal." In *American History: Retrospect and Prospect*, edited by George A. Billias and Gerald N. Grob. New York: Free Press, 1971.

Coram, Robert. "Political Inquiries, etc." In *Essays on Education in The Early Republic*, edited by Frederick Rudolph, pp. 79–145. Cambridge: Harvard University Press, 1965.

Cowing, Cecil B. *The Great Awakening and the American Revolution: Colonial Thought in the Eighteenth Century*. Chicago: Rand McNally and Company, 1971.

Creighton, Charles. *A History of Epidemics in Britain*. London: Frank Cass and Company, 1965.

Cremin, Lawrence A. *American Education: The Colonial Experience, 1607–1783*. New York: Harper and Row, 1970.

Crofut, Florence S. Marcy. *Guide to the History and the Historic Sites of Connecticut*. 2 vols. New Haven: Yale University Press, 1937.

Curry, Richard O., and Brown, Thomas W. *Conspiracy: The Fear of Subversion in American History*. New York: Holt, Rinehart and Winston, 1972.

Curti, Merle. *The Growth of American Thought*. New York: Harper and Row, 1964.

———. *The Roots of American Loyalty*. New York: Columbia University Press, 1946.

———. *The Social Ideas of American Educators*. Patterson, N.J.: Pageant Books, 1959.

Curti, Merle; Shryock, Richard H.; Cochran, Thomas C.; and Harrington, Fred Harvey. *A History of American Civilization*. New York: Harper and Brothers, 1953.

Cutler, William W., III. "Status, Values and the Education of the Poor: The Trustees of the New York Public School Society, 1805–1853." *American Quarterly* 24 (1972): 69–85.

Dauer, Manning. *The Adams Federalists*. Baltimore: Johns Hopkins University Press, 1953.

Davies, W. "The Society of Cincinnati in New England, 1783–1800." *William and Mary Quarterly*, 3d ser. 5 (1948): 3–25.

Davis, David Brion. *The Problem of Slavery in Western Culture*. Ithaca: Cornell University Press, 1966.

———. *The Problem of Slavery in the Age of Revolution, 1770–1823*. Ithaca: Cornell University Press, 1975.

———, ed. *Ante-Bellum Reform*. New York: Harper and Row, 1957.

———, ed. *The Fear of Conspiracy: Images of Un-American Subversion from the Revolution to the Present*. Ithaca, N.Y.: Cornell University Press, 1971.

De Conde, Alexander. *The Quasi-War: The Politics and Diplomacy of the Undeclared War with France, 1797–1801*. New York: Scribner, 1966.

D'Elia, Donald J. *Benjamin Rush: Philosopher of the American Revolution*. Philadelphia: American Philosophical Society, 1974.

De Mause, Lloyd, ed. *The History of Childhood*. New York: Harper and Row, 1975.

Demos, John, and Demos, Virginia. "Adolescence in Historical Perspective." In *The Family in Social-Historical Perspective*, edited by Michael Gordon. New York: St. Martin's Press, 1973.

Destler, Chester. *Joshua Coit: American Federalist*. Middletown, Conn.: Wesleyan University Press, 1962.

Dietze, Gottfried. *The Federalist: A Classic on Federalism and Free Government*. Baltimore: Johns Hopkins University Press, 1960.

Dolan, Jay P. *The Immigrant Church: New York's Irish and German Catholics, 1815–1865*. Baltimore: Johns Hopkins University Press, 1975.

[Dunlap, William]. "The Diary of William Dunlap." In *New York Historical Society, Collections, 1929*, pp. 20–22.

Eddy, Bob. "The *Courant* Took a Chance." *The Quill* 52 (1964): 12.

Edgerton, Franklin. "Notes on Early American Work in Linguistics." *Proceedings of the American Philosophical Society* 87 (1944): 25–34.

Edwards, Newton. *The School in the American Social Order*. 2d ed. Boston: Houghton Mifflin Co., 1963.

Elkins, Stanley, and McKitrick, Eric. *The Founding Fathers: Young Men of the Revolution*. Washington, D.C.: Service Center for Teachers of History, 1962.

Ellis, Joseph. "Habits of Mind and an American Enlightenment." *American Quarterly* 28 (1976): 150–64.

Elson, Ruth Miller. "American Schoolbooks and 'Culture' in the Nineteenth Century." *Mississippi Valley Historical Review* 46 (1959): 411–34.

———. *Guardians of Tradition: American Schoolbooks of the Nineteenth Century*. Lincoln, Nebr.: University of Nebraska Press, 1964.

Erikson, Erik H. *Childhood and Society*. New York: W. W. Norton, 1950.

———. *Identity, Youth and Crisis*. New York: W. W. Norton, 1968.

———. "The Problem of Ego Identity." *Journal of the American Psychoanalytic Association* 4 (1956): 58–121.

———. *Young Man Luther: A Study in Psychoanalysis and History*. New York: W. W. Norton, 1958.

Evans, Bergen. "Noah Webster Had the Same Troubles." *New York Times Magazine*, 13 May 1962, pp. 11, 77, 79–80.

Fischer, David Hackett. "America: A Social History. Volume 1. The Main Lines of the Subject, 1650–1975." Unpublished, 1974.

———. *The Revolution of American Conservatism: The Federalist Party in the Era of Jeffersonian Democracy*. New York: Harper and Row, 1965.

Fiske, John. *The Critical Period of American History, 1783–1789*. New York: Appleton, 1888.

Fitzpatrick, John C., ed. *The Writings of George Washington from the Original Manuscript Sources, 1745–1799*. 39 vols. Washington, D.C.: U.S. Government Printing Office, 1931–44.

Flexner, Eleanor. *Century of Struggle*. Cambridge: Harvard University Press, 1950.

Foner, Eric. *Tom Paine and Revolutionary America*. New York: Oxford University Press, 1976.

Ford, Arthur L. *Joel Barlow*. New York: Twayne, 1971.

Ford, Emily E. F. *Notes on the Life of Noah Webster*. 2 vols. New York: [privately printed], 1912.

Ford, Paul Leicester, ed. *The New England Primer*. New York: Teacher's College, Columbia University, 1962.

Formisano, Ronald P. "Deferential-Participant Politics: The Early Republic's Political Culture, 1789–1840." *American Political Science Review* 69 (1975): 473–87.

Foster, Charles I. *An Errand of Mercy: The Evangelical United Front, 1790–1837*. Chapel Hill: University of North Carolina Press, 1960.

———. "The Urban Missionary Movement, 1814–1837." *Pennsylvania Magazine of History and Biography* 85 (1951): 46–65.

[Fowler, William]. "Memoir." *A Dictionary of the English Language*, revised edition. New York: Huntington and Savage, 1845.

Fox, Dixon Ryan. "The Protestant Counter-Reformation in America." *New York History* 16 (1935): 19–35.

Franklin, Benjamin. *Autobiography and Other Writings*. Edited with an Introduction by Russel B. Nye. Boston: Riverside Press of Houghton Mifflin Co., 1958.

Freud, Sigmund. *Beyond the Pleasure Principle*. Translated by James Strachey. New York: Bantam, 1959.

———. *Civilization and Its Discontents*. Translated by James Strachey. New York: W. W. Norton, 1961.

———. *Totem and Taboo: Some Points of Agreement between the Mental Lives of Savages and Neurotics*. Translated by James Strachey. New York: W. W. Norton, 1950.

Friedman, Lawrence J. *Inventors of the Promised Land*. New York: Alfred A. Knopf, 1975.

Friend, Joseph H. "The Development of American Lexicography from Its Beginnings through the Webster–Worcester Dictionary War." Ph.D. dissertation, Indiana University, 1962.

———. *The Development of American Lexicography, 1798–1864*. Paris: Mouton, 1967.

Fromm, Erich. *The Dogma of Christ and Other Essays on Religion, Psychology and Culture*. Greenwich, Conn.: Fawcett, 1955.

———. *Escape from Freedom*. New York: Farrar and Rinehart, 1941.

———. *Psychoanalysis and Religion*. New Haven: Yale University Press, 1950.

———. *The Sane Society*. Greenwich, Conn.: Fawcett, 1955.

Gaustad, Edwin Scott. *The Great Awakening in New England*. Chicago: Quadrangle Books, 1957.

George, Alexander L., and George, Juliette L. *Woodrow Wilson and Colonel House: A Personality Study*. New York: Dover, 1956.

Giltney, John H. "Moses Stuart." Ph.D. dissertation, Yale University, 1956.

Gimmestad, Victor E. *John Trumbull*. New York: Twayne, 1974.

Godzins, Morton. "Political Parties and the Crisis of Succession in the United States: The Case of 1800." In *Political Parties and Political Development*, edited by Joseph La Palombara and Myron Weiner. Princeton: Princeton University Press, 1968.

Good, H. G. *A History of American Education*. New York: Macmillan Co., 1956.

Goodman, Paul. *The Democratic-Republicans of Massachusetts: Politics in a Young Republic*. Cambridge: Harvard University Press, 1964.

———. "The First American Party System." In *The American Party Systems,* edited by William Nisbet Chambers. New York: Oxford University Press, 1967.

Goodrich, Chauncy A. "Life and Writings of Noah Webster. . . ." *American Literary Magazine* (1848): [5]–32

Gordon, James D. *The English Language: An Historical Introduction.* New York: Thomas Y. Crowell, 1972.

Gove, Philip B., ed. *The Role of the Dictionary.* Indianapolis: Bobbs-Merrill Co., 1967.

Granfield, Marcella A. *Meet Dr. Webster.* New York: Vantage Press, 1973.

Gray, Jack C., ed. *Words, Words, Words, and Words about Dictionaries.* San Francisco: Chandler Publishing Co., 1963.

Green, Robert W., ed., *Protestantism, Capitalism, and Social Science: The Weber Thesis Controversy.* 2d ed. Lexington: D. C. Heath, 1973.

Greene, Evarts B. "A Puritan Counter-Reformation in America." *Proceedings of the American Antiquarian Society* 41 (1931): 17–46.

Greene, Jack P. "Autonomy and Stability: New England and the British Colonial Experience in Early Modern America." *Journal of Social History* 7 (1974): 171–94.

Gregory, Winifred. *American Newspapers, 1821–1936.* New York: H. W. Wilson Co., 1937.

Greven, Philip J. *Four Generations: Population, Land, and Family in Colonial Andover, Massachusetts.* Ithaca: Cornell University Press, 1970.

Griffin, Clifford S. "Religious Benevolence as Social Control, 1815–1860." *Mississippi Valley Historical Review* 64 (1957): 423–44.

———. *Their Brother's Keepers: Moral Stewardship in the United States, 1815–1865.* New Brunswick: Rutgers University Press, 1964.

Gusfield, Joseph R. *Symbolic Crusade: Status Politics and the American Temperance Movement.* Urbana: University of Illinois Press, 1966.

Guttmann, Allen. *The Conservative Tradition in America.* New York: Oxford University Press, 1967.

Hall, William H. *West Hartford.* Hartford: James A. Reid, 1930.

Handlin, Oscar. *The History of the United States.* New York: Holt, Rinehart and Winston, 1967.

Hansen, Allen O. *Liberalism and American Education in the Eighteenth Century.* New York: Macmillan Co., 1926.

Hartz, Louis. *The Liberal Tradition in America: An Interpretation of American Political Thought since the Revolution.* New York: Harcourt, Brace and World, 1955.

Hay, Robert. "George Washington: American Moses." *American Quarterly* 21 (1969): 780–91.

Heale, M. J. "Humanitarianism in the Early Republic: The Moral Reformers of New York, 1776–1825." *Journal of American Studies* 2 (1968): 161–75.

Heimart, Alan. *Religion and the American Mind: From the Great Awakening to the Revolution.* Cambridge: Harvard University Press, 1966.

Henretta, James A. *The Evolution of American Society, 1700–1815: An Interdisciplinary Analysis.* Lexington: D. C. Heath, 1973.

Hicks, John D.; Mowry, George E.; and Burke, Robert. *A History of American Democracy.* 3d ed. Boston: Houghton Mifflin Company, 1966.

Hiner, N. Ray. "Adolescence in Eighteenth-Century America." *History of Childhood Quarterly* 3 (1975): 253–80.

Hofstadter, Richard. *Academic Freedom in the Age of the College.* Chicago: University of Chicago Press, 1955.

———. *The Idea of a Party System: The Rise of Legitimate Opposition in the United States, 1780–1840.* Berkeley, Los Angeles: University of California Press, 1972.

———. *The Paranoid Style in American Politics and Other Essays.* New York: Knopf, 1965.

Horney, Karen. *The Neurotic Personality in Our Time.* New York: W. W. Norton, 1937.

———. *New Ways in Psychoanalysis.* New York: W. W. Norton, 1939.

Howard, Leon. *The Connecticut Wits*. Chicago: University of Chicago Press, 1943.

_____. "The Late Eighteenth Century: An Age of Contradictions." In *Transitions in American Literary History*, edited by Harry Hayden Clark. Durham, N.C.: Duke University Press, 1953.

Howe, John R., Jr. *The Changing Political Thought of John Adams*. Princeton, N.J.: Princeton University Press, 1966.

_____. "Republican Thought and the Political Violence of the 1790s." *American Quarterly* 19 (1967): 147–65.

Humphreys, Frank Landon. *Life and Times of David Humphreys*. 2 vols. New York: G. P. Putnam's Sons, 1917.

James, William. *The Varieties of Religious Experience: A Study in Human Nature*. New York: Modern Library, 1902.

Jay, William. *Life of John Jay*. Freeport, N.Y.: Books for Libraries Press, 1972. Reprint of the 1833 edition.

Jensen, Merrill. *The Articles of Confederation*. Madison: University of Wisconsin Press, 1966.

_____. *The New Nation: A History of the United States During the Confederation, 1781–1789*. New York: Alfred A. Knopf, 1965.

Johnson, Allen, and Malone, Dumas, eds. *Dictionary of American Biography*. New York: Charles Scribner's Sons, 1964.

Johnson, Gerald W. *Mount Vernon*. New York: Random House, 1953.

Johnson, Henry P. *Yale and Her Honor-Roll in the American Revolution: 1775–1783*. New York: [privately printed], 1888.

Jones, Howard Mumford. *O, Strange New World: American Culture, The Formative Years*. New York: Viking Press, 1964.

Jordan, Winthrop. "Familial Politics: Thomas Paine and 'The Killing of the King,' 1776." *Journal of American History* 61 (1974): 294–308.

_____. Review of *Thomas Jefferson: An Intimate History*, by Fawn M. Brodie. *William and Mary Quarterly*, 3d ser. 32 (1975): 510.

_____. *White Over Black: American Attitudes Toward the Negro, 1550–1812*. Chapel Hill: University of North Carolina Press, 1968.

Kaestle, Carl F. *The Evolution of an Urban School System: New York City, 1750–1850*. Cambridge: Harvard University Press, 1973.

Katz, Michael B. *Class, Bureaucracy, and Schools: The Illusion of Educational Change in America*. New York: Praeger, 1971.

_____. *The Irony of Early School Reform: Educational Innovation in Mid-Nineteenth-Century Massachusetts*. Cambridge: Harvard University Press, 1973.

_____. "The Origins of Public Education." *History of Education Quarterly* 16 (1976): 381–407.

_____. *School Reform: Past and Present*. New York: Little, Brown, and Co., 1971.

Kelley, Brooks Mather. *Yale: A History*. New Haven: Yale University Press, 1974.

Kerber, Linda. *Federalists in Dissent: Imagery and Ideology in Jeffersonian America*. Ithaca: Cornell University Press, 1970.

Ketcham, Ralph. *From Colony to Country: The Revolution in American Thought, 1750–1820*. Macmillan Co., 1974.

Kiell, Norman, ed. *Psychological Studies of Famous Americans: The Civil War Era*. New York: Twayne, 1964.

King, Charles R. *The Life and Correspondence of Rufus King: Comprising His Letters, Private and Official, His Public Documents, and His Speeches*. New York: Da Capo Press, 1971.

King, Ethel. *The Rainbow in the Sky: Concerning Noah Webster and His Dictionary*. Brooklyn: Theo Gaus' Sons, 1962.

Kobre, Sidney. *Development of American Journalism.* Dubuque, Iowa: William C. Brown, 1969.

Koch, Adrienne, ed. *The American Enlightenment: The Shaping of the American Experiment and a Free Society.* New York: George Braziller, 1965.

Kohn, Hans. *The Idea of Nationalism: A Study in its Origins and Background.* New York: Collier Books, 1967.

Kohn, Richard. *Eagle and Sword: The Federalists and the Creation of the Military Establishment in America, 1783–1802.* New York: Free Press, 1975.

Krapp, George Phillip. *The English Language in America.* 2 vols. New York: Frederick Ungar Publishing Co., 1925, 1960.

————. *Modern English: Its Growth and Present Use.* New York: Charles Scribner's Sons, 1910.

Kraus, Michael. "America and the Utopian Ideal in the Eighteenth Century." *Mississippi Valley Historical Review* 22 (1936): 487–504.

Krout, John Allen, and Fox, Dixon Ryan. *The Completion of Independence, 1790–1830.* New York: Macmillan, 1944.

Kurtz, Stephen C. *The Presidency of John Adams: The Collapse of Federalism, 1795–1800.* Philadelphia: University of Pennsylvania Press, 1957.

Laird, Charlton. "Etymology, Anglo-Saxon, and Noah Webster." *American Speech* 21 (1946): 3–15.

————. *Language in America.* Englewood Cliffs, N.J.: Prentice-Hall, 1970.

Leavitt, Robert Keith. *Noah's Ark: New England Yankees and the Endless Quest: A Short History of the Original Webster Dictionaries, with Particular Reference to their First Hundred Years as Publications of the G.&C. Merriam Company.* Springfield, Mass.: G. and C. Merriam Co., 1947.

Lebeaux, Richard. *Young Man Thoreau.* Amherst: University of Massachusetts Press, 1977.

Lewis, W. David. "The Reformers as Conservatives: Protestant Counter-Subversion in The Early Republic." In *The Development of an American Culture.* Edited by Stanley Coben and Norman Ratner. Englewood Cliffs, N.J.: Prentice-Hall, 1970.

Link, Eugene Perry. *The Democratic-Republican Societies, 1790–1800.* New York: Columbia University Press, 1942.

Litto, Frederic M. "Addison's Cato in the Colonies." *William and Mary Quarterly,* 3d ser. 23 (1966): 431–49.

Littlejohn, David. *Dr. Johnson and Noah Webster: Two Men and Their Dictionaries.* San Francisco: Book Club of California, 1971.

Livermore, Shaw, Jr. "The Early National Period, 1789–1823." In *The Reinterpretation of American History and Culture,* edited by William H. Cartwright and Richard L. Watson, Jr. Washington, D.C.: National Council for the Social Studies, 1973.

Lockridge, Kenneth A. "Land, Population and the Evolution of New England Society, 1630–1790, and an Afterthought." In *Colonial America: Essays in Politics and Social Development,* edited by Stanley Katz, pp. 466–91. Boston: Little, Brown, 1971.

————. *A New England Town: The First Hundred Years.* New York: Norton, 1970.

————. "The Population of Dedham, Massachusetts, 1636–1736. *Economic History Review,* 2d ser. 59 (1966): 339–41.

Lodwig, Richard R., and Barrett, Eugene F. *The Dictionary and the Language.* New York: Hayden Book Company, 1967.

Loucks, Rupert Charles. "Connecticut in the American Revolution." M.A. thesis, University of Wisconsin, 1959.

Lynd, Staughton. *Intellectual Origins of American Radicalism.* New York: Vintage Books, 1968.

MacLeod, Anne Scott. *A Moral Tale: Children's Fiction and American Culture, 1820–1860.* Hamden, Conn.: Archon, 1975.

McCary, J. L., ed. *Psychology of Personality: Six Modern Approaches.* New York: Logos Press, 1956.

McDonald, Forest, and McDonald, Ellen Shapiro, eds. *Confederation and Constitution, 1781–1789.* New York: Harper and Row, 1968.

McKnight, George H. *The Evolution of the English Language: From Chaucer to the Twentieth Century.* New York: Dover, 1968.

Madison, James. *Letters and Other Writings of James Madison[,] Fourth President of the United States.* Philadelphia: J. B. Lippincott, 1867.

Maier, Pauline. "Coming to Terms with Samuel Adams." *American Historical Review* 81 (1976): 12–37.

———. *From Resistance to Revolution: Colonial Radicals and the Development of American Opposition to Britain, 1765–1776.* New York: Alfred A. Knopf, 1972.

Main, Jackson Turner. *The Anti-Federalists: Critics of the Constitution, 1781–1788.* Chapel Hill: University of North Carolina Press, 1961.

Malone, Kemp. "A Linguistic Patriot." *American Speech* 1 (1925): 26–31.

Marx, Leo. *The Machine in the Garden: Technology and the Pastoral Ideal in America.* New York: Oxford University Press, 1964.

Massachusetts Historical Society. *Collections.* Fifth series, volume 3, part 2 (1877).

Mathews, Donald G. "The Second Great Awakening as an Organizing Process, 1780–1830: An Hypothesis." *American Quarterly* 21 (1969): 23–43.

Mathews, Mitford. *The Beginnings of American English.* Chicago: University of Chicago Press, 1931.

———. *A Survey of English Dictionaries.* London: Oxford University Press, 1933.

May, Henry. *The Enlightenment in America.* New York: Oxford University Press, 1976.

May, Rollo. *The Meaning of Anxiety.* New York: Ronald Press, 1950.

Mazlish, Bruce, ed. *Psychoanalysis and History.* Rev. ed. New York: Grosset and Dunlap, 1971.

———. *The Revolutionary Ascetic: Evolution of a Type..* New York: Basic Books, 1976.

Mencken, H. L. *The American Language: An Inquiry into the Development of English in the United States.* New York: Alfred A. Knopf, 1923, 1972.

———. *The American Language; An Inquiry into the Development of English in the United States. Supplement I.* New York: Alfred A. Knopf, 1945.

Messerli, Jonathan. *Horace Mann: A Biography.* New York: Alfred A. Knopf, 1971.

Meyer, Adolph E. *An Educational History of the American People.* New York: McGraw-Hill, 1956, 1967.

Meyer, Donald H. *Democratic Enlightenment.* New York: Basic Books, 1976.

Meyers, Marvin. *The Jacksonian Persuasion: Politics and Belief.* Stanford: Stanford University Press, 1957.

Miles, Edwin A. "The Young American Nation and the Classical World." *Journal of the History of Ideas* 35 (1974): 259–74.

Miller, Douglas T. *The Birth of Modern America, 1820–1850.* New York: Pegasus, 1970.

Miller, John C. *Alexander Hamilton and the Growth of the New Nation.* New York: Harper and Row, 1959.

———. *The Federalist Era, 1789–1801.* New York: Harper and Row, 1960.

———, ed. *The Young Republic, 1789–1815.* New York: Free Press, 1970.

Miller, Perry. "From the Covenant to the Revival." In *The Shaping of American Religion,* edited by J. W. Smith and A. L. Jamison. Princeton: Princeton University Press, 1961.

Miner, Louie May. *Our Rude Forefathers: American Political Verse, 1783–1788.* Cedar Rapids, Iowa: Torch Press, 1937.

Miyakawa, T. Scott. *Protestants and Pioneers: Individualism and Conformity on the American Frontier.* Chicago: University of Chicago Press, 1964.

Mohl, Raymond A. *Poverty in New York, 1783–1825*. New York: Oxford University Press, 1971.

Morgan, Edmund S. "The American Revolution Considered As an Intellectual Movement." In *Paths of American Thought*, edited by Arthur M. Schlesinger, Jr., and Morton G. White. Boston: Little, Brown and Co., 1963.

———. "The Puritan Ethic and the American Revolution." *William and Mary Quarterly*, 3d ser. 24 (1967): 3–43.

Morgan, Forest, ed. *Connecticut as a Colony and as a State, or One of the Original Thirteen*. Hartford: Publishing Society of Connecticut, 1904.

Morgan, John S. *Noah Webster*. Mason–Charters Publishers, 1975.

Morison, Samuel Eliot. *Harrison Gray Otis, 1765–1848: The Urbane Federalist*. Boston: Houghton Mifflin, 1969.

Morris, Richard B. "The Confederation Period and the American Historian." *William and Mary Quarterly*, 3d ser. 13 (1956): 139–56.

Morse, Anson Ely. *The Federalist Party in Massachusetts in 1800*. Princeton: Princeton University Press, 1909.

Moss, Richard James. "The American Response to the French Revolution, 1789–1801." Ph.D. dissertation, Michigan State University, 1974.

Mott, Frank Luther. *American Journalism: A History of Newspapers in the United States through 250 Years, 1690–1940*. New York: Macmillan Co., 1941.

Murray, James A. H. *The Evolution of English Lexicography*. London: Oxford University Press, 1900.

Nagel, Paul C. *One Nation Indivisible: The Union in American Thought, 1776–1861*. New York: Oxford University Press, 1965.

———. *This Sacred Trust: American Nationality, 1798–1888*. New York: Oxford University Press, 1971.

Nash, Gary D. "The American Clergy and the French Revolution." *William and Mary Quarterly*, 3d ser. 22 (1965): 392–412.

Neil, J. Meredith. *Toward a National Taste: America's Quest for Aesthetic Independence*. Honolulu: University of Hawaii Press, 1975.

Neumann, Franz. *The Democratic and Authoritarian State: Essays in Political and Legal History*. Glencoe, Ill.: Free Press, 1957.

Nevins, Allan. *The American States: During and After the Revolution, 1775–1789*. New York: Augustus M. Kelley, 1969.

Newspapers in Microfilm: United States. Washington, D.C.: Library of Congress, 1972.

Nock, Albert Jay. *Jefferson*. New York: Hill and Wang, 1926.

Novak, Steven J. *The Rights of Youth: American Colleges and Student Revolt, 1798–1815*. Cambridge: Harvard University Press, 1977.

Oates, Stephen B. *To Purge This Land with Blood: A Biography of John Brown*. New York: Harper and Row, 1970.

Osler, William. "Some Aspects of Medical Bibliography." *Bulletin of the Association of Medical Librarians* 1 (1902): 151–67.

Osterweis, Rollin G. *Three Centuries of New Haven, 1638–1938*. New Haven: Yale University Press, 1953.

Padover, Saul K. *To Secure These Blessings*. New York: Washington Square Press, 1962.

Partch, Clarence E. "Noah Webster: The Schoolmaster of Our Republic." *Journal of the Rutgers University Library* 2 (1939): [39]–45.

Partridge, Eric. *The Gentle Art of Lexicography*. London: Andre Deutsch, 1963.

Peabody, James Bishop, ed. *John Adams: A Biography in His Own Words*. New York: Newsweek, 1973.

Pearson, Hesketh. *Tom Paine: Friend of Mankind*. New York: Harper and Brothers, 1937.

Pei, Mario. *The Story of the English Language*. Philadelphia: J. B. Lippincott, 1967.

Perkins, Nathan. *A Half-Century Sermon*. Hartford: n.p., 1822.

Persons, Stow. "The Cyclical Theory of History in Eighteenth Century America." *American Quarterly* 6 (1954): 147–68.

Peterson, Merrill D. *The Jefferson Image in The American Mind.* New York: Oxford University Press, 1960.

Platt, Gerald M. "The Sociological Endeavor and Psychoanalytic Thought. *American Quarterly* 28 (1976): 343–59.

Potter, David M. "Nathan Hale and the Ideal of American Union." *Connecticut Antiquarian* 6 (1954): 23–25.

Proudfit, Isabel. *Noah Webster, Father of the Dictionary.* New York: J. Messner, Inc., 1942.

Purcell, Richard J. *Connecticut in Transition: 1775–1818.* Middletown, Conn.: Wesleyan University Press, 1918, 1962.

Pyles, Thomas. *The Origins and Development of the English Language.* New York: Harcourt, Brace and World, 1964.

———. *Words and Ways of American English.* New York: Random House, 1952.

Ravitch, Diane. "The Revisionists Revised: Studies in The Historiography of American Education." *Proceedings of The National Academy of Education* 4 (1977).

Read, Allen Walker. "Noah Webster as a Euphemist." *Dialect Notes* 6 (1934): 385–91.

———. "The Philological Society of New York, 1788." *American Speech* 9 (1934): 131–36.

Reed, Joseph. "Noah Webster's Debt to Samuel Johnson." *American Speech* 37 (1962): 95–105.

Richards, Leonard L. *"Gentlemen of Property and Standing": Anti–Abolition Mobs in Jacksonian America.* New York: Oxford University Press, 1970.

Roazen, Paul. *Freud: Political and Social Thought.* New York: Vintage Books, 1968.

Robbins, Caroline. *Eighteenth-Century Commonwealthman.* Cambridge: Harvard University Press, 1959.

Robison, John. *Proofs of a Conspiracy Against All. . . The Religions and Governments of Europe.* Edinburgh: William Greech, 1797.

Rogin, Michael Paul. *Fathers and Children: Andrew Jackson and the Subjugation of the American Indian.* New York: Alfred A. Knopf, 1975.

Rollins, Richard M. "Adin Ballou and the Perfectionist's Dilemma." *Journal of Church and State* 17 (1975): 459–76.

———. "Noah Webster: Propagandist for the Revolution." *Connecticut History* 18 (1976): 22–43.

———. "Words as Social Control: Noah Webster and the Creation of the *American Dictionary.*" *American Quarterly* 28 (1976): 415–30.

———. Review of *Noah Webster,* by John S. Morgan. *Connecticut History* 18 (1976): 68–72.

Rossiter, Clinton. *Conservatism in America: The Thankless Persuasion.* 2d ed., enlarged. New York: Alfred A. Knopf, 1962.

Roth, David. "Connecticut and the Coming of the Revolution." *Connecticut Review* 7 (1973): 49–65.

Rothman, David J. *The Discovery of the Asylum: Social Order and Disorder in the New Republic.* Boston: Little, Brown and Co., 1971.

Rudolph, Frederick, ed. *Essays on Education in the Early Republic.* Cambridge: Harvard University Press, 1965.

Rusche, Dennis Patrick. "An Empire of Reason: A Study of the Writings of Noah Webster." Ph.D. dissertation, University of Iowa, 1975.

Sahakian, William S., ed. *Psychology of Personality: Readings in Theory.* Chicago: Rand McNally and Company, 1965.

Schaar, John. *Escape from Authority.* New York: Basic Books, 1961.

Schneider, Herbert. *The History of American Philosophy.* New York: Columbia University Press, 1963.

Schultz, Stanley K. *The Culture Factory: Boston Public Schools, 1789–1860*. New York: Oxford University Press, 1973.

Scudder, Horace E. *Noah Webster*. American Men of Letters Series, edited by Charles Dudley Warner. Boston: Houghton Mifflin Co., 1883.

Shalope, Robert E. "Toward a Republican Synthesis: The Emergence of an Understanding of Republicanism in American Historiography." *William and Mary Quarterly*, 3d ser. 29 (1972): 49–80.

Shoemaker, Ervin C. *Noah Webster: Pioneer of Learning*. New York: Columbia University Press, 1936.

Shoemaker, Robert W. "'Democracy' and 'Republic' as Understood in Late Eighteenth-Century America." *American Speech* 61 (1966): 83–95.

Silverman, Kenneth. *Timothy Dwight*. New York: Twayne, 1969.

Sinofsky, Faye; Fitzpatrick, John J.; Potts, Louis W.; and de Mause, Lloyd. "A Bibliography of Psychohistory." *History of Childhood Quarterly: The Journal of Psychohistory* 2 (1975): 517–62.

Sklar, Kathryn Kish. *Catharine Beecher: A Study in American Domesticity*. New Haven: Yale University Press, 1973.

Slater, Rosalie. "Noah Webster's 1828 Dictionary Needed to Restore an American Christian Education in the Home, the Church and the School." In *Noah Webster's First Edition of an American Dictionary of the English Language*, edited by Rosalie Slater. Anaheim, California: Foundation for American Christian Education, 1967.

———. "Noah Webster: Founding Father of American Scholarship and Education." In *Noah Webster's First Edition of an American Dictionary of the English Language*, edited by Rosalie Slater. Anaheim, California: Foundation for American Christian Education, 1967.

Sledd, James A., and Kolb, Gwin J. *Dr. Johnson's Dictionary: Essays in the Biography of a Book*. Chicago: University of Chicago Press, 1955.

Smelser, Marshall. "The Federalist Period as an Age of Passion." *American Quarterly* 10 (1958): 391–419.

———. "The Jacobin Phrenzy: Federalism and the Menace of Liberty, Equality and Fraternity." *Review of Politics* 13 (1951): 457–82.

———. "The Jacobin Phrenzy: The Menace of Monarchy, Plutocracy and Anglophobia, 1789–1798." *Review of Politics* 21 (1959): 239–58.

Smith, Daniel Scott. "The Demographic History of Colonial New England." *Journal of Economic History* 32 (1972): 184–213.

Smith, Eugene. *One Hundred Years of Hartford's Courant from Colonial Times through the Civil War*. New Haven: Yale University Press, 1949.

Smith, Gerald. "Noah Webster's Conservatism." *American Speech* 25 (1950): 101–4.

Smith, Henry Nash. *Virgin Land: The American West as Symbol and Myth*. Cambridge: Harvard University Press, 1950.

Smith, Jonathan. "The Depression of 1785 and Daniel Shays' Rebellion." *William and Mary Quarterly*, 3d ser. 5 (1948): 77–94.

Smith, Page. "Anxiety and Despair." *William and Mary Quarterly*, 3d ser. 26 (1969): 416–24.

———. *John Adams*. 2 vols. Garden City, N.Y.: Doubleday, 1962.

Smith-Rosenberg, Carroll. *Religion and the Rise of The American City: The New York City Mission Movement, 1812–1870*. Ithaca: Cornell University Press, 1971.

Smith, Wilson, ed. *Theories of Education in Early America, 1655–1819*. Indianapolis: Bobbs-Merrill, 1973.

Somkin, Fred. *The Unquiet Eagle: Memory and Desire in the Idea of American Freedom, 1815–1860*. Ithaca: Cornell University Press, 1967.

Spaulding, E. Wilder. "The Connecticut Courant: A Representative Newspaper in the Eighteenth Century." *New England Quarterly* 3 (1930): 443–63.

Spencer, Benjamin T. *The Quest for Nationality.* Syracuse: Syracuse University Press, 1957.

Spinka, Matthew. *A History of The First Church of Christ Congregational, West Hartford, Connecticut.* Hartford: Hartford Seminary Foundation, n.d.

Spurlin, Paul Merrill. *Rousseau in America, 1760–1809.* University: University of Alabama Press, 1969.

Stauffer, Vernon. *New England and the Bavarian Illuminati.* New York: Columbia University Press, 1918.

Steger, Stewart A. *American Dictionaries.* Baltimore: Johns Hopkins University Press, 1913.

Stein, Maurice; Vidich, Arthur J.; and White, David Manning, eds. *Identity and Anxiety: Survival of the Person in Mass Society.* New York: Free Press, 1960.

Storr, Anthony. *The Dynamics of Creation.* New York: Atheneum, 1972.

Stromberg, R. N. "History in the Eighteenth Century." *Journal of the History of Ideas* 12 (1951): 295–304.

Strout, Cushing. "The Uses and Abuses of Psychology in American History." *American Quarterly* 28 (1976): 324–42.

Tate, Thad. W. "The Social Contract in America, 1774–1787: Revolutionary Theory as a Conservative Instrument." *William and Mary Quarterly*, 3d ser. 22 (1965): 376–91.

Thomas, John L. "Romantic Reform in America, 1815–1865." *American Quarterly* 17 (1965): 656–81.

Trumbull, J. Hammond. *Historical Notes on the Constitutions of Connecticut, 1639–1818.* Hartford: Case, Lockwood and Brainard Co., 1901.

Tuveson, Ernest R. *Redeemer Nation: The Idea of America's Millenial Role.* Chicago: University of Chicago Press, 1968.

Van Dusen, Albert E. "Connecticut History to 1763: A Selective Bibliography." *Connecticut History* 17 (1975): 49–55.

Walzer, John F. "A Period of Ambivalence: Eighteenth-Century American Childhood." In *The History of Childhood,* edited by Lloyd de Mause, pp. 351–82. New York: Harper and Row, 1975.

Walzer, Michael. *The Revolution of the Saints: A Study in the Origins of Radical Politics.* Cambridge: Harvard University Press, 1965.

Ward, John William. *Andrew Jackson: Symbol for an Age.* New York: Oxford University Press, 1955.

Warfel, Harry R. "The Centenary of Noah Webster's Bible." *New England Quarterly* 8 (1934): 578–82.

————. *Noah Webster: Schoolmaster to America.* New York: Macmillan, 1936.

————, ed. *The Letters of Noah Webster.* New York: Library Publishers, 1953.

Warfel, Ruth Farquhar, and Warfel, Harry R. *Poems by Noah Webster.* College Park, Md.: Harruth Lefraw, 1936.

Warthin, Aldred S. "Noah Webster as Epidemiologist." *Journal of the American Medical Association* 80 (1923): 755–64.

Weber, Max. *The Protestant Ethic and the Spirit of Capitalism.* New York: Scribner's, 1958.

Wells, Ronald. *Dictionaries and the Authoritarian Tradition: A Study in English Usage and Lexicography.* Paris: Mouton, 1973.

Welter, Rush. *The Mind of America, 1820–1860.* New York: Columbia University Press, 1975.

————. "Reason, Revolutionary and Otherwise: The Enlightenment in America." *Reviews in American History* 5 (1977): 321–25.

Wheelis, Allen. *The Quest for Identity.* New York: W. W. Norton, 1958.

Williams, Raymond. *Culture and Society, 1780–1850*. New York: Columbia University Press, 1958.

Wilson, Joan Hoff. "The Illusion of Change: Women and the American Revolution." In *The American Revolution: Explorations in the History of American Radicalism*, edited by Alfred Young. De Kalb: Northern Illinois University Press, 1976.

Wilson, Kenneth G.; Hendrickson, R. H.; and Taylor, Peter Alan. *Harbrace Guide to Dictionaries*. New York: Harcourt, Brace and World, 1963.

Winslow, Charles-Edward Amory. *The Conquest of Epidemic Disease: A Chapter in the History of Ideas*. Princeton, N.J.: Princeton University Press, 1943.

————. "The Epidemiology of Noah Webster." *Transactions of the Connecticut Academy of Arts and Sciences* 32 (1934): 23–109.

Wolcott, Oliver. *Memoirs of the Administrations of Washington and John Adams*. New York: Van Norden, 1846.

Wolman, Benjamin, ed. *The Psychoanalytic Interpretation of History*. New York: Harpers, 1971.

Wood, Gordon S. *The Creation of the American Republic, 1776–1787*. Chapel Hill: University of North Carolina Press, 1969.

————, ed. *The Rising Glory of America*. New York: George Braziller, 1971.

Woodress, James. *A Yankee's Odyssey: The Life of Joel Barlow*. Philadelphia: Lippincott, 1958.

Wyss, Deter. *Psychoanalytic Schools from the Beginning to the Present*. Translated by Gerald Onn. New York: Jason Aronson, 1973.

Zeichner, Otto. *Connecticut's Years of Controversy, 1750–1776*. Chapel Hill: University of North Carolina Press, 1949.

Zunder, Theodore. *The Early Days of Joel Barlow*. New Haven: Yale University Press, 1934.

————. "Noah Webster and the *Conquest of Canaan*." *American Literature* 1 (1929): 200–202.

————. "Noah Webster as a Student Orator." *Yale Alumni Weekly* 36 (1926): 225.

Index

suffrage, 99–100. *See also* univeral white male suffrage

Tallyrand, 83
Tappan, David, 96
Tetard, John Peter, 21
Thacher, Samuel Cooper, 95
Tracy, Uriah, 96
"true republicanism," 74–75
Trumbull, John, 34, 60

universal white male suffrage, 21

Value of the Bible, 140
Van Rensselaer, Stephen, 108
Victoria, queen of England, 127
"The Voice of Wisdom," 140
Voltaire, 81

Walker, Judge, 94
Warfel, Harry R., 125
Washington, George, 7, 15, 16, 17, 24, 42, 45, 47, 52, 72, 77, 100, 126
Weber, Max, 11
Webster, Abraham, 14
Webster, Daniel, 124
Webster, John, 8
Webster, Mercy Steele, 8
Webster, Noah, Jr.: and Alien and Sedition Acts, 102; *American Magazine*, editor of, 56–60; and American Revolution, 24, 51, 86; and Amherst College, 120, 125; Anglo-Saxon, knowledge of, 128; anthologists, criticized by, 95; on asceticism, 29; attacked in press, 84; *Brief History of Epidemic and Pestilential Diseases, A*, writes, 89; Cato, pseudonym, 29; childhood of, 8–10; on church and state, 31, 81, 110; on class distinctions, 30; "Closed Christian Utopian Corporate Community," desire for, 108; on colonization, 68; and commutation controversy, 42–44; and Confederation, problems of, 40; on the Constitution, 53–54; and the Constitutional Convention, 51–52; on contractualism in politics, 27; on corruption in America, 83; on cultural nationalism and language, 47, 63; death of, 143; defines words, 132–37; "demoralizing," invention of, 80; dictionary finished, 123; dictionary

sent to Queen Victoria, 127; *Dissertations on the English Language*, 61–64, 66, 129; on economics, 64–65; on education, 12, 19–20, 33–37, 58–59, 119–20; on election frequency 32, 53; and election of 1800, 101–2; and election of 1840, 140; on enlightenment, 15–17; on equal distribution of property, 30, 53; and etymology, 62–63, 129–31; and evangelical Protestantism, conversion to, 113; *Examination of the Leading Principles of the Federal Constitution, An*, 53; on faction, 80, 83; on family, importance of, 19, 25, 61, 112; on French Revolution, 65, 77, 79–81; and Genet, Edmund, 76; Goshen, New York, moves to, 20–22; *Grammatical Institute of the English Language*, 34–37, 46, 52; Greenleaf, Rebecca, meets, 52; on guillotine, 77–78; and Hartford Convention, 126; Hickory, Giles, pseudonym, 56–57; on history, 29, 79, 83; *History of the United States* 118; *Holy Bible*, edits, 114, 117; identity, problems of, 21–22; on industrialization, 66; and jacobinism, 83, 85, 98, 132; Jefferson, attacks, 102–3; on language and cultural nationalism, 47, 63; on language as similar to England's, 126; as lawyer, 19–20; on linguistic reform, 125; *Little Reader's Assistant*, 66; and Middletown Convention, 39–40, 43, 52, 67, 87, 88, 114; and modern personality structure, 25; on nature of man, 77–78, 97, 108; New England, moves to in 1798, 86; *New England Primer*, edits, 109; and pessimism, 140; Philadelphia, leaves in 1787, 55; Price, Richard, discusses influence of, 28; *Prompter, The*, 96–97; on property, equal distribution of, 30, 53; on "public spirit," 111; and Quiet Christian concept, 114–21; 124, 132–38; 143; and rejection by father, love, section, 22; on religion and government, 81, 110; and religious beliefs, 11, 30–31, 113–17; on religious toleration, 30; *Revolution in France, The*, 78–81; on Rousseau, debt to, 28; as schoolteacher, 19–20; on self-interest as political concept, 44; and Shays' Rebellion, 12, 40, 48–50, 52, 72, 88,